Gertrude Kistler Memorial Library

Rosemont, Pa.

Presented in memory of
Mary Joan Gain Smith, '33
by
Mr. & Mrs. John Connelly

Charlotte Brontë: The Self Conceived

Richmond del. 1850.

HELENE MOGLEN

Charlotte Brontë
The Self Conceived

THE UNIVERSITY OF WISCONSIN PRESS

Published 1984

The University of Wisconsin Press
114 North Murray Street
Madison, Wisconsin 53715

The University of Wisconsin Press, Ltd.
1 Gower Street
London WC1E 6HA, England

First printing by the University of Wisconsin Press
Printed in the United States of America
Originally published in 1976 by W. W. Norton & Company, Inc.

ISBN 0-299-10140-1 cloth; 0-299-10144-4 paper
LC 84-17199

Library of Congress Cataloging in Publication Data

Moglen, Helene, 1936-
    Charlotte Brontë : the self conceived.

    Reprint. Originally published: New York: Norton, c1976.
    Bibliography: pp. 243-247.
    Includes index.
    1. Brontë, Charlotte, 1816-1855. 2. Novelists,
English — 19th century — Biography. 3. Fiction,
Autobiographic. 4. Self in literature. 5. Feminism and
literature. I. Title.
PR4168.M575 1984   823'.8 [B]   84-17199
ISBN 0-299-10140-1
ISBN 0-299-10144-4

To Sig

who

when we were children
helped me to conceive myself
and as we grew to maturity
helped me to realize that self
we had conceived

Contents

Illustrations

Acknowledgments

*T*HE PRECIOUS gift of time was bestowed upon me by the American Council of Learned Societies in the form of a fellowship for the academic year 1973–74. It relieved me of teaching and administrative duties and took me to England: to the British Museum in London, to the Brontë Parsonage Museum at Haworth and, perhaps most importantly, to the Yorkshire moors. At the Parsonage Museum, Mr. Norman Raistrick, the custodian, guided me through the Brontë Society's collection of books and papers and has been of continuing help in sending me necessary material and information.

From the beginning, I have associated my project with the special pleasures and activities that have been part of establishing a new college. To my colleagues at Purchase, who put aside their own work to read and discuss mine, I am affectionately grateful. Interchanging ideas with Evelyn Keller, Marcia Cavell, Bell Chevigny, Geoffrey Field, Myra Jehlen, and Michael O'Loughlin was an interdisciplinary treat and a perpetual reaffirmation of friendship. Carl Resek exerted his decanal powers to find me extra pockets of time, and then insisted that I protect myself against his own forays into them. The students who labored in my two Charlotte Brontë seminars amazed me with their capacity for hard work, delighted me with their enthusiasm, educated me with the freshness of their insights, and confirmed my belief that the book was one worth writing. Isabel Murray refused to be simply an expert typist: she read the novels, checked my sources, stuffed me with candy, and never allowed me to feel discouraged. Lauren Wood, who typed the last draft, met my insanity with good humor and got the job done with patience and intelligence.

I am indebted also to Barbara Gelpi, who read the completed manuscript with extraordinary care and thoroughness and made a number of valuable suggestions. To George Brockway of Norton, I offer the respect due someone who accomplishes what he does with such easy competence.

My sons, Eben, Damon, and Seth, tramped the Yorkshire moors day after rainy day, sharing my curiosity and delight, and remained—in the years since—philosophically tolerant of my "incessant scribbling."

Finally, there are those acts of love which can be recorded but never repaid. Sig, my husband, came home on innumerable evenings, weary of editing other people's books, and surrendered his own thoughts to edit mine: finding the patterns of meaning which hid inside the maze of words; cajoling, reasoning, explaining, teasing—until my best had been done. His dedication was to the utmost clarification of my vision and, as always, to the integrity of thought itself.

Preface

LITERARY BIOGRAPHIES interest me least when they set out to tell exhaustively and "objectively" the history of an individual, tallying dates, genealogies and events, friends and lovers, geographical locations, and the titles of books written and read. Such studies leave one freshly awed by the miracle of the creative process. Art seems to be self-generating, not parented by personality. Often, after reading such a work—tirelessly researched, masterfully organized, representing a martyrdom of sources pursued and handwriting deciphered— one is left with the suspicion that fiction is more satisfying than fact: more competent to capture the mystery and power of a life.

These diligent books are usually compiled by those who believe biography valuable to an understanding of literature but reject the notion that the analysis of an author's work is essential to an understanding of his or her experience. Although their perspective seems opposed to that of the "new critics," who insist that each work of poetry or fiction establishes its own guidelines for study, the two views jointly theorize that biographical and critical explorations are desirably exclusive. Many of us employ this compatibility to nod knowingly in the direction of biography while continuing on our way to the serious business of literary analysis.

There are lives, however, which won't leave one alone: which compel by the psychological problems they raise, which fascinate by their tragic configurations. They promise to reveal the barely submerged secrets of the relationship between art and personality. They whisper confessions of their bondage to social and historical influences. Such lives tempt even the most sceptical to view themselves provisionally as biographers in search of a new form.

For me—Charlotte Brontë's was such a life. It seemed extraordinary, not only in its dramatic power, but in its accessibility. From her childhood, Brontë's fantasies organized themselves into stories which revealed both the shape of a personality struggling for definition and the nature of those forces which conspired to thwart and even to destroy it. Here in the domestic tragedy and the prodigies of juvenile creativity are laid bare the ores from which the profound later works would be refined. An almost unique opportunity for the perception of psychological and artistic formation was afforded.

I saw that there were two dimensions of her too brief self-expression—the life Brontë lived and the life she transmuted into fiction. I perceived the growth of that interaction and knew that its flowering would suggest fresh readings of the novels. It became plain to me that the interaction itself was the critical element. The events of the life could no longer be melodramatically recounted, as they have so often been. The novels could not simply be examined as quirky stages in a developing genre. The centrality of the romantic impulse—the psychosexual and social meaning of the Byronic influence—had to be defined and credited. What emerged was an interpretive critical biography that takes for granted earlier, exhaustive studies, that places chronology at the service of causality, that risks partiality in the interest of emphasis.

Because the nineteenth-century world in which Charlotte Brontë lived is the world which we have ourselves inherited, I discovered that to diagram the process of Brontë's growth was also to explore explicitly formations of the modern female psyche. It was to indicate the nature of the feminist struggle through which men and women today define themselves—both in support and opposition. In our families, in our society, in our political and sexual lives, we are still the victims of the patriarchal forces which protect our economic structures. We continue to reenact our roles in the romantic mythology which embodies and validates that pervasive power. And as we too strive for autonomous definition, we see ourselves reflected in different aspects of Brontë's struggle.

It was for these reasons that I came to write this "life."

But, seeking ostensibly for the "truth," attempting to create a new version of an old literary form, I find that I have done what so many of us always seem to do. I have pursued my own shadow through the beckoning recesses of another's mind, hoping to discover its substance at the journey's end.

Charlotte Brontë: The Self Conceived

CHAPTER ONE

Survival

> Lonely as I am—how should I be if Providence had never given me courage to adopt a career—perseverance to plead through two long, weary years with publishers till they admitted me? How should I be with youth past—sisters lost—a resident in a moorland parish where there is not a single educated family? In that case I should have no world at all: the raven, weary of surveying the deluge and without an ark to return to, would be my type. As it is, something like a hope and motive sustains me still. I wish all your daughters—I wish every woman in England had also a hope and motive: Alas, there are many old maids who have neither.[1]

*C*HARLOTTE BRONTË wrote these words at the age of thirty-three at Haworth Parsonage. The same house still sits atop the Yorkshire hills like a ship amidst huge storm-tossed waves. The family with whom she had voyaged—her mother, her brother, her four sisters, had perished. The bodies of all but one lay in the churchyard beyond. No wonder then that she should summon an image of deluge; of herself a raven-survivor. In six years time, like the wearied raven forced to descend, she too would drown.

The Brontë story is mythic in its power, a dramatization of personal needs and historical forces purged of the prosaic. The children—Maria, Elizabeth, Charlotte, Branwell, Emily, and Anne—are proper tragic figures, products of their society, yet

---

1. Charlotte Brontë to W. S. Williams, July 3, 1849. *The Brontës, Their Lives, Friendships and Correspondence in Four Volumes,* ed. Thomas J. Wise and J. Alexander Symington (New York: Oxford University Press, 1933), III, 6. All subsequent references will be given as "Wise and Symington."

strangers to it. The moors of Yorkshire, with their desolate expanse of heath and sky, are their milieu: the wild beauty well-earned by that company of children who could endure the harsh, intemperate seasons.

A woman of twenty-five, Charlotte Brontë wrote:

> My home is humble and unattractive to strangers, but to me it contains what I shall find nowhere else in the world—the profound, the intense affection which brothers and sisters feel for each other when their minds are cast in the same mold, their ideas drawn from the same source—when they have clung to each other from childhood, and when disputes have never sprung up to divide them. . . .[2]

The parsonage and the moors were the only haven that the young Brontës were to know. In the rest of the world, even in Haworth—the town in which they were set apart as the minister's children—they were insecure and alien. Their fierce devotion to one another and to their home grew out of their isolation and confirmed it. Virtually from infancy, they looked to one another for nurturance and support. Their inability to confess to—perhaps even to allow themselves to feel—the common hostilities of sibling rivalry, locked them into painful dependencies on one another which imprisoned even as they solaced.

Their mother, little more than a shadowy presence in their lives, was a crucial force in death. She bore six children in seven years and in the year and a half which followed Anne's birth, she was bedridden. As Elizabeth Gaskell, Charlotte's biographer, was told by a family servant:

> She was not very anxious to see much of her children, probably because the sight of them, knowing how soon they were to be left motherless, would have agitated her too much. So the little things clung quietly together, for their father was busy in his study and in his parish, or with their mother, and they took their meals alone; sat reading, or whispering low, in the "children's study" or wandered out on the hillside, hand in hand.[3]

One can only imagine how traumatic an effect Mrs. Brontë's long painful illness must have had upon them. And the mystery sur-

---

2. To Henry Nussey, May 9, 1841. Wise and Symington, I, 232.
3. Elizabeth Gaskell, *The Life of Charlotte Brontë* (New York: Dutton, 1971), p. 30. First published 1857.

rounding it, the connection which they might have drawn linking their mother's severe abdominal pains, her childbearing, and her death[4] would have created severe and lasting anxieties of which Charlotte's own lifelong fear of childbearing is but a single example. The actual effect which their mother's death had upon the children's lives—the way in which it touched their minds—is nowhere recorded. But one feels the naiveté of the critics and biographers who have brushed those effects aside, observing that the children were too young and had known their mother too little to have been much moved by the event. The fact that Charlotte speaks only once of Mrs. Brontë in her copious correspondence and journals[5] does not confirm the idea that the memory of her death and dying was so trivial that it could be easily dismissed, but rather suggests that it was so painful that it had to be repressed.

The greater ordeal was still to come. It was the oldest child, Maria, who took their mother's place. She was the "best" of these "good, quiet children": intellectually gifted, humane, and kind; a saint in the judgment of her brother and sisters, adored by her father, enshrined by Charlotte in the portrait of Helen Burns in *Jane Eyre,* a recurrent figure in Branwell's poetry. Her death at the age of twelve (Elizabeth died just a few weeks later) meant to the others the loss of a second mother, better known than the first, perhaps more familiarly—more consciously—loved: a shining ideal, forever fixed, perfect and unattainable.

4. This connection is supported by a recent essay written by Philip Rhodes, an English gynecologist. In "A Medical Appraisal of the Brontës" (*Brontë Society Transactions,* 16, 2 [1971], 102), Dr. Rhodes questions the diagnosis of stomach cancer which was reported by Mrs. Gaskell and accepted ever since. He suggests that it was more likely that Mrs. Brontë died as a result of some chronic disorder consequent upon her rapid childbearing, probably chronic pelvic sepsis together with increasing anemia.

5. When she was thirty-four, Charlotte wrote to her closest friend, Ellen Nussey (February 16, 1850. Wise and Symington, III, 18.)

A few days since, a little incident happened which curiously touched me. Papa put into my hands a little packet of letters, telling me that they were Mamma's, and that I might read them. I did read them, in a frame of mind I cannot describe. The papers were yellow with time, all having been written before I was born. It was strange now to peruse, for the first time, the records of a mind whence my own sprang; and most strange and at once sad and sweet, to find that mind of a truly fine, pure, and elevated order. They were written to Papa before they were married. There is a rectitude, a refinement, a constancy, a modesty, a sense of gentleness about them indescribable. I wish she had lived, and that I had known her.

Again, one imagines. The experience would have been most painfully endured by Charlotte. She and Emily had been sent with the two older girls to the Clergy Daughters' School at Cowan's Bridge. She had watched with full comprehension (the proof is in *Jane Eyre*) Maria's stoical suffering under the harsh regimen there. She had seen her sister's health decline until even the neglectful authorities could no longer ignore the signs of danger. Maria was sent home in the last stages of tuberculosis and died in May. Charlotte was spared the anguished end of the ordeal which Branwell had to bear, but by the time the news of Maria's death had reached Cowan's Bridge, a typhoid epidemic had broken out and Charlotte saw Elizabeth stricken. Now Elizabeth too was sent home, only to die weeks later.

Surrounded by scores of desperately ill children, many of them dying; having to come to terms alone with the fact of Maria's death, the probability of Elizabeth's, the possibility of her own, Charlotte was thrust into a nightmare world of searing, ambivalent feeling. Impotence before circumstances which she could in no way control. Responsibility as the oldest surviving child. And then the guilt and shame which are always the companions of mourners who have been the voyeurs of disaster. Guilt and shame experienced toward the dead whom one has not helped, whom one has allowed to die, whom one has betrayed by remaining alive.[6] The special guilt that Charlotte must have felt at her own pleasure when the epidemic brought to the well children—to her—an alleviation of the usual dreadful routine: a chance to play all day out of doors (as Jane Eyre does) while others inside are dying.

It was an extraordinary burden to carry: this guilt of a child who, having wished for the death of a parent (as most children at some time do) mistakes the wish for the cause. That guilt compounded by the death of a sibling—an older, much admired, always successful sibling who has first competed for nurturance and then herself becomes a nurturing figure, a surrogate mother.

6. See Robert J. Lifton, *History and Human Survival* (New York: Random House, 1970), p. 128. Lifton explains: "For the survivor can never inwardly simply conclude that it was logical and right for him, and not others, to survive. Rather . . . he is bound by an unconscious perception of organic social balance which makes him feel that his survival was made possible by others' deaths: if they had not died, he would have had to, and if he had not survived, someone else would have."

This second death confirming the sense of unworthiness initially aroused by the symbolic rejection of the first. That sense of unworthiness never to be erased.

Guilt, shame, unworthiness, anxiety, insecurity: all were projected onto the hallucinatory visitations from the dead which Charlotte endured throughout her life and recorded in her juvenile fiction, in her journals, and in the novels of her maturity. They are reflected in the recurrent "survivor's dream" which she described as a child to her close friend, Mary Taylor, and which Mary Taylor described, after Brontë's death, to Elizabeth Gaskell.

> She used to speak of her two elder sisters, Maria and Elizabeth, who died at Cowan Bridge. I used to believe them to have been wonders of talent and kindness. She told me, early one morning, that she had just been dreaming: she had been told that she was wanted in the drawing room, and it was Maria and Elizabeth. I was eager for her to go on, and when she said there was no more, I said, "But go on! *make it out.* I know you can." She said she would not; she wished she had not dreamed, for it did not go on nicely; they were changed; they had forgotten what they used to care for. They were very fashionably dressed, and began criticising the room, etc.[7]

While anxiety and fear found expression in dream and transmutation in the games and imaginings of childhood, the events which had given them form remained too threatening to be directly faced.

Reunited at Haworth after their sisters' deaths, the four children began their long journey of escape. Experience had taught them to expect the worst of an alien and hostile world. Never after would they be able to meet strangers with anything less than suspicion. Agonizingly shy and withdrawn, they clung together, drawing a circle round themselves. Inside its limits they allowed their minds to stretch, their imaginations to grow. Here they revealed themselves to one another in a fantasy language which they alone could understand.

The boundaries of that world were inviolable. Even those who shared their home were excluded. There was an aunt, a strict Calvinist, who came to live with them. Possessed of a rigid and

7. Wise and Symington, I, 91.

unyielding nature, she attempted to take charge of their souls but succeeded primarily in looking after their bodies. Of their emotional conflicts, of their intellectual and creative achievements, she seems to have remained largely ignorant. In their servant, Tabby, they found an affectionate but necessarily distanced presence. Only their father touched them in an important way—and only he had a formative influence upon their secret world and its development.

Like many another Victorian patriarch, Patrick Brontë bound his children to him by the strength of a fiercely dominating personality balanced by an undeniable capacity for love. His wit amused them, his intelligence stimulated them, his reading and writing shaped their aspirations and formed their tastes. An Irishman by birth, the eldest of ten children, Patrick had been carried to Cambridge by ambition and curiosity; to the Anglican ministry by ambition and self-discipline. He was suited to his profession by unwavering principles and a moral fiber which was durable. Of more importance to his children, there was in him as well the shadow of a failed writer. In the nine years of his marriage, he had published a volume of religious poetry and two didactic and sentimental novels intended for the "common reader." The writer's need and aspiration had to some degree been his. The imaginative territory which his son and daughters explored was terrain over which he himself had wandered.

In matters of education, Patrick Brontë had apparently been influenced by the theories of Rousseau. He believed in the importance of freedom and the advantages of an active out-of-door life. While he served as the children's tutor, he left them largely to their own devices—attending to his ministerial duties, taking his meals by himself.[8] He shared with them, to an unusual extent, his views, his journals, and his library. Although he was a committed Tory, he nevertheless reserved the right to follow his own conscience and reach his own conclusions. To be informed of both sides of every issue he subscribed to Tory and Whig newspapers. His own love of independence and his sympathy with the working classes had liberalized his political views.[9] He was more

8. Throughout his life, Patrick Brontë ate his meals alone, apparently because of a persistent and probably nervous stomach disorder.

9. It is interesting to note that Brontë supported the first reform bill of 1832. His position was too liberal for his children—they opposed it—but that

flexible too in sexual matters than was common for his time and spoke up vigorously against the unjust treatment of women. He went so far on one occasion as to advise an ill-used wife to leave her husband.[10]

From conversations with their father, the children acquired a love of debate and argument. From him they derived a sense of the centrality of politics in human affairs, the appeal of the military, the lure of power. In his library they first discovered those works which helped form their adolescent interests and fantasies: Homer and Virgil in the original (although only Branwell, the son, was educated in the classics), Milton's works, Johnson's *Lives of the Poets,* Thompson's *Seasons,* Goldsmith's *History of Rome,* Hume's *History of England,* Scott's *Life of Napoleon Bonaparte,* and the works of Cowper, Southey, and—most importantly—of Byron.[11] It was their father also who catalyzed their creative energies, presenting a set of wooden soldiers to Branwell in June 1826, just one year after the deaths of Maria and Elizabeth. The soldiers comprised the dramatis personae for the games, plays, and ultimately the "Glass-Town" literature which first preoccupied and then obsessed the Brontës into adulthood.

Fannie Ratchford has provided an invaluable chronicle of the development of the Brontë juvenilia from the little plays and magazines produced by the four children in collaboration with one another to the sophisticated collections of stories and poems which belonged to two different kingdoms separately conceived: Angria, invented by Charlotte and Branwell, and Gondal, created by Emily and Anne.[12] (The two collaborations determined the configuration of division and companionship which extended to adulthood. Charlotte stood outside of her sisters' secret lives as they were excluded from hers and Branwell's.) The children's fantasies were focused here. Their needs and deprivations found

---

they were influenced by his open-mindedness is suggested in their later writings, most notably in *Shirley.*

10. Annette Hopkins, *The Father of the Brontës* (Baltimore: Johns Hopkins Press, 1958), p. 63. Hopkins also points out that in the baptismal records Patrick Brontë inserted the full parentage of each child instead of indicating just the father's name, as was the custom.

11. Winifred Gerin, *Charlotte Brontë, The Evolution of Genius* (New York: Oxford University Press, 1967), p. 24.

12. Fannie Ratchford, *The Brontë's Web of Childhood* (New York: Russell and Russell, 1964).

form in wishes and dreams which could be shared and structured into art. Mary Taylor, writing of Charlotte's preference for imaginative activity over all other forms of play, explained the process to Gaskell:

> The habit of "making out" interests for themselves, that most children get who have none in actual life was very strong in her. The whole family used to "make out" histories, and invent characters and events. I told her sometimes they were like growing potatoes in a cellar. She said, sadly, "Yes! I know we are!"[13]

Angria had as its hero no lesser a man than Arthur Wellesley, the first duke of Wellington. He was adored by all the children and had long occupied a central position in Charlotte's imagination. She admired him profoundly for his self-control and strong sense of duty, qualities she wished that she could herself possess. But Byron, the second hero who dominated the imaginative lives at Haworth, expressed deeper aspirations; the repressed needs and feared passions of her "other" self. The two men established the polar possibilities of definition both for her and for the heroines of her novels, serving functions not unlike those served by Rochester and St. John Rivers for Jane Eyre.

II

The children's first memorable contact with Byron has been traced back to August, 1825, when, in a *Blackwood's* review of Parry's *Last Days of Lord Byron,* they first learned the circumstances of the poet's death and began fitting his legend into the pattern of the Napoleonic wars which had already kindled their imaginations. From this time "Byron's name was synonomous with everything that was forbidden and daring."[14]

By the time she was thirteen, Charlotte was fully acquainted with Byron's work. In 1829, after reading Branwell's copy of "Childe Harold," she modeled Arthur Wellesley (also known as the Marquis of Douro and the Duke of Zamorna), the duke of Wellington's eldest son, after her understanding of Byron's character. By her fifteenth year, when she was well into her adoles-

13. Gaskell, p. 68.
14. Winifred Gerin, "Byron's Influence on the Brontës," *Keats-Shelley Memorial Bulletin,* 17 (1966), 2.

cence, Zamorna had completely replaced his father as the hero of Angria. This description of him, written several years later, leaves no question about Zamorna's ancestry:

> His figure was toweringly, overbearingly lofty, molded in statue-like perfection, and invested with something I cannot describe—something superb, impetuous, resistless. His hair was intensely black, curled luxuriantly, but the forehead underneath . . . looked white and smooth as ivory. His eyebrows were black and broad, but his long eye-lashes and large clear eyes were deep sepia brown. . . . The upper lip was very short—Grecian—and had a haughty curl. . . . At the first glance I discerned him to be a military man.[15]

As the description suggests, it was Zamorna's sexual magnetism rather than his military exploits that most interested Charlotte, even if the latter were Branwell's primary concern.

In fact, the collaboration between brother and sister had taken an interesting turn during their adolescent years. Branwell continued to take the lead, as he had always done, outlining elaborately complicated plots which Charlotte was able to validate through her growing mastery of characterization. Both were preoccupied with power. But while Branwell's fantasies were still concerned with martial accomplishments, political intrigue, and the building of empires, Charlotte fantasized about social and psychological interaction in a world of wits and beautiful women; about courtships and, increasingly, about seduction and adultery. As Branwell was enraptured by the possibilities of political power, so Charlotte became obsessed with the implications of sexual domination. If Branwell saw that Zamorna's courage and treacherous cunning made it inevitable that he could conquer kingdoms, Charlotte perceived that his capacity for feeling would make it impossible for women to resist him. In creating their characters they were responding to the Byronic vision which represented the Zeitgeist of their time. To understand the effect that Byron had upon them, one must understand this larger cultural phenomenon.

The Byronic hero and Lord Byron the poet—the vision and the man—were inseparable in the public mind. From the time of

15. "My Angria and the Angrians," October 1834, Brontë Parsonage Museum.

Childe Harold's publication in 1812, Byron was—first in England and then throughout Europe—the embodiment of the Romantic movement. In his life and in his work he was its spokesman and its symbol. He represented the possibility of escaping from or rebelling against the pressures exerted by a society in the process of radical change: an increasingly industrialized society which decreasingly valued the individual. It was a society which—as major twentieth-century psychohistorians have pointed out—thwarted the satisfaction of those needs most fundamental to personal happiness: the pleasure principle placed at the service of the performance principle.[16] It was a society which purchased the souls of its members with the metallic coinage of materialism. More spiritual ideals of self-realization would yield to a narrower standard of physical self-interest. The Victorians experienced the full effects of industrialization. The Romantics simply felt the first waves of instability and reacted to them by attempting to assert the ascendancy of the individual and the primacy of feeling. Byron was the supreme embodiment of this effort, standing not only against a dehumanized system of labor but also against traditionally repressive religious, social, and familial institutions. He spoke not only to members of the aristocracy and upper-middle class who shared his educational background and condoned his sexual habits. He spoke also to members of the burgeoning lower-middle class—the small capitalists, tradesmen, and clerks—to all who felt themselves alienated, wasted, and unfulfilled.

Club-footed from birth, morose in public, temperamental and mercurial, Byron seemed to bear the ominous mark of Cain. A descendent of two eccentric and dissolute aristocratic families,

16. See, for example, Sigmund Freud, *Civilization and Its Discontents*, trans. and ed. James Strachey (New York: W. W. Norton, 1961); Herbert Marcuse, *Eros and Civilization* (New York: Vintage Books, 1955); Norman O. Brown, *Life Against Death* (New York: Vintage Books, 1959). Marcuse explains, ". . . the necessity of repression, and of the suffering derived from it, varies with the maturity of civilization, with the extent of the achieved rational mastery of nature and of society. Objectively, the need for instinctual inhibition and restraint depends on the need for toil and delayed satisfaction. . . . (In) the system of institutional authority characteristic of mature civilization, domination becomes increasingly impersonal, objective, universal, and also increasingly rational, effective, productive. At the end, under the rule of the fully developed performance principle, subordination appears as implemented through the social division of labour itself. . . . Society emerges as a lasting and expanding system of useful performances . . ." (pp. 80–81)

living a profligate life while identifying himself with liberal causes (the Nottingham weavers during the Luddite uprisings, Catholic emancipation; lastly, Greek independence) Byron appeared to be divorced from class and even national affiliation. Pursued by women everywhere he went, dropping mistresses like pocket-handkerchiefs, he dared finally to commit the one moral crime which his society fantasized about but would not forgive. He maintained an incestuous relationship with his half-sister, Augusta Leigh, and flaunted it before his wife and friends. Divorced and ostracized, forced to leave England, Byron spent the last eight years of his life living promiscuously and writing in Switzerland and Italy, dying finally in Greece, where he had gone to join the rebellion against the Turks.

Byron's hero was modeled upon the role which the poet himself had chosen to play. Misanthropic and adventurous, he also defined himself as rebel. He not only rejected the ugliness of the new world he saw coming to birth, but also the old repressions of the world from which it had descended. Central to his rebellion was the assertion of a self freed from external limitations and control. Without religion, he proclaimed himself his own God, master of his own fate. Living as an outlaw, he rejected society's claims and rewards, even its punishments. Emerging from a mysterious past, he was without apparent familial ties, most notably, perhaps, without a father. Promethean, he was courageous, proud and ambitious, and asserted as his primary power his ability to shape his own destiny, even if that destiny was death.

Although the Byronic hero is a radical and rebel, he cannot be a revolutionary. Having rejected his culture he exists in isolation. All of his efforts refer essentially to himself: to his own feelings, his own sensations, his own capacities. Because his isolation is unbearable, he undertakes the romantic quest: to resolve aesthetically or erotically the subject-object conflict—obliterating the division between the "I" and the "not-I" by fusing the two in a redemptive state of feeling. To those who were part of Byron's cult, the drive for integration was focused in eroticism. The search by the self for "the other" was intended to culminate in physical and spiritual union. But the effort did not advance beyond narcissism. The result was quite different from the ideal. Instead of the oceanic feeling which allows the self to negate and transcend its own limits, union is realized through a pattern of domination in which the ego masters and absorbs "the other." Metaphysical striving acquires a political form. Questions concerning the structure of reality and modes of knowing are resolved into far more concrete problems of dominance and submission. That such relationships will be sadomasochistic to varying degrees seems inevitable since they are defined by subjugation and the exercise of power.[17] It is in this nexus that the work of Brontë and Byron is joined. The myth of romantic love articulated—as Byron himself acted out and as Brontë's life and works archetypically captured—the sexual fantasies shared by middle- and upper-class men and women. Once scrutinized, the myth discloses those economic and social forces which determine the nature of psychosexual interaction.

The advent of industrialization and the growth of the middle class was accompanied by a more diffuse yet more virulent form of patriarchy than any that had existed before. As men became uniquely responsible for the support of the family, women became "possessions," identified with their "masters' " wealth. The status of the male owner derived from the extent of his woman's leisure time and the degree of her emotional and physical dependence upon him. Sexual relationships followed a similar pattern of dominance and submission. Male power was affirmed through an egoistic, aggressive, even violent sexuality. Female sexuality was passive and self-denying. The woman, by wilfully defining herself as "the exploited," as "victim"; by seeing herself as she was reflected in the male's perception of her, achieved the only kind of control available to her. Mutuality was extraordinarily difficult, if not impossible, to achieve.[18]

17. Gregory Zilborg observes: "I might suggest that future researches into the psychology and origin of the economic factors of human culture might very well prove that property originated in the sadistic act of overcoming the free mother—women may be considered chronologically the first piece of property, in the true sense of the word, in that sense which Ward defined with unique simplicity and brilliance: Property is possession beyond one's immediate needs. It was the possession beyond his immediate, purely sexual needs that man established over women." "Masculine and Feminine: Some Biological and Cultural Aspects," in *Psychoanalysis and Women,* ed. Jean Baker Miller, M.D. (Baltimore: Penguin, 1973), p. 119.

18. The conflicts involved in this extremely complex sadomasochistic relationship are brilliantly, if only half-consciously, revealed in Samul Richardson's mid–eighteenth-century novel, *Clarissa.* Written when the forces of industrialization were beginning to exert pressure upon religious, sexual, social, and familial values, *Clarissa* contains, significantly enough, the first of the

So the reasons for Byron's symbolic importance begin to emerge. The ideal by which Byron attempted to define his life expressed not only personal but collective longings for psychic and social liberation. But the reality of his circumstances betrayed the potency of the forces which obstructed freedom and thwarted realization. In his own relationships with women, and in the relationships which he created for his heroes, the poet expressed the complex destructive and self-destructive attitudes which define romantic love. In him the desire to obliterate the boundaries between the "I" and the "not-I," between the self and "the other," is channeled by a culturally formed and supported sexism. For all his rebelliousness, he was the product of his society—prey to its patriarchal neuroticism. He was open in his disdain of women. He not only avowed his dislike of them, he acted out that dislike in sadistic behavior that ranged from the subtle to the absurd.[19] If he did not himself pursue women, he did rely on their pursuit of him. His vanity was fed by their admiration, but the more they admired, the more he despised them for the weakness they betrayed. The eroticism they offered was not desired because it yielded knowledge of "the other," thereby expanding the limits of the self, but because, in the stimulation of his own sensibilities, he was better able to feel himself feeling. Certainly he preferred the company of men. Here were his intellectual and spiritual equals. And if rumors of homosexuality surrounded him, that reality would have been more appropriate than ironic. If love as mutuality was in fact at all possible it was most likely to be realized with others of his own sex. If love of himself were primary, homosexuality was one expression of that narcissism.

In all likelihood, then, Byron's incestuous love of his sister represented more than a simple act of rebellion: a form of the

---

proto-Byronic heroes—Lovelace. This emphasizes the fact that Byron himself served to focus forces which had been actively at work in the culture for a substantial period of time.

19. Speaking of Byron's attitudes toward women at the time of the publication of *Childe Harold*, Leslie Marchand observes: ". . . he had always been most successful with girls below his intellectual level, with those who had flattered his ego and looked up with awe at his title, and he had come to have a kind of oriental scorn of women as creatures in no way capable of sharing a man's thoughts or feelings." (*Byron: A Biography* [New York: Alfred A. Knopf, 1957], I, 330.)

romantic commitment to the forbidden. It was a perfect compromise, expressive of the romantic impulse, linking implied ideals of narcissism with those of heterosexual love. In his union with Augusta Leigh, Byron was in fact striving to achieve union with himself: attempting to become purely self-dependent by possessing his past in his present, affirming a more complete identity by enveloping and containing his other, complementary self. But to incorporate "the other" is also after all to negate it. No space remains for the female. She can either allow herself to be devoured or she can retreat into isolation.

A form of love which is inseparable from annihilation must threaten the lover as well as the beloved. Byron betrays his fear of his own destructive power when he writes of one of his mistresses:

> . . . the Guiccioli is going into a consumption. Thus it is with everything and everybody for whom I feel anything like a real attachment . . . I never even could keep alive a dog that I liked or liked me.[20]

The romantic rebellion which has as its urge the desire to reorder reality in a transcendent unity has as its effect sadism or solipsism. Erotic love, ideally the neutralizer of power, proves instead to be power's most lethal weapon.

The road that points to freedom is paved in fantasy. At its end lies disillusionment. The rebel builds the guillotine for his own beheading. Byron, the symbol of romanticism, was ironically a neoclassicist. His affinity was with the eighteenth century. Theoretically searching for an antiauthoritarian system of values, Byron's great giftedness was as a satirist. In assuming this essentially conservative stance, he wedded himself to his society—criticizing but never denying it altogether. It is not surprising that his life was characterized by frustration, cynicism, and remorse, that his death was a gesture toward liberty and a veiled suicide. He mounted the revolution and betrayed it, reenacting the plight of most revolutionaries who are defeated by their identification with the power they strive to overthrow.[21]

20. Quoted in Peter Quennell, *Byron in Italy* (London: Collins, 1951), p. 156.

21. "In every revolution, there seems to have been a historical moment when the struggle against domination might have been victorious—but the moment passed. An element of *self-defeat* seems to be involved in this dynamic

As children, Charlotte and Branwell participated in Byron's mass romantic dream-wish. Identifying with the striving, they were unaware of the contradictions. They adored the hero and never tried to analyze the man. For them, the heroic fantasy of romantic love concretized in their writing was particularly powerful. They were not able to recognize its dangers because they had minimal contact with a reality that could offer a corrective perspective. To disengage themselves from delusion, they would have had to understand and control in their own lives the social and psychosexual forces which were acting through them. For Branwell, this was impossible. His identification with the romantic hero was immediate, total, and ultimately fatal. His self-destruction of course assumed a parodic form: he was a pitiable Manfred. But although his conflict was domesticated, its outlines were familiar and its end predictable. He was trapped in the mythological mode as Byron had been himself. Charlotte's problem was more complex. Because she was female, her identification with their beloved, Byronic Zamorna was equivocal. She could not, after all, *be* the fantasized hero. She was, in fact, "the other." The dream by which she was fascinated could not contain her. The need for psychic expression propelled her from the paralysis of myth into the surging reality of history and the complexities of society. For her, the creation of Angria initiated a long and painful process of self-investigation which did finally yield to discovery and knowledge: to a true if tragic freedom.

III

Branwell was a victim of the romantic illusion as it was molded by the mythologies of Victorian life—for the Brontë family, with all its eccentricities, was prophetically Victorian in its

---

(regardless of the validity of such reasons as the prematurity and inequality of forces). In this sense, every revolution had also been a betrayed revolution.

Freud's hypothesis on the origin and the perpetuation of guilt feelings elucidates, in psychological terms, this sociological dynamic: It explains the 'identification' of those who revolt with the power against which they revolt." (Marcuse, pp. 82–83.)

Fred Weinstein and Gerald Platt, in *The Wish to Be Free* (Berkeley: University of California Press, 1969), concern themselves with the insecurities that naturally accompany an attack on a contemporary system of values and the anxieties which are part of an attempt to build a system of values from within.

structures and patterns of interaction. He was the gifted only son of a powerful, domineering father: the adored only brother of three adoring sisters:

> If Branwell Brontë was born with an extravagant sense of the high destiny he could achieve, he was not alone in holding it; it was fostered and fanned by all those who stood nearest to him and who, from the beginning, made a distinction in his treatment from that of his sisters. In this, it should hastily be added, his sisters themselves wholeheartedly shared, neither questioning nor seeking to undermine the position accorded their only brother. The little girls might receive the petting of servants, the confidence and attention of their father, but it was Branwell who was the main purpose, the fond hope and pride of that bereaved father's heart.[22]

As in most Victorian families, the girls did not share in the freedom and absence of discipline which characterized their brother's childhood and adolescence. Theirs was the awareness and habitual practice of duties and obligations thought to be appropriate to the lives of women.

> . . . any one passing by the kitchen door, might have seen (Emily) studying German out of an open book, propped up before her, as she kneaded the dough; but no study, however interesting, interfered with the goodness of the bread, which was always light and excellent. Books were, indeed, a very common sight in that kitchen; the girls were taught by their father—theoretically and by their aunt practically, that to take part in the household work was, in their position, women's simple duty; but in their careful employment of time, they found many an odd five minutes for reading while watching the cakes, and managed the union of two kinds of employment better than King Alfred.[23]

What they could only do in their spare time and what they could only fantasize about, Branwell—the male, the son, the brother—could become. He could be their effective agent in the world, well worth the sacrifice of personal achievement.

From his family and his admiring friends in the little village of Haworth, Branwell derived a sense of his own position which

22. Winifred Gerin, *Branwell Brontë* (London: Thomas Nelson and Sons, 1961), p. 2.
23. Gaskell, p. 91.

was as inflated as the self-image which he synthesized from his reading and writing. Neither was tested externally. Although he, as the Brontë male, was always intended to represent the others in the active competitive world beyond the parsonage, he was the least fitted to venture outside the threshold of his imagination. While his sisters had been forced—first at Cowan Bridge, later at Miss Wooler's school at Roe Head—to measure their illusions against reality, Mr. Brontë would not trust Branwell's education to any direction but his own. The course of study he followed emphasized the heroic example and the military ideal. The father's reverence for the real and fictitious heroes of history and literature was echoed in the son's admiration of Napolean and Wellington. That Branwell's reading provided his private and literary fantasies is suggested by the titles of his first two "books": "My Battell Book," written when he was nine, and "History of the Rebellion in my Army," a product of his eleventh year. The themes of these early attempts reemerged in more complex and intricate forms in his adolescent fiction, but they never really changed. In a similar way, his heroes remained much the same throughout his literary career, although his identification with them became more intimate as his worldly ambitions were thwarted.

One is forced to ask how this isolated, protected boy—stunted in size, ignorant of the sophisticated world—could formulate in personal terms the heroic ideal which was fundamental to his concept of masculine effectiveness. The compromise he reached with the help of his family might seem at first to have been eminently sensible. He focused his hopes on his giftedness as an artist. Like his sisters, he aspired to being a painter. Unlike them, his aspirations were taken seriously—more seriously than his talent warranted. The admiration of his family had weakened him for the task of testing himself against the formidable model which had been defined by them and by his own illusions. To match this model he would have had to expand himself tenfold. The fragile threads with which we are all bound together frayed through as Branwell first rubbed against the abrasive world outside.

To sacrifice for his success was, of course, part of the responsibility of the women. His aunt drew from her small store of savings an amount which would be adequate to subsidize his journey to London and his education there at the schools of the Royal Academy of Arts. It was also part of Charlotte's professed obligation to take upon herself the hateful task of governess-teacher at Roe Head, so that she could contribute to Branwell's support.

But others' sacrifices could not substitute for personal self-confidence. How unheroic and sad a tale it is: this history of Branwell's brief stay in London, his inability to present for judgment the best of his work which he had brought with him: his inability to do anything, apparently, but drink away his money, miserably aware of his own failure and cowardice.[24] How unlike his revered heroes he must have felt when he returned to the security of his home—to his father, his sisters, the friends in his tiny village—telling vague tales about robbers who had set upon him and stolen everything he had. At nineteen he was overwhelmed by the world of possibilities which lay beyond Haworth. He had received a blow from which he would never recover. Failure followed failure. Branwell turned from painting to sculpture. The unsuccessful sculptor became a careless and lazy tutor. The tutor gave way to a debauched railway clerk, ultimately dismissed for a default in his accounts. His last tutoring job culminated in an adulterous affair with his student's mother, raging dismissal by the deceived husband, a horrible decline and miserable death. Through it all Branwell never surrendered his romantic aspirations, although the forms into which they were translated became increasingly parodic: bizarre actualizations of nightmare.

In his obsession with boxing, Branwell continued to express the need to prove himself physically, to find a substitute for heroic exploits and military trials. Gambling provided his only excitement. Alcohol and eventually opium were his primary means of escape. As he became increasingly absorbed in his fantasy-worlds, even his ties to his family were gnawed. His guilt and sense of inadequacy, as well as their disapproval, alienated him. He had lost his childhood and could not find his place as a man:

> Yes—now at last I've reached my native home,
> And all who love me joy to see me come . . .
> I have seen my Father full of honoured days,

---

24. See Gerin's account of this stage of Branwell's life, in *Branwell Brontë*, pp. 95–110.

Whom last I saw adorned with manhood's grace . . .
                . . . I have seen her too
The first I loved on earth—the first I knew—
She who was wont above that very bed
To bend with blessing o'er my helpless head,
I have seen my sister—I have seen them all—
All but myself. They have lost me past recall,
As I have them. And vainly have I come
Three thousand leagues—my Home is not my Home.[25]

Feeling himself inadequate to the roles defined for him as only son and brother and unable to translate his fantasy-self into reality, Branwell increasingly identified with his fictive hero, the rebellious Northangerland—Zamorna's rival, a more mature version of the "Rogue" of his childhood. He could not confront real people or real feelings. Mary Taylor, Charlotte's extraordinary girlhood friend, a feminist and radical, terrified him into flight by falling in love with him. Charlotte writes of the events to Ellen Nussey:

> Did I not once tell you of an instance of a Relative of mine who cared for a young lady till he began to suspect that she cared more for him and then instantly conceived a sort of contempt for her? You know to what I allude—never as you value your ears mention the circumstance—But I have two studies—*you* are my study for the success of a quiet, tranquil character. Mary is my study—for the contempt, the remorse—the misconstruction which followed the development of feelings in themselves noble, warm—generous—devoted and profound—but which being too freely revealed—too frankly bestowed—are not estimated at their real value—God bless her—I never hope to see in this world a character more truly noble—she would *die* willingly for one she loved—her intellect and her attainments are of the very highest standard yet I doubt whether Mary will ever marry.[26]

Mary's love did indeed represent the ultimate threat to the instability of romantic subjectivity: a threat of equality. From her there would have been insupportable expectations and demands.

25. From Branwell's poem, "The Wanderer," later retitled "Sir Henry Tunstall," published in Mrs. Oliphant's *Annals of a Publishing House* (1897) and in the *DeQuincey Memorials* in 1891.
26. November 20, 1840. Wise and Symington, I, 221–22.

It was preferable to him to play at being his own hero,
Northangerland; to indulge, as Byron had, in adulterous games
which never had to be won: to court a woman who—married—
was unattainable, although she held out the promise of ideal
union. And so he "fell in love" with Lydia Robinson, the mother
of the boy he tutored. It was an outrageous business, but he
fiercely seized the opportunity which had been offered him to
give everything to love and, finding it inadequate, to die. The fact
that Mrs. Robinson was apparently incapable of feeling, that
when her husband died she rejected Branwell completely—and
dishonestly—in order to marry an "eligible" old man; this all
demonstrated the self-destructive nature of his delusions and his
behavior.

In the three years that followed his separation from Lydia
Robinson and preceded his death, Branwell was finally able to
bring to fruition in himself a demonic if perversely domestic version of the Byronic hero. Although he plays the part of rebel in
the Brontë myth, his situation was marked by agonizing dependence. He was dependent upon alcohol and opium, the primary
causes of his death. He was dependent upon his sisters who
nursed him, paid his debts, and provided an audience for his
melodrama of disintegration—representing in their horror and
disapproval, the "society" of which he saw himself as victim.
But most of all he was dependent upon his father. Of all the emotional dependencies which he had not been able to outgrow, this
was the most profound:

> I know only that it is time for me to be something when I am
> nothing. That my Father cannot have long to live, and that
> when he dies, my evening, which is already twilight, will
> become night—That I shall then have a constitution so strong
> that it will keep me years in torture and despair when I should
> every hour pray that I might die.[27]

He played at the oedipal battle as he had played at love. There
was never any contest, although there were absurd charades of violent rebellion:

> For some time before his death he had attacks of delirium
> tremens of the most frightful character; he slept in his father's

27. To J. B. Leyland, January 24, 1847. Wise and Symington, II, 124.

room, and he would sometimes declare that either he or his father should be dead before morning. The trembling sisters,
sick with fright, would implore their father not to expose himself to this danger; but Mr. Brontë is no timid man, and perhaps he felt that he could possibly influence his son to some
self-restraint, more by showing trust in him than by showing
fear. The sisters often listened for the report of a pistol in the
dead of night, till watchful eye and hearkening ear grew heavy
and dull with the perpetual strain upon their nerves. In the
mornings young Brontë would saunter out, saying with a
drunkard's incontinence of speech, "The poor old man and I
have had a terrible night of it; he does his best—the poor old
man: but it's all over with me . . ."[28]

The urge to self-destruction was supreme. He died in his father's
arms.

IV

The course which Branwell's life followed profoundly affected Charlotte's personal and artistic development. Initially,
she defined herself almost exclusively in terms of their sym-
biosis. In its way, their relationship was as incestuous as was
Byron's with Augusta Leigh. Theirs was not an incest of body
but of mind: an incest of the imagination. In the intense privacy
of shared fantasy, their identities were fused. Eventually, in order
to free herself, Charlotte would find it necessary to initiate a violent separation which helped to destroy the pattern of Branwell's
self-image and rend the fabric of his life. It seemed that nothing
less than this could release her from the bonds woven by the con-
centration of their familial situation. In the course of their relationship, Charlotte's art offered her the means of exploring and
expressing aspects of her feeling for Branwell which she could
not consciously accept. Their collaborative efforts were tunneled
by dark passageways through which Charlotte burrowed in search
of hidden sources of illumination which could irradiate her consciousness.

Ellen Nussey, reminiscing about the nature of Charlotte's attachment to Branwell when she and Charlotte were adolescents at
the Roe Head School, recalls:

28. Gaskell, pp. 197–98.

> . . . he was *then* a very dear brother, as dear to Charlotte as
> her own soul; they were in perfect accord of taste and feeling,
> and it was mutual delight to be together. . . . . Happy, indeed,
> she then was, in Himself, for she, with her own enthusiasms,
> looked forward to what her brother's great promise and talent
> might effect.[29]

To accept unquestioningly the reality of such complete harmony,
such complacent idolatry, is impossible, although one can accept
the appearance of its existence on a conscious level. The complementary ambivalence which we suspect is indeed found in Charlotte's writing, rather than in her friendly confidences or overt behavior.

Her initial criticisms are humorous and tolerant. At the age of
thirteen Charlotte had produced a volume entitled "Characters of
the Great Men of the Present Time," authored by "Captain
Tree," one of the many male personae she adopted in her juvenile writings. In the characters of Captain Bud and Young Salt
the Rhymer, she drew the first two of a series of satirical portraits
of Branwell, exaggerating those faults with which she was all too
familiar: his tendency to bombast, his poetic effusions, his "tire-
some gravity," his nervous disposition, and inflamed imagination.[30]

By this time Charlotte had taken the first crucial steps toward
independence, but the early recognitions which she made and the
minimal criticism which she allowed herself had little actual effect upon her relationship with Branwell or upon her sense of herself within that relationship. Rational analysis is generally inadequate to psychic defense. Branwell could, after all, be forgiven
his flaws. Flaws—even vices—were central to the romantic concept of masculinity, It was part of the female's role to understand
and overlook. Patience, understanding, tolerance, duty—these
were aspects of the self-abnegating personality which comple-
mented the idolatrous needs of the masculine posture.[31] Much

29. "Reminiscences of Charlotte Brontë by 'E,' " *Scribner's Monthly,* II
(1871), quoted in Wise and Symington, I, 106.

30. Ratchford, pp. 28–29.

31. I have no desire to further the debate about the nature and sources of
female masochism. My intention is not to discuss pathological states but to indicate, in a nonclinical way, general patterns of psychosexual interaction. I accept the point of view of many contemporary psychoanalysts—some of them
quite traditional—who describe masochism as part of an adaptational apparatus

stronger than rational analysis were the social forces which inhib-
ited even normal levels of female aggression and stunted wom-
en's intellectual and psychic growth; forces which defined marriage as women's only appropriate occupation and nurturance as
their only mode of relation.[32]

Already plagued by the survivor's sense of inadequacy and
guilt, Charlotte must easily have fallen prey to masochistic submission. She would have embraced the domination of her father
and brother, accepted the social pressures as interpreted by her
aunt. She would have recognized the wisdom of purchasing love
with self-denial. Then, feeling exploited, she would have turned
the anger back upon herself transmuting it to self-doubt, finding
that preferable to being alienated from those upon whom she was
so painfully dependent.[33]

Both Mary Taylor and Ellen Nussey remembered most viv-
idly their friend's extraordinary "sense of duty"—that quality
she so admired in the duke of Wellington. Both recalled how conscientiously she studied at Roe Head, never playing with the
other children, avoiding competitive activity, ever mindful of the
expense of her education, intent on becoming a governess—a job

rather than an instinctual drive. See, for example: Irving Bieber, M.D., "The
Meaning of Masochism," *American Journal of Psychotherapy*, 7 (1953),
443–48; Marcia Cavell, "Since 1924: Toward a New Psychopathology of
Women," *Woman and Analysis,* ed. Jean Strouse (New York: Grossman,
1974); Helene Deutsch, *The Psychology of Women*, I (New York: Bantam,
1973).

32. John Stuart Mill wrote in 1869 in *The Subjugation of Women:* "All the
moralities tell women that it is their duty and all the current sentimentalities that
it is their nature to live for others; to make complete abnegation of themselves,
and to have no life but in their affections." Women's psychological plight was
intensified by their economic dependence and many social Darwinians (Freudians came later) rationalized the belief in women's biological and intellectual
inferiority.

33. "Masochism is not an instinct; it is an adaptational device. The pain,
or its equivalents, is never sought or self-inflicted for the pleasure in the pain,
per se . . . the apparent pleasure is both a facade to cover up the intense underlying hostile responses consequent to the masochistic act, and an attempt at
self-conviction that the sustained injury is not painful but even pleasurable, to
prevent the expression of this hostility. Hostility always accompanies the masochistic act and is directed toward the feared person from whom the injury is expected and for whom the defensive masochistic act is being performed. Since
this hostility frequently cannot be openly expressed, it feeds back by being
turned inwards and increases his masochism." (Bieber, p. 447.) See also Karen
Horney, "The Problem of Female Masochism," *Psychoanalysis and Women*,
ed. Jean Baker Miller, M.D. (Baltimore: Penguin Books, 1973).

she dreaded except for the fact that it would allow her to maintain herself and help the others, particularly Branwell. Ellen Nussey's account of Charlotte's single attempt at self-assertion, her single public expression of a desire *not* to be "good," is profoundly moving:

> The last day Charlotte was at school she seemed to realize what a sedate, hard-working season it had been to her. She said, "I should for once like to feel *out and out* a school-girl; I wish something would happen. Let us run round the fruit-garden (running was what she never did); perhaps we shall meet some one, or we may have a fine for trespass." She evidently was longing for some never-to-be forgotten incident. Nothing, however, arose from her little enterprise. She had to leave school as calmly and quietly as she had there lived.[34]

Similar fears inform a dream of her early adolescence. It was recorded in one of her "little books," and is described by Lucile Dooley, an early biographer:

> (She speaks) of finding herself in a cave under the ocean, of feeling the terror of the walls heaving and cracking, of the floods about to overwhelm her. Then the scene changed to a desert and a roaring lion rushed toward her while she remained rooted to the spot.[35]

Both the dream and the thwarted schoolgirl experience suggest the extraordinary repression which characterized Charlotte's inner life and colored her behavior—the flimsiness of her defense against the attacks of the external world. The point would seem to be that in these adolescent years Charlotte, overwhelmed by her sense of inadequacy, denied her needs, repressed her anger, and withdrew into a womblike world of fantasy. There in Angria the raging lion of sexuality could be controlled in the same process of sublimation which made all of her desires and anxieties, her guilt and her fear, manageable.

The dream image is compelling. This secret fantasy world became her second Eden and she protected the repressed self which dwelt within it from any contact with a threatening reality. Her

34. Wise and Symington, I, 100.
35. Lucile Dooley, "Psychoanalysis of Charlotte Brontë as a Type of the Woman of Genius," *The American Journal of Psychology*, 31 (July 1920), 243.

tiny, cramped handwriting, virtually unreadable, is the most direct clue to Charlotte's relation to her work. She kept her stories secret from her friends. Only Mary was told of the "magazines" the children wrote and she was never shown any of them.[36] It was Branwell alone who shared this interior space: her vital self. Towards him, free of care and responsibility, beloved, so full of promise in these years, her feelings must have been increasingly ambivalent: resentment tinging, then suffusing, dependence. It was not simply that Branwell, although younger, was, as a male, the one sibling with whom she could not compete. It was not simply that he was the "other," better self who sealed her failure because she could bind herself to him only by denying her own ego. It was also that he further appropriated her identity as her collaborator and became an integral part of the guilt which she experienced in response to the repressed fantasy life of which her writing was an expression.

The important adolescent crisis of feeling occurred when Charlotte returned to the Roe Head School in 1835 at age nineteen, now as a teacher-governess. Emily accompanied her as a student paid for by Charlotte's services. When Emily's homesickness became intense, Charlotte sent her back to Haworth and arranged for Anne to take her place. Despairing as she was herself, sympathetic as she felt to her sister's needs, she was driven still by the same compulsions that had driven her in childhood. As she confessed to Ellen: "I am sad—very sad—at the thoughts of leaving home; but duty—necessity—these are stern mistresses, who will not be disobeyed."[37] But the psychic effort began to have its physical effect. Although Gaskell reports that "Charlotte's life at Miss Wooler's was a very happy one, until her health failed,"[38] the fragments of a journal which Charlotte kept during these years suggested that her profound unhappiness was the cause and not the effect of her failing health.

Mary Taylor, describing Charlotte at this time, says, "She seemed to have no interest or pleasure beyond the feeling of duty, and when she could get, used to sit alone, and "make out."[39] Ostensibly the conflict was as Winifred Gerin describes it: "be-

36. Gaskell, p. 66.
37. July 6, 1835. Quoted in Gaskell, p. 89.
38. Gaskell, p. 91.
39. Gaskell, p. 97.

tween two fiercely striving forces within her soul; the urge to create and the determination to do her duty.''[40] In fact, there was a deeper conflict which derived from Charlotte's intense preoccupation with her fantasy life, with her feelings of guilt at the nature of her creation and, perhaps, with her growing consciousness of her ambivalence toward Branwell.

As always before, Branwell's function was to establish the outlines of their plots, but now Charlotte—isolated, homesick, thwarted—had to wait for occasional letters or infrequent visits to discover how Branwell had disposed of their characters; how he had, on some level, disposed of *her*. In 1836, for example, he writes to tell Charlotte that he has decided to kill Mary Percy, Zamorna's wife. It is the only act of aggression that Zamorna imagines as effective against his treacherous father-in-law, Northangerland. He will, in the gallant Byronic style, reject Mary (whom, he does, of course, love) so that she will die slowly, agonizingly, of a broken heart, while her father helplessly looks on.

It is an ingenious plan, but it overlooks one thing: Charlotte's great devotion to Mary, with whom she closely identifies. Charlotte, writing in her journal of this event, betrays no anger (she never, at this point in their lives, speaks angrily of Branwell). Her tones are those of great sorrow and impotence:

> I wonder if Branwell has really killed the Duchess. Is she dead? Is she buried? Is she alone in the cold earth on this dreary night with the ponderous coffin plate on her breast under the black pavement of a church in a vault closed up with lime and mortar. Nobody where she lies—she who was watched through months of suffering—as she lay on her bed of state. Now quite forsaken because her eyes are closed, her lips sealed and her limbs cold and rigid . . . a set of wretched thoughts are rising in my mind. I hope she's alive still partly because I can't abide to think how hopelessly and cheerlessly she must have died. . . .[41]

Certainly her awareness of the inequality of their collaboration must have intensified her suffering during this period of isolation: a period of three years' separation from the sources of herself.

40. Gerin, *Charlotte Brontë*, p. 100.
41. Roe Head Journal, unpublished. Bonnell Collection: Brontë Parsonage Museum.

I'm just going to write because I cannot help it. . . . There is a
voice, there is an impulse that wakens up that dormant power
which smites torpidity I sometimes think dead. That wind
pouring in impetuous currents through the air, sounding
wildly, unremittingly from hour to hour, deepening its tone as
the night advances, coming not in gusts, but with a rapid, gath-
ering, stormy swell, that wind I know is heard at this moment
far away on the moors at Haworth. Branwell and Emily hear it
and as it sweeps over our house down the church-yard and
round the old church, they think perhaps of me and Anne—
glorious! that blast was mighty. It reminded me of Northangerland, there was something so merciless in the heavier rush, that
made the very house groan as if it could scarce bear this accel-
eration of impetus. O it has wakened a feeling that I cannot satisfy—a thousand wishes rose at its call which must die with
me for they will never be fulfilled. Now I should be agonized if
I had not the dream to repose on—its existence, its forms, its
scenes do fill a little of the craving vacancy.

The reality of the school overwhelms her with its alien nature:

Stupidity the atmosphere, schoolbooks the employment, asses
the society: What in all this is there to remind me of the divine,
silent, unseen land of thought, dim now, and indefinite as the
dream of a dream, the shadow of a shade?

Here at last she can express her anger at the necessity of "doing
her duty," even her "rage," directed overtly at the students, but
derived from her sense of fragmentation:

The Thought came over me: Am I to spend all the best part of
my life in this wretched bondage, forcibly suppressing my rage
at the idleness, the apathy and the hyperbolical and most asi-
nine stupidity of these fat-headed oafs, and on compulsion assuming an air of kindness, patience and assiduity? Must I from
day to day sit chained to this chair, prisoned within these four
bare walls, while these glorious summer suns are burning in
heaven and the year is revolving in its richest glow, and declar-
ing at the close of every summer day, the time I am losing will
never come again.

But the demands of her job are not adequate to explain her inability to write freely. Her physical distance from Haworth is not adequate to explain the psychological distance she experiences.

> And now once more on a dull Saturday afternoon, I sit down to
> try to summon around me the dim shadows, not of coming
> events but of incidents long departed, of feelings, of pleasures,
> whose exquisite relish I sometimes fear it will never be my lot
> again to taste. How few would believe that from sources purely
> imaginary such happiness could be derived! Pen cannot portray
> the deep interest of the scenes, of the continued train of events
> I have witnessed in that little room with the narrow bed and
> bare white-washed walls twenty miles away. What a treasure is
> thought! What a privilege is reverie! I am thankful I have the
> power of solacing myself with the dream of creations whose
> reality I shall never behold. May I never lose that power, may I
> never feel it grow weaker.

Her desire now is to escape: to live in that cave under the ocean—
cherishing the kernel of herself that is the poet-dreamer. She
would share her sanctuary with those "creations," her other
selves, tempting in their unreality. But: "I cannot write of them
except in total solitude I scarce think of them." There is a
forbidden quality about this world that derives from its immoral
and sexual nature: from the adulterous adventures of Northangerland and Zamorna; the passionate desires of her heroines. She can
only allow herself to explore it freely when she is hidden from
public scrutiny—at Haworth, where she doesn't feel the pressure
of the ocean beating against the walls of her cavern.

The letters written to Ellen Nussey from Roe Head during this
period, suggest the extent to which Charlotte was subject to extremes of shame and guilt:

> Don't deceive yourself by imagining I have a bit of real
> goodness about me—my darling. If I were like you, I should
> have my face Zion-ward, though prejudice and error might oc-
> casionally fling a mist over the glorious vision before me—*but
> I am not like you.* If you knew my thoughts, the dreams that
> absorb me, and the fiery imagination that at times eats me up,
> and makes me feel society, as it is, wretchedly insipid, you
> would pity and I dare say despise me.[42]

Later in the same year she writes more specifically of the self-en-
forced repression and its cost:

> . . . I have some qualities that make me very miserable,
> some feelings that you can have no participation in—that few,

42. May 10, 1836. Wise and Symington, I, 139.

very few, people in the world can at all understand. I don't pride myself on these peculiarities. I strive to conceal and suppress them as much as I can; but they burst out sometimes, and then those who see the explosion despise me, and I hate myself for days afterwards. . . .[43]

The crisis of conscience briefly sought religious expression.

I *do* wish to be better than I am. I pray fervently sometimes to be made so. I have stings of conscience, visitings of remorse, glimpses of holy, of inexpressible things, which formerly I used to be a stranger to: it may all die away, and I may be in utter midnight, but I implore a merciful Redeemer, that, if this be the dawn of the Gospel, it may still brighten to a perfect day. . . . I am in that state of horrid, gloomy uncertainty that, at this moment, I would submit to be old, grey-haired, to have passed all my youthful days of enjoyment, and to be settling on the verge of the grave, if I could only therefore ensure the prospect of reconciliation to God, and redemption through His Son's merit.[44]

But Charlotte could return only briefly to the harsh religion of her aunt. The conventional form of sublimation embraced by Ellen was inappropriate to her needs. Surely some relief derived from the journal entries and the agonized letters, all filled with veiled allusions and confessions, guilt, renunciation, and a burning sense of unworthiness: ". . . it seems as if some fatality stood between you and me. I am not good enough for you, and you must be kept from the contamination of too intimate society."[45] But it was only in Angria that the real confrontation could occur. That confrontation's form is reflected in the remarkable change that took place in the fiction during this same time.

Between 1836 and 1839, at Haworth for holidays or brief respites from teaching and governess duties, Brontë wrote her last five Angrian stories, the last of her juvenilia. "Passing Events," "Julia," "Mina Laury," "Henry Hastings," and "Caroline Vernon" were all produced independently. They were completely her own. The tales are crucial to an understanding of Brontë's personal and artistic development, bridging as they do the fantasies of the child-woman and the conscious, self-exploring art of the adult. All are responses to the increased pressure

43. Roe Head, 1836. Wise and Symington, I, 141.
44. Roe Head, 1836. Wise and Symington, I, 140.
45. To Ellen Nussey, December 29, 1837. Quoted in Gaskell, p. 108.

she felt to free herself from her paralyzing relationship with Branwell and to overcome the deeply disturbing effects of her sexual fantasies. All are exercises in confrontation, keyed at different levels, employing varieties of technique. They suggest a new, if painfully achieved, mastery.

To a limited extent, Charlotte explored the confusion of her own feelings about Branwell by developing further, in these stories, Zamorna's relationship with Northangerland, the persona and alter ego which Branwell had adopted in earlier tales. Attempting to out-Byron his Byronic hero, Branwell seems to have projected onto the outrageously immoral Northangerland— Zamorna's father-in-law and treacherous minister—his own guilt at his betrayal of his family's hopes as well as some complex elements of his oedipal conflict. Charlotte emphasizes the tensions of the Zamorna-Northangerland relationship, bending them to her own purpose. She underlines the attraction and repulsion which bind the two men in a reciprocal erosion. She explores the way in which the desire of each for power is thwarted—particularly in Zamorna's case—by a desire for the approval and love of the other. She suggests—most movingly in "Caroline Vernon"— the persistent and troubling effect which loving bonds of the past have upon a deteriorating relationship. The emotional ties and crucial rivalries that so complicate the feelings of parent and child reflect the sibling conflicts she knows so well. Brontë's ability to define these conflicts along with her inability to resolve them, suggest the depth both of her knowledge and her doubt.

In her choice of narrative voice, Brontë attempts a more direct confrontation. In four of the five stories ("Mina Laury" is the only exception) Brontë continues to develop for herself the persona of Zamorna's younger brother, Charles Towneshend: disenfranchized, powerless, a cynical victim of the circumstances of his birth and of Zamorna's heedless cruelty. His introduction dates back to 1833, to a book entitled "Arthuriana," which deals with Charles's critical view of Zamorna. Fannie Ratchford comments on the interest of this work:

> The increasing antagonism between the two reflects a growing conflict within Charlotte herself, as her conscience condemns while her romantic imagination rejoices in the moral lapses of her hero. To satisfy conscience she shaped Lord Charles into a

yet more precise instrument of censure through which she roundly denounces the sin that made her hero glorious.[46]

In these late tales, the earlier tendency intensifies. Charles is alternately repelled and attracted by his tyrannical older brother. The ironic, witty tone which he sometimes adopts in describing Zamorna's exploits, successfully transports the hero from the amorality of the Byronic world to a more recognizable universe of values. The problem is that Brontë cannot maintain this aspect of Charles's tone consistently. An explanation can be found in the nature of her projection. Charles is a part of herself, the superego cast as a man (a woman in this mythology would be merely the shadow of powerlessness). Zamorna is identified with her own deepest desires while also representing Branwell. Her bondage and her unsuccessful attempt at liberation are, in this way, simultaneously expressed. While the chronological relation to Branwell is inverted, the affective relationship is maintained, i.e., although cast as a male, she is—as the *younger* brother—completely vulnerable. Conscience is as inadequate to the economy of her personality as she herself is impotent before Branwell.

At the same time that Brontë is testing the strengths and inadequacies of this most crucial of all her relationships, she is beginning to confront more directly and more analytically the sexual fantasies which have dominated her private life. Writing independently during this period, Brontë for the first time thrusts both Zamorna and Northangerland into a series of explicit and adulterous love affairs.

As always before, fantasies reveal frustrations and yearnings rather than realities. Brontë's circumstances and absence of self-esteem have made her despair of the possibility that she could herself ever in fact be loved. But at the same time that she writes to Ellen Nussey that she will never marry, she is projecting in her stories the illusion of the "great love," the sexuality that overwhelms and solves all of life's problems. The configuration of this illusion is typically masochistic.

> In the constellation of pathological dependency, the individual or individuals depended on are generally perceived by the patient to be supermen or superwomen. The need to endow these

46. Ratchford, p. 71.

individuals with magical power arises in part from the patient's belief that no ordinary mortal like himself can solve his problems or do the things that he is so thoroughly unable to do. Another basis for such endowment is the attempt to recreate a mother or father figure in order to act out or work out problems originally related to these figures.[47]

The pathology which Irving Bieber describes would commonly be found in women raised in patriarchal families, subject to the values of patriarchal societies. Certainly it seems predictable of Brontë—the guilty "survivor," the submissive daughter, the adoring sister—and predictable also of those surrogate selves: her heroines.

The concept of romantic love which informs these late stories is traditionally Byronic. The relationships described are conventionally sadomasochistic. The male is possessive, tyrannical, capable of casual, defensive cruelty. The woman is submissive, adoring, disinterested: deriving pleasure from the pain of an unequal attachment. This passage from "Julia," written in 1837, suggests the dominant elements of the mythology:

> . . . Fury was the feeling at his heart, he desired something that he could not have . . . he imagined the bliss but could not attain it. . . . Recollection showed him her image as he had seen it a hundred times—young, pallid, seldom smiling, waiting his approach in a salon of gorgeous state. . . . The Duke thought he at that hour looked down on her fair cheek resting on his shoulder, met the adoration of her eyes, felt the beating of her heart against his circling arm, saw the pulse flutter on her heaving breast, beheld the folds of satin disclosing her exquisite form. With his whole enthusiastic soul he loved her. . . . It had been to him the delight of his life at times to satisfy and soothe her intense idolatry—he was in the mood for that benevolent office now . . .[48]

Brontë still identifies with her heroine's "intense idolatry" and is appealed to by the selfish domination of the male. But she has begun to struggle against the force of that appeal. She has started to question the desirability of that identification. The mild irony

---

47. Bieber, p. 444. Horney makes a similar observation in "The Problem of Female Masochism," p. 32.

48. "Julia," *Five Novelettes,* ed. Winifred Gerin (London: The Folio Press, 1971), p. 113.

of the final observation ("It had been to him the delight of his life at times to satisfy and soothe her intense idolatry—he was in the mood for that benevolent office now") undercuts the serious romantic tone of the section which precedes it. Psychological analysis has begun to accompany mute sympathy and, although the two attitudes are still maintained in conjunction with one another, the first suggests the direction which will dominate the next three novelettes of this period (1837–39): "Mina Laury," "Caroline Vernon," and "Henry Hastings." These are marked by a maturing consciousness which attempts to bring chaotic emotionality under moral and psychological control.[49]

Although Brontë's sympathies remain confused and ambiguous in these tales, the focus of her interest changes. For example, while she can no longer invest Zamorna and Northangerland with the old romantic idealism, she is still appealed to—as she was in "Julia"—by their masculine selfishness, their cynicism and gratuitous cruelty. But this becomes less important because it is no longer the heroes who occupy her attention. It is the appeal itself. Unable now to embrace wholeheartedly the concept of romantic love, she is still not willing to apply the scorn of Victorian sensibility to her own psychosexual insights. She attempts instead to understand the nature of infatuation. She attempts, in fact, to penetrate the complexities of the masochistic personality, groping for the meaning of her own femininity and sexuality. It is the birth of a consciousness which will stunningly dominate the process of the mature novels.

The unhappiness of Brontë's heroines permeates these stories. They suffer, all of them, because their lovers are unfaithful and capricious. They suffer because they are deserted. But they suffer most of all in their dependence upon Zamorna, a male who, himself profoundly flawed, must define and affirm them. Rejection fulfills their expectations, confirms their doubts. Deprived of sense of self, they cannot accept responsibility: moral choice is impossible (in "Caroline Vernon," for example, we are told that "conscience was feeble"). Love for them cannot be completion. It is a means of self-abnegation, a rationalization of self-denial. Her women are defined by their noble capacity for love; but they never love or esteem themselves. They depend

49. Winifred Gerin cites this change of emphasis in her article, "Byron's Influence on the Brontës," p. 9.

upon their dependency. For them, the greatest horror is not the
physical loss of their lovers—but the psychological loss: to have
autonomy thrust upon them—to be forced back into the void of
the self. Alone, they barely exist. This complex of attitudes is the
female version—the obverse side—of the male romantic experience: the compulsion to see everything through the lens of the
self until all reality disappears in the mysterious terrain of one's
own personality.

In the novelettes, Zamorna distributes his wife and mistresses
about the countryside, placing them in castles where they sit like
so many enchanted princesses before their mirrors, carefully pre-
serving their lover's image of them, until he chooses to return and
bring them back to life. He describes Caroline Vernon's feelings
about her incarceration ("I placed her where she is safe and
happy") with the same painful accuracy that he uses to describe
his wife's devotion:

> When did I ever tyrannize over Mary? Ask herself, ask her at
> this moment, when she is as much exasperated against me as
> she ever was in her life. Tell her to leave me. She will not
> speak to me or look at me, but see what her answer would be to
> that.[50]

Mary Percy, Mina Laury, and Caroline Vernon are not simply
Zamorna's victims. They victimize themselves since they alone
can unlock their castle doors to enter a world of mature responsibility. Charlotte perceives their dilemma but she does not yet
know where they can find the requisite keys.

The ambiguities and conflicts of the female predicament are
more fully explored in "Mina Laury." In fascinating ways, Mina
combines spiritual strength with emotional weakness: independence of mind with psychic submission. Having played an idealized Claire Claremont of Zamorna's Byron, she accompanied
her lover into exile, cared for his child, became part of the political intrigues that surrounded him—a confidante and agent of
those most highly placed: "So clever and earnest was she in all
she said and did that the haughty Aristocrats did not hesitate to
communicate to her often on matters of first rate importance."[51]
But despite the fact that Mina achieves a position of her own, she

50. "Caroline Vernon," *Five Novelettes,* p. 310.
51. "Passing Events," ibid., pp. 43–44.

does not experience herself as an independent entity. She accepts the role she plays as a duty: "Had her life been different, she would not have interfered in such matters. She did not interfere now—she only served."[52] She has known only one lover in her life and to him, to Zamorna, she is completely faithful. She describes the effect upon her of the infatuation which overwhelmed her from the beginning:

> I lost the power of properly appreciating the value of the world's opinion, of discerning the difference between right and wrong.[53]

She defines herself as Zamorna's property. She sees herself as his object. She exists only as she exists for him: denying her own capacities, her potential, her integrity:

> Strong-minded beyond her sex—active, energetic, accomplished in all other points of view—here she was as weak as a child—she lost her identity—her very way of life was swallowed up in that of another.[54]

She accepts, even embraces, humiliation: "Shame and reproach have no effect on me. I do not care for being called a camp follower."[55] It is enough for her to feel "the condescending touch" of Zamorna's hand, to accept his embrace "as a slave ought to take the caress of a Sultan." [56] She lives in a state of thralldom: a woman obsessed.[57]

> She had but one idea—Zamorna, Zamorna—! It had grown up with her—become part of her nature—absence—coldness—to-

52. "Mina Laury," ibid., p. 142.
53. "Mina Laury," p. 147.
54. Ibid., p. 165.
55. "Passing Events," p. 44.
56. Ibid., p. 46.
57. An observation of Freud's is interesting in this context: "The maiden whose desire for love has for so long and with such difficulty been held in check, in whom the influences of environment and education have formed resistances, will take the man who gratifies her longing, and thereby overcomes her resistances, into a close and lasting relationship which will never be available to any other man. The experience brings about a state of thralldom in the woman that assures the man lasting and undisturbed possession of her and makes her able to withstand new impressions and temptations from without." "The Taboo of Virginity," *Collected Papers,* trans. Joan Riviere (New York: Basic Books, 1959), 4, 217. Freud traces this condition of thralldom to the loss of virginity in women and the overcoming of impotence in men (p. 218).

tal neglect—for long periods together—went for nothing—she could no more feel alienation from him than she could from herself—[58]

In fact, it is because she is alienated from herself that she so dreads alienation from him. It is because she experiences herself as incomplete and unworthy that she looks to him to fill her emptiness. She is a completely male-identified woman—"female acquaintance she never sought"—and only to Zamorna, who rejects her autonomy (not to Lord Hartford, for example, who would offer her marriage and adoration) can she ascribe the magical power that will affirm her being.

Brontë uncompromisingly emphasizes the irrationality of Mina's infatuation by presenting its object as a comic figure. In the late story, Zamorna has passed his prime and has become the "great blithering king of Angria." His heroic dimensions have gotten out of hand. He is a "man mountain" whose political adventures have been replaced by mealtime quibbling. His once treacherous prime minister father-in-law is reduced to parental nagging: "I wish you would masticate your food better."[59] But if Brontë can place the hero in a new, essentially antiromantic perspective, she is still unable to suggest what can be done to prevent or overcome the heroine's infatuation. She does not yet see how the intensity of need and feeling might be constructively channeled. Still, she deals with these problems more fruitfully in "Henry Hastings," the most developed of the last short novels. The success here derives from her emphasis upon the functioning of the masochistic female personality in a context which is real and immediate to her: the relationship of sister to brother.

The "dissipated and drunken mushroom," Henry Hastings, had been created by Branwell after he returned from his disastrous stay in London in 1837. Through this new persona, Branwell expressed his growing guilt and impotence as well as his alienation from his family.

> Besides, conscience with withering sting was constantly striking into my heart—king, country and cause forsaken, old associations severed, friendships torn away—and had I not received a letter from my father coldly saying he and all at home

58. "Mina Laury," p. 143.
59. Ibid., p. 128.

had cut me for ever and ever, all which matters, like hot sweet-
meats, the more and more incited me to drink.[60]

In "Julia," Brontë merely appropriates Branwell's character,
portraying him as a shiftless, vain, and unstable alcoholic. In
"Henry Hastings" she develops the hero further, rejecting Branwell's early definition of him as simply a debased traitor and mur-
derer. She provides him with a motive, explaining how the extraordinary rise in his fortunes—a function of his giftedness and
heroism—had negatively affected his character and initiated his
ruin. But Hastings is not at the center of the story. That position
is occupied by his sister, Elizabeth, who, fully recognizing her
brother's flaws and degradation, risks everything she values to
save his life:

> It was very odd that his sister did not think a pin the worse of
> him for all his dishonor: it is private moments not public in-
> famy that degrade a man in the opinion of his relations. Miss
> Hastings had heard him cursed by every mouth, saw him de-
> nounced in every newspaper, still he was the same brother to her
> he had always been—still she beheld his actions through a me-
> dium peculiar to herself. She saw him go away with a trium-
> phant Hope—that his future actions would nobly blot out the
> calumny of his enemies. Yet after all she knew he was an
> unredeemed villain—human nature is full of inconsistencies—
> natural affection is a thing never rooted out where it has once
> existed.[61]

The heroine is defined, as the other heroines had been, by her
self-sacrifice. In Elizabeth's case, however, self-sacrifice seems
to be a function of choice and a source of strength rather than the
sterile result of blind idolatry as it was with Mina Laury.

This is the first of her stories in which Brontë models her
heroine upon herself. In this respect, "Henry Hastings" is the
forerunner of the mature novels. Elizabeth is—like Brontë, like
Jane Eyre, like Lucy Snowe—"plain and undersized."

> Young indeed she was—but not handsome—she had a fair,
> rather wan complexion, dark hair smoothly combed in two
> plain folds from her forehead—features capable of much

60. Fragment, dated July 12, 1837. Brontë Parsonage Museum.
61. "Henry Hastings," *Five Novelettes*, p. 242.

varied expression and a quick wandering eye of singular and by no means common-place significance.[62]

She is possessed of that odd mixture of qualities which makes Jane Eyre so appealing a heroine. Serious and thoughtful, she is also humorous. Shy, she is fiercely proud. Retiring, she can be moved easily to passion:

> . . . still the exclusive proud being thought she had not met with a single individual equal to herself in mind, and therefore not one whom she could love . . . , she was one who scorned respect . . . she was always burning for warmer, closer attachment.[63]

In her presentation of Elizabeth's situation, Brontë places fantasy at the service of analysis, beginning to transmute the dream into art. For example, one level of the story seems to draw upon her sense of her own and Branwell's rivalry for their father's love. Hastings's transgressions place Elizabeth in a situation of open competition in which she can, for the first time, be victorious as the "good" albeit female child. But Brontë recognizes that the urge to punish the father may be stronger, and more real, than the urge to claim the love of which he has deprived her—love, therefore, that may not exist. After Henry has been painfully disowned by his father because of his treasonous activities, Elizabeth chooses to come to his defense and is therefore cast out as well. Not able to reject her brother openly, she joins him in the rebellion against the paternal authority. This too is a kind of victory. She is superior to father *and* brother. In her fidelity she proves that it is *her* love for Henry which is most enduring. Tested, she claims the prize. The sister's sacrifice totally vindicates her own character and exposes her brother's, without creating an incredible reconciliation with the father which would be unacceptable to the psyche. The family romance, we find, has many levels.[64]

Given these terms, Elizabeth's commitment to her brother is *not* an enslavement. Rather it frees her as a rebel from the traditional role within the family. It frees her from the rivalry for parental approval. It frees her even from the problems accom-

62. "Henry Hastings," p. 181.
63. Ibid., pp. 243–44.
64. As we shall see, Charlotte did—for her own reasons—accept the role of the "good child," and became Branwell's most vehement judge. Still, like Elizabeth, she was freed by her brother's deterioration.

panying the brother-sister relationship, for, between them, no relationship at all is now possible. Henry's weakness of character is proof against her fidelity. Always spoiled and self-centered, he has become soured by guilt.

It is in this way that Elizabeth has independence thrust upon her. Without conventional supports she must discover her own values and role. She has to test herself in areas which define her, quite terrifyingly, as a person rather than as a woman. She becomes a successful teacher and schoolmistress. The sense of self which is actualized by her dedication to Henry gives her enough self-confidence to transform her in the eyes of others. Her intelligence and capacity for feeling illuminate her from within.

Sir William Percy is one of those who fall in love with her but, because of his position and his pride, he can offer her only the small satisfactions and large humiliations of an illicit relationship. Although she longs for love and is attracted to him "with an intensity of romantic feeling that very few people in this world can form the remotest conception of,"[65] Elizabeth rejects him, as Jane will later reject Rochester. It is a courageous act, for she has no more hope than do Brontë's later heroines, than Brontë does herself, that she can derive important alternate satisfactions from the teaching that makes her financially independent:

> She spent her mornings in her drawing-room surrounded by her class and not wearily toiling to impart the dry rudiments of knowledge to yawning, obstinate children—a thing she hated and for which her sharp, irritable temper rendered her wholly unfit.[66]

It is finally by her integrity, her disillusionment, and her extraordinary loneliness that she is defined.

> Sometimes, when she was alone of an evening, walking through her handsome drawing room by twilight, she would think of home—long for home, till she cried passionately at the conviction that she would see it no more. So wild was her longing that where she looked out on the dusky sky, between the curtains of her bay-window . . . fancy seemed to trace on the horizon, the blue outlines of the moors.[67]

65. "Henry Hastings," p. 294.
66. Ibid., p. 243.
67. Ibid., p. 244.

Here, in the development of Elizabeth Hastings, Brontë begins the painful work of her maturity.

Biographers have been quick to comment on the irony which emerges from a comparison of Elizabeth's fidelity to Henry and Charlotte's later rejection of Branwell. But they have been blind to the central albeit disguised point of "Henry Hastings": that Branwell's disintegration was essential to Charlotte's discovery of herself; that his failure was necessary if she was to succeed; that her separation from him, begun at this point in her life, expressed at this stage of her work, allowed her to begin to reject as well the universe of mythic values which had locked her into the artistic and personal infantilism by which Branwell had been trapped. Charlotte, with her heroine, cannot avoid looking back but, with Elizabeth, she realizes that she cannot return. Her "Farewell to Angria" (written at the end of 1839, when she was twenty-two) is profoundly moving. It suggests that self-knowledge can only be sought within a historical reality that denies escape into fantasy but encourages the discovery of the truth buried in the dream.

> I have now written a great many books and for a long time have dwelt on the same characters and scenes and subjects. I have shown my landscapes in every variety of shade and light which morning, noon, and evening—the rising, the meridian, and the setting sun can bestow upon them. Sometimes I have filled the air with the whitened tempest of winter: snow has embossed the dark arms of the beech and oak and filled with drifts the parks of the lowlands or the mountain-pass of wilder districts. Again, the same mansion with its woods, the same moor with its glens, has been softly colored with the tints of moonlight in summer, and in the warmest June night the trees have clustered their full-plumed heads over glades flushed with flowers. So it is with persons. My readers have been habituated to one set of features, which they have seen now in profile, now in full face, now in outline, and again in finished painting,—varied but by the thought or feeling or temper or age; lit with love, flushed with passion, shaded with grief, kindled with ecstasy; in meditation and mirth, in sorrow and scorn and rapture; with the round outline of childhood, the beauty and fulness of youth, the strength of manhood, and the furrows of thoughtful decline;—but we must change, for the eye is tired of the picture so oft recurring and now so familiar.

Yet do not urge me too fast, reader: it is not easy to dismiss from my imagination the images which have filled it so long; they were my friends and my intimate acquaintances, and I could with little labour describe to you the faces, the voices, the actions, of those who peopled my thoughts by day, and not seldom stole strangely even into my dreams by night. When I depart from these I feel almost as if I stood on the threshold of a home and were bidding farewell to its inmates. When I try to conjure up new inmates I feel as if I had got into a distant country where every face was unknown and the character of all the population an enigma which it would take much study to comprehend and much talent to expound. Still, I long to quit for awhile that burning clime where we have sojourned too long—its skies flame—the glow of sunset is always upon it—the mind would cease from excitement and turn now to a cooler region where the dawn breaks grey and sober, and the coming day for a time at least is subdued by clouds.[68]

IV

Although Brontë's descent from the "burning clime" of her fantastic imaginings to the "cooler region" of mature self-knowledge and artistic control began in the emotional crisis of 1839, it was several years before she understood its implications and its cost. What she had divined in the experience of her heroines, she had to comprehend in her own life. She had to emerge from the swaddling of societal mythology and the richly projective fantasy self. To penetrate that constricting wrap she had to find in herself the sources of the mysterious romantic conspiracy, suffer the agony of disillusionment, and struggle toward the freedom implicit in uninsulated reality. Ultimately, the initial trauma passed, she had to examine the scars of confrontation on her own masochistic personality, replacing rationalization with reason. This was to be her personal and artistic goal. It provided the motivating force and the form of her fictions.

The duties which she felt it necessary to assume did not augur well for her undertaking. In 1839, while she was creating Elizabeth Hastings and bidding farewell to Angria, she was beginning a series of trials which might well have sent her scurrying back to

68. *Legends of Angria,* compiled by Fannie Ratchford and William De-Vane (New Haven: Yale University Press, 1933), p. 316.

the security of her fantasies. For three months she was a governess in the family of a Mr. and Mrs. Sedgewick of Yorkshire. She had virtually no relationship with Mr. Sedgewick but, writing to Ellen of her situation, she reveals herself to be drawn to her new "master"—astonishingly attracted to the role of submissive woman when it is played opposite that of a domineering man:

> One of the pleasantest afternoons I have spent here—indeed, the only one at all pleasant—was when Mr. ____ walked out with his children, and I had orders to follow a little behind. As he strolled on through his fields, with his magnificent Newfoundland dog at his side, he looked very like what a frank, wealthy Conservative gentleman ought to be.[69]

But while she still accepted domination within the context of male-female interaction, she was withered by her powerlessness in the broader circumstances of her life. The fear of inadequacy which had marked her childhood was validated now. Occupying, as all governesses did, an undefined area between the domestic servants and the members of the family, she had neither friends nor rights. Even her relationship to the children for whom she cared was ambiguous and demeaning. The pain of her situation, the humiliation which she felt as a result of her servitude and, above all, the anger and resentment which she could not overtly express and which she therefore turned against herself—all of this is suggested in a letter which she wrote to Ellen a couple of years later when she was again a governess, now to the children of Mr. and Mrs. John White:

> But no one but myself can tell how hard a governess's work is to me—for no one but myself is aware how utterly averse my whole mind and nature are to the employment. Do not think that I fail to blame myself for this, or that I leave any means unemployed to conquer this feeling. Some of my greatest difficulties lie in things that would appear to you comparatively trivial. I find it so hard to repel the rude familiarity of children. I find it so difficult to ask either servants or mistress for anything I want, however much I want it. It is less pain to me to endure the greatest inconvenience than to request its removal.[70]

69. June 8, 1839. Quoted in Gaskell, p. 115.
70. March 3, 1841. Wise and Symington, I, 226.

There were few enough alternatives for a young woman who had to be self-supporting. The obvious one was marriage. But in 1839 Charlotte still shared her heroines' romantic dreams of love and was unwilling to compromise. In writing to Ellen of her second proposal of marriage (her first had been made by Ellen's brother, Henry, in the same year) she explained:

> I had a kindly leaning towards him, because he is an amiable and well-disposed man. Yet I had not, and could not have, that intense attachment which would make me willing to die for him; and if ever I marry, it must be in that light of adoration that I will regard my husband. Ten to one I shall never have the chance again; but n'importe.[71]

If her sentiments remained the same during the following year, her tone changed compellingly;

> Do not be over-persuaded to marry a man you can never respect—I do not say *love;* because, I think, if you can respect a person before marriage, moderate love at least will come after; and as to intense *passion,* I am convinced that is no desirable feeling. In the first place, it seldom or never meets with a requittal; and in the second place, if it did, the feeling would be only temporary: it would last the honeymoon, and then, perhaps, give place to disgust, or indifference worse, perhaps, than disgust. Certainly, this would be the case on the man's part; and on the woman's—God help her, if she is left to love passionately and alone.
> I am tolerably well-convinced that I shall never marry at all. Reason tells me so, and I am not so utterly the slave of feeling but that I can *occasionally hear* her voice.[72]

The intensity of her idealism provided the measure of her frustration and disappointment. The depth of her need, her absence of self-confidence, her growing despair: all determined the degree of her scepticism. The fate of her childhood heroines, with whom she had identified so closely, had been confirmed in her own limited experience by Branwell's treatment of Mary Taylor. The strains combined to produce a stance of surprising militancy.

> No young lady should fall in love till the offer has been made, accepted—the marriage ceremony performed and the first half-

71. March 12, 1839. Wise and Symington, I, 174.
72. May 15, 1840. Wise and Symington, I, 206–7.

> year of wedded life has passed away—a woman may then
> begin to love, but with great precaution—very coolly—very
> rationally—If she ever loves so much that a harsh word or a
> cold look from her husband cuts her to the heart—she is a
> fool—if she ever loves so much that her husband's will is her
> law—and that she has got into a habit of watching his looks in
> order that she may anticipate his wishes she will soon be a ne-
> glected fool—Did I not tell you of an instance of a relative of
> mine who cared for a young lady till he began to suspect that
> she cared more for him and then instantly conceived a sort of
> contempt for her?[73]

But, as events were to prove, Charlotte was in fact neither sceptic
nor militant. Experience found her to be as susceptible to infatuation and as vulnerable to rejection, as were Mary Percy or Mina
Laury. Brussels replaced Angria as the scene of her ordeal. It was
here—to the Pensionnat Heger—that she and Emily came to pre-
pare themselves to open, with Anne, a school of their own. It was
a venture which could free them in time from the bondage of the
governess role.

Now twenty-six years old, Charlotte had undeniably tired of
the constricted life she led. Intellectually, emotionally, psychologically, and sexually she longed for an opportunity to grow, to
learn, to experience. A few months before she left for Brussels,
she had written to Ellen:

> . . . Mary's letter spoke of some of the pictures and Cathe-
> drals she had seen—pictures the most exquisite—and cathe-
> drals the most venerable—I hardly know what swelled to my
> throat as I read her letter—such a vehement impatience of re-
> straint and steady work. . . . Such a strong wish for wings—
> wings such as wealth can furnish—such an urgent thirst to
> see—to know—to learn—something seemed to expand boldly
> for a minute—I was tantalized with the consciousness of fac-
> ulties unexercised—then all collapsed and I despaired.[74]

Her feeling for M. Heger, headmaster of the school in Brussels,
offered her those wings, and in the nine months of her first stay
there, she began to understand what it meant to fly.

It would seem at first that M. Heger had little in common with
the Byronic heroes of Brontë's adolescent fantasies but the simi-

73. November 20, 1840. Wise and Symington, I, 221.
74. August 7, 1841. Wise and Symington, I, 218.

larities are actually striking. The schoolmaster might indeed have been Zamorna, transplanted to a domestic setting. The death of his young first wife and child in a cholera epidemic had left him not only with a haunting past, but also with a rather morose and gloomy presence. A domineering man, possessed of a quick temper, he used his position and his personality as weapons: substitutes for reason, excuses for petty tyrannies. But he was also a man who could inspire devotion by virtue of his warmth and patience.[75] Not least of all, he was a gifted teacher: knowledgeable and insightful, appreciative of his serious students, responsive to their intellectual and emotional requirements. He exploited the teacher-student relationship, with its undisputed hierarchy of power, its always latent sexuality, its allowance for dependence—even idolatry—without humiliation. All of this provided a channeling of psychosexual forces acceptable within the Victorian culture. The friendship with Heger provided Brontë with a viable transition between her relationships with her father and brother and the more mature heterosexual interaction of which she was becoming capable. Revealingly, Brontë writes to Ellen, after she has had time to accustom herself to the regimen of the Hegers:

> I was twenty-six years old a week or two since; and at this ripe time of life I am a school-girl, and, on the whole, very happy in that capacity. It felt very strange at first to submit to authority instead of exercising it—to obey orders instead of giving them: but I like that state of things. I returned to it with the same avidity that a cow, that has long been kept on dry hay, returns to fresh grass. Don't laugh at my simile. It is natural to me to submit and very unnatural to command.[76]

Recognizing Charlotte and Emily's giftedness, Heger devised a new technique for teaching them French by emphasizing the spirit and rhythm of the text rather than simple grammatical rules. The technique must have made Charlotte more aware of her own literary style.[77] Then too, Heger's comments on her composi-

75. See Gerin, *Charlotte Brontë*, p. 194.
76. May, 1842. Wise and Symington, I, 260.
77. ``. . . he proposed to read to them some of the master-pieces of the most celebrated French authors . . . and having thus impressed the complete effect of the whole, to analyze the parts with them, pointing out in what such or such an author excell'd and where were the blemishes . . . he hoped thereby to help them catch 'the echo of a style.' '' (Gaskell, pp. 151–52).

tions represented the first objective criticism of her writing that she had ever received. Beside this informed interest and intellectual stimulation, Charlotte's feelings of alienation from the other students, her dislike of Catholics, even her persistent self-consciousness seemed trivial indeed. She was questioning herself; stretching and growing in a world which no longer seemed to demand abnegation.

When Charlotte and Emily were called home in November of 1842 because of their aunt's death, it was unthinkable to Charlotte that she would remain at Haworth. Their status at the school had already changed. In return for their board and studies in French and German, Emily was teaching music, Charlotte English. Now, in addition, M. Heger offered them a salary if they would return.[78] Never happy away from Haworth, never charmed as Charlotte was, by Heger, Emily welcomed the opportunity to take her aunt's place at home. But Charlotte sped back to Brussels, compelled by feelings which had little to do with M. Heger's generous terms of employment. Almost three years later, Brontë wrote of this compulsion to Ellen:

> I returned to Brussels after aunt's death against my conscience, prompted by what then seemed an irresistible impulse. I was punished for my selfish folly by a total withdrawal for more than two years of happiness and peace of mind . . .[79]

The words could have been spoken by Mina Laury of her involvement with Zamorna. But if the words seem similar, the nature of the involvement was not. In fact, it was the necessity of the difference which made Charlotte's involvement possible at all. The relationship between Charlotte and Heger, *could* exist only in some shadowy world that blurred fantasy and reality. The attraction and the protection from the attraction were simultaneously present. The sources of conflict were submerged, but its power became increasingly more difficult to deny.

When she returned to the Pensionnat, Brontë came to know Heger better than she had before. Teaching him and his brother-in-law English, she established herself in a position of greater equality with him. Heger spoke to her more openly, loaned her

---

78. See Gerin, *Charlotte Brontë,* pp. 180–215 for a complete account of these months in Brussels.

79. October 14, 1846. Wise and Symington, II, 115.

books, showed her the more elusive—and attractive—aspects of his personality as well as the admirable qualities of his mind. But to know him better was to want to know him intimately; to feel closer to him was to understand the great gulf which separated them. The letters written during the spring of her return suggest both her increasing sense of isolation and her increasing confusion.

> As I told you before, M. and Madame Heger are the only two persons in the house for whom I really experience regard and esteem, and, of course, I cannot always be with them, nor even often. They told me, when I first returned, that I was to consider their sitting-room my sitting-room also, and to go there whenever I was not engaged in the schoolroom. This, however, I cannot do. In the daytime it is a public room, where music masters and mistresses are constantly passing in and out; and in the evening I will not and ought not to intrude on M. and Madame Heger and their children. Thus I am a good deal by myself out of school hours; but that does not signify.[80]

Hotly denying rumors that she has been drawn back to Brussels by a love affair, she adds—with a degree of ambiguity and defensiveness that is characteristic of her at this time:

> . . . if these charitable people knew the total seclusion of the life I lead—that I never exchange a word with any other man than Monsieur Heger and seldom indeed with him—they would perhaps cease to suppose that any such chimerical and groundless notion influenced my proceedings . . . not that it is a crime to marry—or a crime to wish to be married—but it is an imbecility which I reject with contempt—for women who have neither fortune nor beauty—to make marriage the principal object of their wishes and hopes and the aim of all their actions—not to be able to convince themselves that they are unattractive—and that they had better be quiet and think of other things than wedlock . . .

To Branwell, she admits—albeit unconsciously—that the world around her has become as affectless as has her relationship with Heger: an image of her psychic state:

> I perceive that I grow exceedingly misanthropic and sour . . . nobody ever gets into a passion here. Such a thing is not

80. To Ellen Nussey, March 6, 1843. Wise and Symington, I, 293.

known. The phlegm that thickens their blood is too gluey to
boil. They are very false in their relations with each other, but
they rarely quarrel, and friendship is a folly they are unac-
quainted with. The black swan, M. Heger, is the only sole
veritable exception to this rule (for Madame always cool and
always reasoning, is not quite an exception). But I rarely speak
to Monsieur now, for not being a pupil I have little or nothing
to do with him. From time to time he shows his kindheart-
edness by loading me with books, so that I am still indebted to
him for all the pleasure or amusement I have.[81]

Her pride can barely protect her from recognition. But she, like
the heroines of her adolescence, finds solace in her own capacity
for patience, for understanding, for constancy.

There seems to be little doubt that Brontë's schoolgirl attachment to M. Heger was perceived by his wife, who deftly but
surely saw to it that Brontë would not be misled about the degree
or nature of her husband's interest. For them, withdrawal must
have seemed a matter of necessity. The reputation of the school
was at stake. It was a kindness to encourage her to develop new
friendships. But of course Brontë experienced withdrawal as rejection. The martyrdom of her isolation provided her with the
only comfort possible. Here was her castle and she had imprisoned herself within it.

Of late days, M. and Mme. Heger rarely speak to me, and I really don't pretend to care a fig for anybody else in the es-
tablishment. You are not to suppose by that expression that I
am under the influence of *warm* affection for Mme. Heger. I
am convinced that she does not like me—why, I can't tell, nor
do I think she herself has any definite reason for the aversion;
but for one thing, she cannot comprehend why I do not make
intimate friends of Mesdames Blanches, Sophie and Hausse.
M. Heger is wondrously influenced by Madame, and I should
not wonder if he disapproves very much of my unamiable want
of sociability. He has already given me a brief lecture on universal *bienveillance,* and, perceiving that I don't improve in
consequence, I fancy he has taken me as a person to be let
alone—left to the error of her ways: and consequently he has in
a great measure withdrawn the light of his countenance, and I
get on from day to day in a Robinson-Crusoe-like condition—

81. May 1, 1843. Wise and Symington, I, 296–97.

very lonely . . . except the loss of M. Heger's good will (if I
have lost it) I care for none of 'em.[82]

The agonies of the next six months made the denial mechanism
increasingly ineffective so that, in a letter written to Ellen in
November, she betrays—although she does not entirely give
away—her awareness of Madame Heger's motivation: "I fancy I
begin to perceive the reason of this mighty distance and reserve:
it sometimes makes me laugh, and at other times nearly cry.
When I am sure of it I will tell it you."[83] It is impossible to deny
the romantic and fundamentally sexual nature of Brontë's interest, although her biographers have politely averted their heads in
order to avoid the recognition.[84] It is also difficult to ignore the
similarity of Brontë's attachment to Heger and those idolatrous
attachments which had entrapped her heroines. It is perhaps sentimentality—more likely, prudery—that leads Winifred Gerin to
assert that Charlotte's love was "innocent," that "what tortured
her was a love that could neither be expressed, returned, or understood by any living soul."[85] In reality, her love *was* understood quite well by Madame Heger. It was this which Brontë
could not forgive. Truly, hers was not an adulterous wish denied,
but rather one which was repressed and never fully confronted.
All of her longings for love, for release, for fulfillment, for
growth, were focused on Heger. This was not a tragic trick of fate
but a psychological necessity. One cites with some confidence,
the phenomena of Victorian repression and sexual fear. But one
also speculates that the impossibility of reciprocation in fact
provided an appropriate outlet for Brontë's masochistic tendencies. How else can one explain the extraordinary passivity which
allowed her to remain for months in a humiliating situation, not
simply unable to fight her dependence upon her "maitre" but
consistently constructing circumstances that would support and
intensify that dependence? Why else couldn't she force herself to
leave Brussels, suffering as she was from severe depressions and

82. To Emily Brontë, May 29, 1843. Wise and Symington, I, 299.
83. November 15, 1843. Wise and Symington, I, 309.
84. This was easier to do before the publication of Charlotte's letters to
Heger in 1913, but even such distinguished biographers as Fannie Ratchford
and, to a lesser extent, Winifred Gerin, who wrote well after the material was
available, did not confront the issue.
85. Gerin, *Charlotte Brontë*, p. 24.

general malaise?[86] Made desperate at last, she turned her anger upon the students, the teachers, Madame Heger, herself—but she never turned it against "the professor." To him she would not allow herself to show the rage of disappointment. This she would probably not even have allowed herself to feel.

> I suffered much before I left Brussels. I think, however long I live, I shall not forget what the parting with M. Heger cost me; it grieved me so much to grieve him, who has been so true, so kind, and disinterested a friend.[87]

How self-deluded was she? How could she have believed her "dear master" to have been so grieved if he had, in fact, rejected her with such consistent coldness? Was it only a last spurt of friendliness on his part, emanating from relief, that made Brontë believe, when she left Brussels in January of 1844, that she and Heger were still good friends, that he would send one of his daughters to the school which she hoped now to open; that he would write to her, that there was still the possibility of communication, that she could look to him for continued support?

In fact, we know that there was some correspondence between them after Brontë returned to Haworth, that Heger sent her advice—as he told Elizabeth Gaskell—"about her character, studies, mode of life."[88] These letters have not survived, but letters written to others of his students have been preserved. They suggest—as does the passage from a letter to a student quoted below—another perspective which must be added to those habitually applied to "Charlotte's infatuation":

> At the end of your nice letter, which is in front of me, you say, "I remain your *little* friend ——" Allow me to disapprove of a phrase too humble to be sincere; you are not little in my eyes, neither in size, nor age nor reason; nor by the affection you have inspired in me and in my family. We feel this as strongly as ever though you are far from us. "If that is true," you will say to me, "why have you been so slow in answering

86. Gerin suggests that Brontë ultimately decided to leave Brussels only after she had received a strong letter from Mary Taylor urging her to do so. (*Charlotte Brontë*, p. 252). Appealing as this theory is, it can remain only conjecture since Mary Taylor destroyed all of Brontë's correspondence.

87. To Ellen Nussey, January 23, 1844. Wise and Symington, II, 3.

88. Elizabeth Gaskell to Ellen Nussey, July 9, 1856. Wise and Symington, IV, 201–3.

me?'' Why? It will be easy for me to show that although it is
true that I have not written, I have nevertheless answered you
frequently and at length, and this is how. Letters and the post
are not, luckily, the only means of communication, or the best,
between people who are really fond of one another: I am refer-
ring to the telephone, which allows one to speak, to have conversations, from a distance. I have something better than that. I
only have to think of you to see you. I often give myself the
pleasure when my duties are over, when the light fades. I post-
pone lighting the gas lamp in my library, I sit down, smoking
my cigar, and with a hearty will I evoke your image—and you
come (without wishing to, I dare say) but I see you, I talk with
you—you, with that little air, affectionate undoubtedly, but independent and resolute, firmly determined not to allow any
opinion without being previously convinced, demanding to be
convinced before allowing yourself to submit—in fact, just as I
knew you, my dear M—— —and as I have esteemed and
loved you.

In thinking it over you will have no difficulty in admitting
that you yourself have experienced a hundred times that which
I tell you about communication between two distant hearts, in-
stantaneous, without paper, without pen, or words, or messenger, etc., a hundred times without noticing it, without its having attracted your attention, without anything extraordinary.[89]

Winifred Gerin, thinking of the letters preserved by many of
Heger's students, muses on the qualities of those which he might
have written, indeed probably did write, to Charlotte herself:
"How delightful they could have been, had no fear of Charlotte's
misunderstanding their kindness existed in the writer's mind
. . ."[90] How delightful indeed! And there can be little question
of "poor Charlotte's" susceptibility. Heger's theory of spiritual
or magnetic communication (he must have shared it with other
favored students) appears in a somewhat startling, implicitly sexual, but still recognizable form in *Jane Eyre,* when the heroine
hears Rochester's voice calling to her. But then one asks—particularly in an age more aware of the sexual power games played

89. Translation of original letter from M. Heger to Meta Mossman, November 21, 1887, by courtesy of Walter Cunliffe, Esq. Quoted in Winifred
Gerin, *Charlotte Brontë,* pp. 262–63. Gerin explains, in a note, that "Meta
adored him," but she does not draw any parallels between Meta's feelings and
Charlotte's.

90. Gerin, *Charlotte Brontë,* p. 261.

by male professors with female students—"How many of Heger's little 'friends' would not have been susceptible to letters such as this one?" "How many would not have woven fantasies around the affectionate references, the playful, complimentary tone, the masculine manipulation?" And if this is the role that Heger played in his correspondence, what role did he play—unconsciously, of course—in the classroom? How many students, more or less masochistic than Charlotte, but subject still to similar social and psychosexual pressures, might have created fantasies equally disturbing if less consuming and not so naively tested? In short, how unique was Brontë's response? To what extent was her infatuation, accepted for so long at face value, simply another manifestation of the sexual politics pervasive in Victorian society: more insidious because it was socially validated?

Of course, there was a difference. The circumstances of her life and—most of all—the peculiarity of her art, made it impossible for her to lightly play the games that many other women of her time were used to playing. Her imagination had already begun to carry her to deeper levels of consciousness. Once physically separated from Heger, she was freer to return to these. The distinction between fantasy and reality blurred. The letters she wrote to him contained the romantic language and tone she had perfected in the Angrian tales. The degree of intensity was not one which Heger could allow. It was certainly not one he could share. It blasted the surface of "conventional interaction." It grasped implication by the throat. He discontinued the correspondence. The letters which she writes then, in an attempt to penetrate his silence, are heartbreaking in the degree of vulnerability they reveal; in their need and, ultimately, in their despair.

In the first of the letters which greets his silence, she mentions that she must abandon altogether her aspirations as a writer: aspirations which he had not apparently encouraged.

> . . . now my sight is too weak to write. —Were I to write much I should become blind. This weakness of sight is a terrible hindrance to me. Otherwise, do you know what I should do Monsieur? —I should write a book, and I should dedicate it to my literature master—to the only master I ever had—to you Monsieur.[91]

91. July 24, 1844. Wise and Symington, II, 13.

The passage is oddly compelling. In no other letter written at this time does Charlotte mention her "failing sight" as a serious problem.[92] Indeed, one is tempted to dismiss the reference as a transparent plea for sympathy or to accept it as one of the many hysterical symptoms which accompanied the depressions of Brontë's mature years. Certainly, the cataract condition which threatened to deprive her father of his vision must have preoccupied her. It might well have created fears linked to the guilt which accompanied her repressed love for Heger. Blindness was, after all, the punishment she later meted out to Rochester, the adulterer.

The connection that Charlotte makes between her "failing sight" and the difficulty she finds in writing, seems to support this line of interpretation. At this crucial point in her life Charlotte truly does not want to "see" clearly the situation which obsesses her. If she could not confront it, she could not write about it, and her obsession prevented her writing about anything else. Furthermore, how could the adoring student write a book which would be worthy of dedication to her "master"? The relationship is predicated upon a presumption of inequality. How could she risk a judgment which would involve not only her work but her "self"?

In October, a brief note to him reveals that, in her agony of frustrated watching and waiting, she has decided that her letters might not have reached him. It is convenient for her to believe that "Madame" has intercepted his mail, but, when she sends another letter to him by personal messenger and still receives no reply, she can deceive herself no longer. Then she betrays the depth of her suffering and dependence:

> Day and night I find neither rest nor peace. If I sleep I am disturbed by tormenting dreams in which I see you, always severe, always grave, always incensed against me.
> Forgive me then, Monsieur, if I adopt the course of writ-

92. Gaskell acknowledges that it is probable that even her sisters and most intimate friends didn't know of her ultimate dread of blindness, but the biographer tries to rationalize the fears expressed to Heger: "Long-continued ill-health, a deranged condition of the liver, her close application to minute drawing and writing in her younger days, her now habitual sleeplessness at nights, the many bitter noiseless tears she shed over Branwell's mysterious and distressing conduct—all these causes were telling on her poor eyes . . ." (Gaskell, p. 191).

ing to you again. How can I endure life if I make no effort to
ease its sufferings? . . .

　All I know is that I cannot, that I will not, resign myself to
lose wholly the friendship of my master. I would rather suffer
the greatest physical pain than always have my heart lacerated
by smarting regrets. . . .

　I shall not reread this letter. I send it as I have written it.
Nevertheless, I have a hidden Consciousness that some people,
cold and commonsense, in reading it would say—"She is talk-
ing nonsense." I would avenge myself on such persons in no
other way than by wishing them one single day of the torments
which I have suffered for eight months. We should then see if
they would not talk nonsense too.[93]

Three months later, in a letter to Ellen Nussey, she would reveal
the bitterness which this attachment had created:

Ten years ago, I should have laughed at your account of the
blunder you made in mistaking the bachelor doctor for a married man. I should have certainly thought you scrupulous over-
much—and wondered how you could possibly regret being
civil to a decent individual merely because he happened to be
single instead of double. Now, however, I can perceive that
your scruples are founded on common-sense. I know that if
women wish to escape the stigma of husband-seeking, they
must act and look like marble or clay—cold—expressionless,
bloodless—for every appearance of feeling of joy—sorrow,
friendliness, antipathy, admiration—disgust, are alike construed by the world into an attempt to hook a husband.[94]

Her knowledge did not change her behavior. The bitterness could
not effect the power of the attachment. It only made the agony of
her deprivation greater. Still, the last of the existing letters to
Heger does reveal some change: resignation perhaps; perhaps
weary self-knowledge.

I tell you frankly that I have tried meanwhile to forget you, for
the remembrance of a person whom one thinks never to see
again, and whom, nevertheless, one greatly esteems, frets too
much the mind: and when one has suffered that kind of anxiety
for a year or two, one is ready to do anything to find peace
once more. I have done everything; I have sought occupations:

93. January 8, 1845. Wise and Symington, II, 23.
94. April 2, 1845. Wise and Symington, II, 30.

I have denied myself absolutely the pleasure of speaking about you—even to Emily: but I have been able to conquer neither my regrets nor my impatience. That, indeed, is humiliating—to be unable to control one's own thoughts, to be the slave of a regret, of a memory, the slave of a fixed and dominant idea which lords it over the mind. Why cannot I have just as much friendship for you, as you for me—neither more nor less? Then should I be so tranquil, so free—I could keep silence then for ten years without an effort.[95]

Brontë had come again to question the motives of infatuation. She had explored them six years earlier in Mina Laury, Mary Percy, and Caroline Vernon. The problem now is pressingly her own. Her situation is humiliating. She is powerless: enslaved not by Heger but by herself: by her obsession, her need. She is one of her own imprisoned princesses. Always dependent upon others to confirm her value—to confirm her very identity—she had found in Heger the possibilities not only of recognition but of growth. That promise veiled the degradation of her dependence and made her thralldom seem quite different from that of her heroines. But by the time she wrote this last letter she must have known it to have been the same:

To forbid me to write to you, to refuse to answer me, would be to tear from me my only joy on earth, to deprive me of my last privilege—a privilege I never shall consent willingly to surrender.[96]

His undeniable rejection of her destroyed whatever shred of self-confidence might have been left to her by her father, by Branwell, by the masters and mistresses for whom she had worked as a governess and teacher. Gradually, all around her, the props upon which her life had been built—however tenuously—were being removed. Branwell's illness was paralleled by the mental collapse of Ellen Nussey's brother, George. Her father's impending blindness made the primary authority figure in her life vulnerable and dependent. Heger's apparent inhumanity was the harshest but by no means the only blast at the foundation of the patriarchal structure which had protected and fostered her weakness. To her old teacher, employer, and friend, Miss Wooler, she wrote:

95. November 18, 1845. Wise and Symington, II, 69–70.
96. Wise and Symington, II, 70.

> You ask me if I do not think men are strange beings—I do in-
> deed. I have often thought so—and I think too that the mode of
> bringing them up is strange, they are not half-sufficiently
> guarded from temptation—girls are protected as if they were
> something very frail and silly indeed while boys are turned
> loose on the world as if they—of all beings in existence, were
> the wisest and least liable to be led astray.[97]

Her growing cynicism phrased her questions. It could not invent
answers. Where should she turn? Mary Taylor had decided to
emigrate to New Zealand. She alone of all the women Brontë
knew could provide a model of independent thought and be a
goad to action. But their lives had prepared them to follow different routes. Mary had been raised to rebel. Charlotte had
merely survived.

After she had returned from Brussels, Brontë had written to
Ellen Nussey:

> I do not know whether you feel as I do, but there are times now
> when it appears to me as if all my ideas and feelings, except a
> few friendships and affections, are changed from what they
> used to be; something in me which used to be enthusiasm is
> tamed down and broken. I have few illusions; what I wish for
> now is active exertion—a stake in life.[98]

During the next year, her fevered letters to Heger and her misery
at his withdrawal demonstrated that she had kept more illusions
than she had imagined. But finally rejection left her too unsure to
define herself through her own efforts. Broken and weak as she
was, she had to withdraw into the old caverns of her childhood:
obligation, duty, self-sacrifice. Suffering was her lot—perhaps
her punishment. But it was also, in its familiarity, her security;
for the waters again threatened to break down the walls and
sweep her away. The toll taken by that dreadful year is described
in a letter by Mary Taylor to Elizabeth Gaskell:

> When I last saw Charlotte [January 1845], she told me she had
> quite decided to stay at home. She owned she did not like it.
> Her health was weak; She said she should like any change at
> first, as she had liked Brussels at first, and she thought that
> there must be some possibility for some people of having a life

97. January 30, 1846. Wise and Symington, II, 77.
98. January 23, 1844. Wise and Symington, II, 3.

> of more variety and more communion with human kind, but she saw none for her. I told her very warmly that she ought not to stay at home in solitude, and weak health would ruin her, that she would never recover it. Such a dark shadow came over her face when I said, "Think of what you'll be five years hence," that I stopped and said, "Don't cry Charlotte." She did not cry, but went on walking up and down the room, and said in a little while, "But I intend to stay, Polly."[99]

Brontë did remain at Haworth. But her fate was not the one which Mary Taylor saw written on her face. She once again survived and ultimately she was, in a sense, reborn. The process of her salvation was inevitable. It had been shadowed with the accuracy of psychological insight and self-knowledge in the story of Elizabeth Hastings. A feminist Victorian creation myth had been subconsciously conceived and was now realized. The sister-mother was fed by the wasted skeleton of the brother-child. As Elizabeth had found her strength in Henry's weakness, this phoenix also rose from the ashes of dissolution: Charlotte's renewal was made possible by Branwell's disintegration. Her own obsession, her guilt, her humiliation were given concrete form in Branwell's illicit affair with Lydia Robinson. Heger's rejection was acted out in Lydia's denial. And in Branwell's long and terrible decline, *there* was the punishment which she would never have to accept.

Brontë's biographers have noted with some surprise and not a little displeasure her inability to sympathize with Branwell's pain. They have observed, with Winifred Gerin, that "it was Branwell's crowning misfortune that his own calamity should coincide with Charlotte's."[100] None have seen that if it was Branwell's misfortune it was Charlotte's salvation. Emily and Anne—close comrades from their childhood—could afford to hope for their brother's regeneration. Patrick Brontë could weep for his lost son. They could all see his situation with some objectivity and, therefore, they could pity him. But once again Branwell had shown himself to Charlotte as her "other self." Now he had realized what she had known only in fantasy. She had worshiped, as Branwell had, and in shame she had hidden herself away at Haworth:

99. Gaskell, p. 190.
100. Gerin, *Branwell Brontë*, p. 245.

> Idolater I kneeled to an idol cut in rock!
> I might have slashed my flesh and drawn my
>   heart's best blood:
> The Granite God had felt no tenderness, no shock;
> My Baal had not seen nor heard nor understood.
> In dark remorse I rose; I rose in darker shame;
> Self-condemned I withdrew to an exile from
>   my kind;
> A solitude I sought where mortal never came
> Hoping in its wilds forgetfulness to find.[101]

But there was an important difference between them. Branwell had given in to temptation. Charlotte had not:

> Have I not fled that I may conquer?
> Crost the dark sea in firmest faith
> That I at last might plant my anchor
> Where love cannot prevail to death?[102]

Charlotte chose to forget (if her choice was unconscious, it was also essential) that Branwell had been given the opportunity which she had been denied. Rejecting Branwell, she could reject her own humiliation and guilt. It was not his degradation that appalled her. It was the fact that he had acted out her most secret and forbidden desires. How else can one account for the priggish, self-righteous tone of the letters of this period:

> Branwell still remains at home, and while *he* is here, *you* shall not come. I am more confirmed in that resolution the more I see of him. I wish that I could say one word to you in his favour, but I cannot, therefore I will hold my tongue.[103]

> You say well in speaking of Branwell that no sufferings are so awful as those brought on by dissipation—Alas! I see the truth of this observation daily proved—Ann and Mercy must have a weary and burdensome life of it—in waiting upon their unhappy brother—it seems grievous indeed that those who have not sinned should suffer so largely.[104]

---

101. From "He saw my heart's woe," undated, in *The Poems of Charlotte and Patrick Branwell Brontë*, ed. Wise and Symington (New York: Oxford University Press, 1934), p. 241.
102. "Reason," undated, ibid., p. 241.
103. To Ellen Nussey, November 4, 1845. Wise and Symington, II, 66.
104. To Ellen Nussey, December 31, 1845. Wise and Symington, II, 74.

Branwell offers no prospect of hope—he professes to be too ill to think of seeking for employment—he makes comfort scant at home.[105]

You ask about Branwell; he never thinks of seeking employment and I begin to fear he has rendered himself incapable of filling any respectable station in life, besides, if money were at his disposal he would use it only to his own injury—the faculty of self-government is, I fear, almost destroyed in him . . .[106]

The death of Mr. Robinson, which took place about three weeks or a month ago, served Branwell for a pretext to throw all about him into hubbub and confusion with his emotions, etc., etc.[107]

And, finally, after his death: this ambiguous letter to Williams:

The removal of our only brother must necessarily be regarded by us rather in the light of a mercy than a chastisement. Branwell was his father's and his sisters' pride and hope in boyhood, but since manhood, the case has been otherwise. It has been our lot to see him take a wrong bent; to hope, expect, wait his return to the right path; to know the sickness of hope deferred, the dismay of prayer baffled; to experience despair at last—and now to behold the sudden early obscure close of what might have been a noble career.

I do not weep from a sense of bereavement—there is no prop withdrawn, no consolation torn away, no dear companion lost—but for the wreck of talent, the ruin of promise, the untimely dreary extinction of what might have been a burning and shining light. My brother was a year my junior. I had aspirations and ambitions for him once, long ago—they have perished mournfully. Nothing remains of him but a memory of errors and sufferings. There is such a bitterness of pity for his life and death, such a yearning for the emptiness of his whole existence as I cannot describe. I trust time will allay these feelings.[108]

Branwell's life had become for Charlotte the external form of her fantasy-wish. In her rejection of him, her transcendence was

---

105. To Ellen Nussey, January 23, 1846. Wise and Symington, II, 75.
106. To Miss Wooler, January 30, 1846. Wise and Symington, II, 77.
107. To Ellen Nussey, June 17, 1846. Wise and Symington, II, 96.
108. To W. S. Williams, October 2, 1895. Wise and Symington, II, 261.

made possible. Upon his hopelessness, Charlotte was at last able to build her future and despite the fact that the effective cause of her growing self-confidence was, in part, the neurotic projection of her own guilt, it moved her in the direction of separation and health. With Elizabeth Hastings she could become independent and directed. She could begin to assume responsibility.

Branwell's crisis developed as the cataracts which darkened Patrick Brontë's vision thickened. Her father's growing blindness loosened the bonds of the other symbiotic relationship which had been so destructive in Charlotte's life. The situation of dependence had radically altered, as she suggests in a letter written to M. Heger in 1845:

> My father is well but his sight is almost gone. He can neither read nor write. . . . My father allows me to read to him. I write for him; he shows me, too, more confidence than he has ever shown before, and that is a great consolation.[109]

It is not inappropriate that this woman, whose masochistic dependence and passivity had evolved within the strictures of a patriarchal Victorian family, should find the sources of freedom in the moral and physical disintegration of her brother and in the growing blindness of her father.[110] Only thus could her ego survive at all. But freedom had also to be developed from within. A female child, a survivor, she had turned from the overwhelming terrors of reality to the imagined world of Angria. Rejecting those fantasies, she had reluctantly reached out to life. But the forces which shaped her fantasies made of her life a prison from which she could only escape—once partially freed—by returning again to art: an art which, as it became increasingly mature, became increasingly self-conscious and analytical. Here the haunting, regressive fantasies could be laid to rest. The key to the enchanted castle could be cast.

109. November 18, 1845. Wise and Symington, II, 70.
110. Although the surgical removal of Mr. Brontë's cataracts in August, 1846, successfully restored his vision, Charlotte remained aware for the rest of her life, of her father's increasing physical and emotional dependence upon her and used this dependence as a reason, or an excuse, for remaining at Haworth.

CHAPTER TWO

The Professor: *Androgyny and the Search for Self*

I gave, at first attention close;
    Then interest warm ensued;
From interest, as improvement rose
    Succeeded gratitude.

Obedience was no effort soon,
    And Labour was no pain;
If tired, a word, a glance alone
    Would give me strength again

From others of the studious band,
    Ere long he singled me;
But only by more close demand
    And sterner urgency.

The task he from another took,
    From me he did reject;
He would no slight omission brook,
    And suffer no defect.

If my companions went astray,
    He scarce their wanderings blamed;
If I but falter'd in the way,
    His anger fiercely flam'd.

When sickness stay'd awhile my course,
    He seemed impatient still,
Because his pupil's flagging force
    Could not obey his will.

One day when summoned to the bed
    Where pain and I did strive,

I heard him, as he bent his head,
    Say, God, she *must* revive!

I felt his hand, with gentle stress,
    A moment laid on mine,
And wished to mark my consciousness
    By some responsive sign.

But pow'rless then to speak or move,
    I only felt, within,
The sense of Hope, the strength of Love,
    Their healing work begin.

And as he from the room withdrew,
    My heart his steps pursued;
I long'd to prove, by efforts new,
    My speechless gratitude.

When once again I took my place
    Long vacant, in the class,
Th'unfrequent smile across his face
    Did for one moment pass.

The lessons done: the signal made
    Of glad release and play
He, as he passed, an instant stay'd,
    One kindly word to say

"Jane, till to-morrow you are free
    From tedious task and rule;
This afternoon I must not see
    That yet pale face in school.

Seek in the garden-shades a seat,
    Far from the play-ground din;
The sun is warm, the air is sweet:
    Stay till I call you in."

A long and pleasant afternoon
    I passed in those green bowers;
All silent, tranquil, and alone
    With birds, and bees, and flowers.

Yet, when my master's voice I heard
    Call, from the window, "Jane!"
I entered, joyful, at the word,
    The busy house again.

He, in the hall, paced up and down;
  He paused as I passed by;
His forehead stern relaxed its frown:
  He raised his deep-set eye.

"Not quite so pale," he murmered low.
  "Now, Jane, go rest awhile."
And as I smiled, his smoothened brow
  Returned as glad a smile.

My perfect health restored, he took
  His mien austere again;
And, as before, he would not brook
  The slightest fault from Jane.

The longest task, the hardest theme
  Fell to my share as erst,
And still I toiled to place my name
  In every study first.

He yet begrudged and stinted praise,
  But I had learnt to read
The secret meaning of his face,
  And that was my best meed.

Even when his hasty temper spoke
  In tones that sorrow stirred,
My grief was lulled as soon as woke
  By some relenting word.

And when he lent some precious book,
  Or gave some fragrant flower,
I did not quail to Envy's look,
  Upheld by Pleasure's power.

At last our school ranks took their ground;
  The hard-fought field I won;
The prize, a laurel wreath, was bound
  My throbbing forehead on.

Low at my master's knee I bent,
  The offered crown to meet;
Its green leaves through my temples sent
  A thrill as wild as sweet.

The strong pulse of Ambition struck
  In every vein I owned;

At the same instant, bleeding broke
     A secret, inward would.

The hour of triumph was to me
     The hour of sorrow sore;
A day hence I must cross the sea,
     Ne'er to recross it more.

An hour hence, in my master's room,
     I with him sat alone,
And told him what a dreary gloom
     O'er joy had parting thrown.

He little said; the time was brief,
     The ship was soon to sail,
And while I sobbed in bitter grief,
     My master but looked pale.

They called in haste; he bade me go,
     Then snatched me back again;
He held me fast and murmered low,
     "Why will they part us, Jane?

"Were you not happy in my care?
     Did I not faithful prove?
Will others to my darling bear
     As true, as deep a love?

"O God, watch o'er my foster child!
     O guard her gentle head!
When winds are high and tempests wild
     Protection round her spread!

"They call again; leave then my breast;
     Quit thy true shelter, Jane;
But when deceived, repulsed, opprest,
     Come home to me again!"

THIS POEM, which appears near the conclusion of Charlotte Brontë's first novel, *The Professor,* is not laudable for its literary qualities.[1] Its importance lies rather in the clarity of its presentation of Brontë's fantasy relationship with Heger. While the formal and thematic elements of the poem are naive,

1. The "Jane" poem was apparently written in 1845; a year before Brontë wrote *The Professor* and the last year of her abortive correspondence with Heger.

extraordinary tension is unconsciously created between the surface reality and the sexuality which underlies it. The interaction of master and pupil is ambiguous. Jane's desire for sexual submission is expressed in humble "obedience" and "gratitude," while the teacher's demanding discipline masks a dominating and frustrated passion. He is both father and lover: she is mistress and daughter. Jane's critical illness elicits a longed-for and ambiguously loving response. The moment of recognition heralds separation instead of the impossible consummation. Finally, their parting is effected by an unnamed enemy (Madame Heger, society, conscience) and is made bearable by the contradictory promise of reconciliation at the end.

This fantasy, variously imaged and developed, recurs in all four of Brontë's novels. Her compulsive reworking of the same themes demonstrates the degree of difficulty she experienced in resolving the conflict with Heger. It also suggests the extent to which that conflict was associated implicitly with attitudes toward her own sexuality, her father, Branwell, and her work. In *The Professor* the fantasy provides the novel's motivating impulses, but not its substance. The form of the fantasy is presented but its energy is suppressed. The distance between the crafted fiction and the emotional energy which informs it, measure the gulf between Brontë's obsession and her capacity for self-analysis.

The "Jane" poem reveals as it veils, functioning on the level of dream as had Brontë's juvenile writing. The novel, on the other hand, intentionally represses and obscures the free play of imagination. Its structure is that of the *Bildungsroman,* conventional in form and subject. Ostensibly it carries the hero, William Crimsworth, from innocence to experience, tracing his development from orphaned outsider (the friendless younger brother bereft of status, wealth, and professional competence) to respectable schoolmaster and "paterfamilias." His initiation involves him in a troubling personal relationship with two elder men— Hunsden, the wealthy mill owner, and Pellet, the successful Belgian school director, both of whom are foils intended to help him in his self-definition. He has one abortive "romantic" relationship with Zoraïde Reuter, a Belgian schoolmistress modeled on Mme. Heger. Her failings instruct him in the genuine value of Frances Henri, the poor young student whom he eventually marries. The hero's progress is praiseworthy and archetypic in form, but there is only formal pattern, deprived of genuinely depicted struggle or conflict.

It is interesting, therefore, that Crimsworth should observe, when he discovers the "Jane" poem among Frances's papers:

> [The lines were] not the writer's own experience, but a composition by portions of that experience suggested. Thus while egotism was avoided, the fancy was expressed and, of course, satisfied.[2]

Crimsworth's comment is, in fact, more appropriate to the process which has produced the story in which he figures than it is to the poem which he describes. The struggle between willed feeling and felt truth has taken place well beneath the surface of this novel and the characters emerge from it curiously flattened and dispassionate: shadow versions of their poetic counterparts.

A comparison of the themes in the novel with those of the poem is instructive. In the novel, Crimsworth is the peremptory master, bestowing criticism more easily than praise upon his adoring pupil. He shows his regard for Frances by the stringency of the demands he makes upon her: a game which disguises and prefigures their psychosexual interaction. They are separated, as are the Jane of the poem and her "master," by an "enemy," the jealous Mlle. Reuter. Finally, their moment of reconciliation takes place when Frances is in the throes of deepest despair and loneliness after the death of her last living relative.

The outlines of the recurrent fantasy can be discerned but reading the story one finds that the images are not suggestive— simply blurred. Emotion, where it exists at all, is stifled or disjointed. In a perverse way, Brontë has managed to withhold her characters in order to withhold herself, all the while pursuing a well-defined aesthetic plan which she carefully explains to the reader:

> Novelists should never allow themselves to weary of the study of real life. If they observed this duty conscientiously, they would give us fewer pictures checkered with vivid contrasts of light and shade; they would seldom elevate their heroes and heroines to the height of rapture—still seldomer sink them to

2. Charlotte Brontë, *The Professor* (New York: Oxford University Press, 1967), p. 208. All subsequent references are to this edition and will be given in the text.

the depths of despair; for if we rarely taste the fullness of joy in this life, we yet more rarely savour the acrid bitterness of hopeless anguish . . . (p. 150)

In writing her first novel, Brontë found security in following these guidelines conscientiously. First in her "Farewell to Angria" and later in the "Preface" she wrote for *The Professor*,[3] she made it clear that she had rejected the mythic dimensions of the romantic world:

> I had not indeed published anything before I commenced *The Professor*, but in many a crude effort, destroyed almost as soon as composed, I have got over any such taste as I might once have had for ornamented and redundant composition, and come to prefer what was plain and homely. (p. v)

Unfortunately, she did not understand the options available to her as a "realistic" writer. She did not recognize the potential richness of the psychological insights which had distinguished her early writings from Branwell's: the range and subtlety which a mastery of the psychological perspective would contribute to the "plain and homely" order of life which she had seized upon as her appropriate subject. She did not yet know how crucial some of the old techniques could be in helping her to order psychic chaos while transforming obsession into art. Mistakenly, she purges her fiction of the most compelling tensions of the juvenilia. What remains are unresolved personal and artistic conflicts —an uneasy and, at times, disastrous attempt to wed old and new characters and situations. What is most interesting in this novel, therefore, are its flaws: the subterranean eruption of materials which will become the foci of Brontë's later work.

Although the plot seems to follow the traditional formula of the education of the hero, Crimsworth's growth is not organic. He achieves complacency rather than wisdom. Life seems to happen to him. He has only been moved through time and space. His orphaned childhood is briefly mentioned, never discussed. Reference is made to his quarrel with the aristocratic uncles who have, not ungrudgingly, subsidized his education. His past remains largely an unexplored mystery. We watch his catastrophic ap-

3. The "Preface" was first printed with the permission of Arthur Bell Nicholls, Charlotte's husband, in a posthumous edition of the novel published by Smith, Elder in 1857.

prenticeship to his mill-owner brother, Edward, and are curiously unmoved by it. One is a passive victim: the other a villain without motive. Their underlying resentments are reminiscent of the hostility between Zamorna and Charles, even Zamorna and Northangerland, but while the causes are equally ambiguous, all the passion is gone. Rejecting or, rather, rejected by business as a way of life, Crimsworth happens upon the position of teacher, first in a boys' school in Brussels and later in the girls' school which adjoins it. He is briefly tempted by Mlle. Reuter, the headmistress, but proof of her emotional unreliability immediately precedes his discovery of Frances, the Anglo-Swiss pupilmistress who ultimately resolves all of his conflicts: sexual, professional, even national. His economic difficulties are swept away by good fortune and it remains for him only to marry the still adoring young student with whom he lives happily ever after. The story is neither engaging nor convincing.

Unsatisfactory as a hero, Crimsworth is equally disappointing as the narrator. Standing at the narrative center of the novel, he represents its most crucial problem. Never realized as a fully dimensioned character, Crimsworth is unable to develop a clear narrative voice. Never conscious of his own experience on any but the most immediate level, he is unable to bring to the events he describes a vital complexity of vision.[4] Crimsworth explains, presents, and describes his experience, but his words seem undisturbed by the pressures of life. In *Villette,* the same narrative distance will be perceived as the functioning of a neurotic personality. But here, because the elements of character are never integrated, distance is felt as a lapse of art in much the same way that Brontë's inability to establish a consistent stance for Crimsworth in relation to the reader[5] is interpreted as a sign of novelistic inexperience.

4. It seems hardly necessary to mention Brontë's misjudgment in beginning the novel with Crimsworth's letter to his old friend Charles. Charles, along with the epistolary device, disappears from sight after the first chapter. The relationship, so briefly outlined, seems to look back to the friendship between William Percy and Charles Towneshend and prefigures Crimsworth's ambivalent relationship with Yorke Hunsden.

5. He withholds information, unexpectedly inserting material relevant to the past, but not mentioned at an appropriate time. He also includes material which seems to add bulk but not substance to the story.

II

Generally, the crudities of plot development reflect the inadequate concept of character which results from Brontë's personal insecurity. She cannot create a persona with whom she identifies her own point of view nor can she adopt an ironic stance without knowing who she is or what she wishes to represent. She is caught in a bind: unable to analyze the facts of her situation while urgently wishing to explore its implications for her as a woman, a sister, a daughter, a lover, a writer. In her need to find ways of expressing her anger and frustration and in her desire to create alternative modes of action, she rummages among bits and scraps of the past and tries to synthesize an image of her potential self. The fascinating, unresolved—barely conscious—conflicts that existed among the Angrians are fused with the superficial events that cloak the trauma of Brussels. Searching for focus Brontë projects herself into her story and becomes a force for fragmentation rather than synthesis. In effect, she divides herself among the three central figures—Crimsworth, Frances, and Hunsden—who are alternate versions of one another, all problematical because they are all incomplete; all unconscious of their own motivations and dependent upon one another for definition. The technique Brontë employs foreshadows the allegorical process of inquiry she will use so effectively in *Jane Eyre*. If she had clearly conceived the central protagonist, she would have been able to project his growth onto other well-articulated characters who could have been fully developed themselves while articulating aspects of ther hero's internal struggle. (Jane Eyre's relationship to Rochester and St. John Rivers offers an obvious example.) But because Brontë had not fully grasped the nature of her hero nor the purpose of his quest, because she had not conceived him as a fully separable and distinct character, she is led to suspend the three in uneasy balance, truncating their progress and leaving them incomplete.

The superficial similarities of Crimsworth, Frances, and Hunsden have been noted as well as their similarities to the novelist herself. All are physically plain, energetic, independent, high-minded. All are argumentative, priggish, embarassingly honest.[6] All are extremely vulnerable and their vulnerability is protected by postures which are variously sarcastic, ironic and, in Hunsden's case, cynical. They are not people who, in the best of circumstances, would communicate easily with others. They are locked within their own suspicions and fears. Given the odd blurring of identity boundaries, the failure of their interaction is assured. Dialogue therefore approximates monologue and discussions are dramatized interior debates in which one aspect of Brontë's personality seeks ascendancy over the others.

We assume that Brontë chose to use a male narrator for reasons similar to those which had dictated the same decision for her in the past: that she is still bound to the ambivalent attitudes of adolescence and accepts automatically the male point of view as the "official" perspective. Never having encountered a "heroine" in her personal, cultural, or political experience—or, for that matter, in literature—it was difficult for her to conceive of any woman as the focus of a work of fiction. Even in those late stories, Mina Laury, Elizabeth Hastings, and Caroline Vernon are seen through the eyes of either Charles Towneshend or an omniscient sexless narrator. Not one of them speaks for herself. Furthermore, although these heroines' conflicts are analyzed with unusual insight and subtlety, their lives are justified and their personalities validated, by the man they love: the "hero." In order to use a woman as the locus of consciousness, Brontë had to reexamine her deepest assumptions. Therefore the inconsistency of her characterizations, and particularly the ambiguous treatment of Crimsworth, must not simply be accepted as indications of artistic incompetence but are rather indications that the reexamination had already, rather uncertainly, begun.

William Crimsworth is her transitional hero: a bridge between her identification with a male persona and her commitment to a female "voice." He is, at times, feminized: almost androgynous. One notices at once his propensity for "feeling," his close identification with his mother and his extreme sensitivity: all met with cynicism by the other male characters—Hunsden, Pellet, and Edward. Of more importance is his initial position of powerlessness which makes him seem most "feminine" to the reader and to himself. An orphaned outsider, without money, deprived

6. See Charles Burkhart, *Charlotte Brontë, A Psychosexual Study of Her Novels* (London: Gollancz, 1973), pp. 50–51.

of social status, he describes himself as "a single lean cormorant, standing mateless and shelterless on poverty's bleak cliff" (p. 189). The image is reminiscent of Brontë's description of herself as "a solitary raven surveying the deluge." Standing lonely at a dance given by his elder brother and master, Edward, Crimsworth betrays his confusion of sexual identity when he observes, "I looked weary, solitary, kept down like some desolate tutor or governess" (p. 18). The confusion persists during his early experience in Brussels, and is revealed by the language and imagery he uses to describe Mlle. Reuter's pursuit of him:

> Still she persevered, and at last, I am bound to confess it, her finger, essaying, proving every atom of the casket, touched its secret spring, and for a moment the lid sprung open; she laid her hand on the jewel within, whether she stole and broke it, or whether the lid shut again with a snap on her fingers, read on, and you shall know. (p. 97)

She is the seducer. He is her passive victim: virginal. For Brontë, gender seems quite astonishingly—if only half-consciously—to be a semantic symbol denoting power in much the same way as "blackness" is, in Jean Genet's play, *The Blacks,* a matter of relative position rather than a color.[7] The perception of sexual role as status will be emphasized more in the writing of *Jane Eyre* and *Shirley.* Still, the terms are established here, in the sense which emerges from Crimsworth's attitude toward his social position and in his relationship with Edward, his older brother.

Although it is difficult to take Edward seriously as a character (he is a cardboard, melodramatic villain) he is important as a representative of a developing class which is antithetical to personal humane values: a product and prophet of industrialization. Crimsworth, looking down from the hills upon his brother's mill, must remind himself to

> Look at the sooty smoke in that hollow, and know that there is your post! There you cannot dream, you cannot speculate and theorize—there you shall out and work. (p. 11)

7. In his introduction to *The Blacks,* Genet asks, "What exactly is a black? First of all, what's his color?" (*The Blacks: A Clown Show,* trans. Bernard Frechtman [New York: Grove Press, 1960]). In the play within his play, the black man who achieves ascendancy is no longer "black" but "white" and his victim, his subordinate, is "black" whatever his "real," apparent color.

In the mill, William's education, his intelligence, his sensitivity count for nothing. They may be experienced as threatening to others, but they are not considered useful. They relegate William to a lower class in a society which is becoming increasingly stratified, a society in which the master-owner has crucial power over his economic inferiors.

Edward's attitude toward his wife is typical of his materialistic orientation. She is his possession, a sign of his status, valueless in herself, part of his "image"—the object of his benevolence when he is successful, the object of his sadistic rage when his position is threatened. And she allows herself to be so defined. Her virtues are "social," synthesized to please. She is deprived of intellect and will. Crimsworth recognizes that she is only a plaything, not an appropriate mate. His choice must be of a different sort, he thinks, for he knows that in a man's life there must be "November seasons of disaster, when a man's hearth and home would be cold indeed, without the clear, cheering gleam of intellect" (p. 9). Crimsworth's woman will still have to satisfy the needs of her dominating male but Crimsworth considers his own needs to be of a higher order of value than his brother's.

In this, as in other ways, Crimsworth would regard himself as an intellectual, not standing in opposition to the class society which rejects him, but placing himself outside it altogether. However, his position must be supported psychologically since it cannot be supported socially. The capacity to define himself through love and meaningful work are necessary conditions of his self-confidence. Significantly, Crimsworth can realize himself in these ways only by leaving England. Crimsworth knows that the social system is too inflexible to accommodate him and he feels that he must put his brother behind him, for Edward cannot help but triumph in his own milieu, despite momentary failures and temporary setbacks.

With magical power characteristic of fairy tale and repression (but not conducive to plot credibility) Crimsworth does, in fact, erase his older brother from his mind and, as a foreign professor in Brussels, achieves a privileged status which places him above the middle-class businessman, his students, and—of course— women. When he does finally return to England, it will be to establish, with Frances, a school of his own: a fulfillment of an ambition which dominated Brontë's own life. The school's success allows him to be accepted, because of his intellectual achievements, by members of the upper class and thus to be placed in a position superior to that of the bourgeoisie.[8] In this way Crimsworth becomes the hero of a fantasy shared, with appropriate variations, by intellectuals and artists who found themselves increasingly deprived of social status in the nineteenth century. The compromised nature of this novel's resolution must have had its source in Brontë's own social insecurity, revealed recurrently in the writer's life and work.

Crimsworth's psychological development from alienated younger brother to successful "maitre" establishes a pattern which is faithfully followed by the heroines of the next three novels: most faithfully by Lucy Snowe. Initially, Crimsworth is virtually immobilized by the "cold disdain" of his guardians' attitude toward him. In fact, having known neither joy nor liberty in his life, Crimsworth accepts disdain as his due. Hunsden accurately describes the effect of this sense of inferiority:

> You see beauty always turning its back on you; you are mortified and then you sneer. I verily believe that all that is desirable on earth—wealth, reputation, love—will forever to you be the ripe grapes of the high trellis: you'll look up at them; they will tantalize in you the lust of the eye; but they are out of reach: you have not the address to fetch a ladder, and you'll go away calling them sour. (p. 195)

To deal with his extreme vulnerability, Crimsworth has become passive. It is his passivity which allows him to stay at the mill, tolerating Edward's sadism, defining his situation as a conflict between duty and the need for freedom; giving in, as Brontë does herself, to the "fetish of perseverance" (p. 24). Only after Edward initiates a violent argument with him, can he justify his departure, reassuring himself that "I had not forced circumstances; circumstances had freed me" (p. 39).

Although other characters refer to Crimsworth's sensitivity, it is not his sensitivity to which the reader responds. It is his coldness and defensiveness. That Brontë cannot make the reader aware of his sensitivity and defensiveness simultaneously—as

8. This point is made by Tom Winnifrith, *The Brontës, and Their Background: Romance and Reality* (New York: Macmillan, 1973), p. 156.

she will in *Villette* with Lucy Snowe—is a failure of her art. Nevertheless, she does demonstrate persuasively the way in which Crimsworth, by withholding himself, makes of his vulnerability a weapon.

When Crimsworth first arrives at Edward's house, seeking a livelihood from a brother whom he has not seen for many years, he wonders whether he should "feel free to show something of my real nature" (p. 7) to Edward and his wife. He is anxious to establish a relationship with them, yet he is fearful of the rejection his past has taught him to expect. Fortunately, as he comes to feel when he learns the cruelty of his brother's nature, he does not betray to them his deeper, more authentic self. But the tendency to withdraw that protects him from Edward, makes him unexpectedly attractive to others. It piques Hunsden's curiosity and makes the older man his patron. It stimulates Mlle. Reuter's interest and makes of her his seductress. It manipulates Frances's love and earns him her half-fearful adoration. In short, his reticence ironically brings him into a world of relationships in which he finds that he must attempt to face himself. Most urgently, he must confront the fears surrounding his own sexuality. To define these, Brontë—caught up in the subconscious complexities of her androgynous vision—must have used as a model the more familiar female fear of penetration to conceive the male fear of castration. They are two aspects of the horror of the loss of the self to the "other." The connection to the ambivalence of the Byronic hero is evident—and fascinating.

At the beginning of the novel, we are told that, despite his uncles' urgings, he would not marry "the large and well-modeled statue, Sarah" (p. 2), who seems to be a precursor of Rochester's Berthe. For Crimsworth, sexually desirable women are small and delicate: completely unthreatening. Because he is repelled by an active sensuality which demands response, his feelings about Zoraïde Reuter are ambivalent. Extremely attracted to her, he tries to deny his attraction by imagining the aftereffects of a marriage based upon sensuality:

> . . . when passion cooled, how dreadful to find a lump of wax and wood layed in my bosom, a half idiot clasped in my arms, and to remember that I had made of this my equal—nay, my idol—to know that I must pass the rest of my dreary life with a creature incapable of understanding what I said, of ap-

> preciating what I thought, or of sympathizing with what I felt.
> (p. 100)

To the reader, who might well admire the schoolmistress's intelligence and spirit, Crimsworth's judgment might seem harsh (its egotism does not bear mentioning). The very excessiveness of his language seems to suggest that he fears Zoraïde's sexuality. His problem is resolved when he discovers (unconvincingly) that she has been flirting with him while maintaining an engagement to Pellet. Condemning her duplicity, he can rationalize his rejection of her sexual aggressiveness. But her subservient response to his rejection teaches him a lesson which relieves his sexual anxieties more effectively and teaches him the path to confident masculinity.

> Servility creates despotism. This slavish homage, instead of softening my heart, only pampered whatever was stern and exacting in its mood. The very circumstances of her hovering around me like a fascinated bird, seemed to transform me into a rigid pillar of stone. (p. 120)

Again, the image is compelling. His "manhood" is aroused at last and it is inevitably identified with power:

> I had ever hated a tyrant; and, behold, the possession of a slave, self-given, went near to transform me into what I abhorred! There was at once a sort of low gratification in receiving this luscious incense from an attractive and still young worshiper; and an irritating sense of degradation in the very experience of the pleasure. When she stole about me with the soft step of a slave, I felt at once barbarous and sensual as a pasha. (p. 175)

This aspect of their relationship awakens in him the self-confidence essential to his assertion of the masculine "virtues." He tells us that Zoraïde's interest in him "had proved that I *could* impress" (p. 196) and, although the credibility of the plot suffers from the easy transference of his affections from Mlle. Reuter to Frances, there is a logic in the presentation which, if it does not reflect *well* upon him does, in fact, reflect truthfully.

Crimsworth's aggressive masculinity is supported by the role he is encouraged to play in the schoolroom. Here is a new world with a hierarchical structure that can accommodate his intellectual achievements as Edward's world did not. He appropriates the au-

thority and power inherent in his position with extraordinary
avidity. The primary satisfaction which he derives from teaching
is the display of his own intellectual superiority. (The immaturity
he betrays in his attitude towards his students is not censured by
Brontë. On the contrary, it seems rather to express the bitterness
she herself experienced as a privileged, Protestant student and
teacher at the Pensionnat Heger.) All the Belgians with whom
Crimsworth comes into contact are dull and stubborn: their intellectual facilities are weak; their animal propensities strong. His
male students have "short memories, dense intelligences, feeble
reflective powers" (p. 60). He finds bullying to be the only viable
approach he can adopt toward them: "I offered them but one alternative—submission and acknowledgment of error, or igno-
minious expulsion" (p. 61). The girls whom he teaches are flirta-
tious, sensual, dishonest, and equally stupid. Those possessed of
any intelligence have had their minds and souls warped by their
religion. Thus, although his adversaries emerge as astonishingly
unworthy, his sense of his own superiority is marvelously
strengthened.

Frances offers him an appealing opportunity to show off his
late-blossoming, newly male ego. She is worthy of him although,
or perhaps because, she is still his inferior:

> The toil worn, fagged, probably irritable tutor, blind almost to
> beauty, insensible to airs and graces, glories chiefly in certain
> mental qualities: application, love of knowledge, natural ca-
> pacity, docility, truthfulness, gratefulness, are the charms that
> attract his notice and win his regard. (p. 112)

In his relationship with Frances there is a nod to a principle of
mutual respect which distinguishes the intellectual basis of *their*
feeling from the materialism of Edward's marriage. With *her,*
Crimsworth's need for power is refined: rationalized and controlled. A subtly expressed domination replaces both the raw arrogance of the classroom pose and the sadism of his approach to
Zoraïde. The romantic myth is placed within the context of
teacher-student interaction.

> The reproofs suited her best of all: while I scolded she would
> chip away with her pen-knife and a pencil or a pen; fidgeting a
> little, pouting a little, defending herself by monosyllables; and
> when I deprived her of the pen or pencil, fearing it would be all
> cut away, and while I interdicted even the monosyllabic de-

fence for the purpose of working up a subdued excitement a little higher, she would at last raise her eyes and give me a certain glance, sweetened with gaiety, and pointed with defiance, which, to speak truth, thrilled me as nothing had ever done, and made me in a fashion (though happily she did not know it), her subject, if not her slave. (pp. 168–69)

Crimsworth can "risk" himself emotionally, because Frances does not threaten him sexually. She is a dependent child, waiting to be aroused. Idealizing her, he completely denies her sexual nature. The richly metaphoric language he uses to describe his attachment suggests again the motivating force of sublimation:

[She is] my ideal of the shrine in which to seal my stores of love; personification of discretion and forethought, of diligence and perseverance, of self-denial and self-control—those guardians, those trusty keepers of the gift I long to confer on her—the gift of all my affections. . . . (p. 160)

Crimsworth's analysis of the attraction is also revealing. (It is most revealing, perhaps, of Brontë's inability to separate herself from her narrator. Her representation of Rochester's sexual fears will be far more sophisticated.)

It is true Frances' mental points had been the first to interest me, and they still retained the strongest hold on my preference; but I liked the graces of her person, too. I derived a pleasure, purely material, from contemplating the clearness of her brown eyes, the fairness of her fine skin, the purity of her well-set teeth, the proportion of her delicate form; and that pleasure I could ill have dispensed with. It appeared then, that I too was a sensualist in my temperate and fastidious way. (p. 217)

That temperance and fastidiousness are not adequate to calm Crimsworth's fear of sexuality is revealed in the severe attack of depression which immediately follows his declaration of love and proposal of marriage.[9]

9. Experiences such as this one which is attributed to Crimsworth were familiar to Brontë and recurred throughout her life as they recur in her novels. She described one of these painful interludes in a letter to Miss Wooler (undated fragment, circa November 1846; Wise and Symington, II, 117), in which she recalls her experiences as a teacher at Roe Head. It's interesting that she should use imprisonment in a subterranean dungeon—the image from her adolescent dream—as a central image in her description:

I pity Mr. Thomas from my heart. For ten years—he has now, I think, been a sufferer from nervous complaints—for ten years he has felt the tyranny of

Crimsworth naively attributes the resurgence of "hypochon-dria" (earlier experiences are associated with his lonely orphaned childhood) to a lack of food and rest. It is clear, however, that the cause must be sought elsewhere: in his fear of sexual initiation; his fear of a commitment which will make him vulnerable, in his fear of impotence which will belie the fantasy-self which emerged from his relationship with Zoraïde, in his fear of failure which will negate the professional good fortune of his profes-sorial appointment. The veneer which is his aggressive Byronic masculinity is easily shattered. Hypochondria appears before him as a woman, of course: tempting him into a "grey darkness"; lur-ing him to death. It is the insecurity of his childhood reborn in the challenges of maturity. She is the mother who died, the woman he would marry, the female component of his being. She tempts him with passivity, withdrawal, negation. However complex and obscure the route followed by Brontë in defining the implications of Crimsworth's psychosexual anxieties, by whatever process the fear of penetration was extended to suggest the fear of castration, it seems that this marked the beginning of a new level of compre-hension of the Byronic hero.

The illness which lasts for two weeks is similar to the ordeals later endured by Jane Eyre, Carolyn Helstone, and Lucy Snowe. For all, recovery marks a psychic rebirth: an entry into a new life. Crimsworth emerges from the darkness of hypochondria into a sunny and elevated "place" in society. He exchanges the helpless-ness of the orphaned child for the secure power of the patriarch: husband, father, "maître." Ultimately, as the director of an En-glish school (no longer an alienated foreigner) he will stand be-

---

Hypochondria—a most dreadful doom, far worse than that of a man with healthy nerves buried for the same length of time in a subterranean dungeon—I endured it but a year—and assuredly I can never forget the concentrated anguish of certain insufferable moments and the heavy gloom of many living hours—besides the preternatural horror which seemed to clothe existence and Nature—and which made life a continual waking Nightmare—under such circumstances the morbid nerves can know neither peace nor enjoyment—whatever touches—pierces them—sensation for them is all suffering. A weary, burdened, nervous patience consequently become to those about them—they know this and it infuses a new gall cor-rosive in its extreme attitude into their bitter cup—when I was at Dewsbury Moor—I could have been no better company for you than a stalking ghost—

tween the upper and middle classes, with access to the first and superior to the second.

Although orderly, the resolution remains unconvincing. While Crimsworth's identity crisis has theoretically yielded maturity, while his achieved status has defined him unalterably as male—still, Brontë's art has not made him human. The reader who is informed of his development is aware of external change rather than organic process. He moves but never flowers. The *idea* of Crimsworth's progress is fascinating because of Brontë's unconscious revelations. But to the extent that the artistic, psychological, and social perspectives are conscious, they can only be described as naive.

Frances cannot be realized as a fictive character if Crimsworth is not. She is the other side of his experience: conditioned by his definition of her and the victim, as is he, of Brontë's ambiguous and even contradictory vision. Her relationship with her "maître" does force upon her a condition of fragmentation which is potentially valid: the fragmentation of a woman who seeks for independence in life and feels dependent in love. On one hand, she reveals herself, in her immediate responses to Crimsworth's marriage proposal, to be childish and immature:

> You have always made me happy; I like to hear you speak; I like to see you; I like to be near you; I believe you are very good, and very superior; I know you are stern to those who are careless and idle, but you are kind, very kind to the attentive and industrious, even if they are not clever. Monsieur, I should be *glad* to live with you always— . . . (p. 214)

But she demonstrates, at the same time, a commanding desire for freedom and an adult understanding of the needs of her own personality.

> Think of my marrying you to be kept by you, Monsieur! I could not do it; and how dull my days would be! You would be away teaching in close, noisy school-rooms from morning till evening, and I should be lingering at home, unemployed and solitary; I should get depressed and sullen, and you would soon tire of me. (p. 216)

The fragmentation is never realized on the novel's surface as part of the character's psychological conflict. Brontë—apparently trapped in the depths of her own ambivalence—neither allows the conflict to penetrate Frances's consciousness nor to affect her life. By maintaining a larger perspective which is male-oriented, Brontë offers a superficial and unconvincing solution. Frances does not have to *earn* her independence. It is not necessary for her to discover its source within herself. Instead, her freedom is given to her and sustained by Crimsworth, who magnanimously explains:

> I put no obstacle in her way; raised no objection; I knew she was not one who could live quiescent and inactive, or even comparatively inactive. Duties she must have to fulfill, and important duties; work to do—and exciting, absorbing, profitable work; strong faculties stirred in her frame, and they demanded full nourishment, free exercise: mine was not the hand ever to starve or cramp them; no, I delighted in offering them sustenance and in clearing wide a space for action. (p. 237)

That freedom awarded rather than claimed is simply another form of imprisonment, that the price of Frances's professional liberation is personal servitude, becomes clear to the reader although it is not perceived by Frances, since it is not perceived in these terms by Brontë herself. As Madame, the directress, Frances is "a stately and elegant woman," dignified, vigilant, rather cool, worthy of respect. But at six o'clock "the lady-directress vanished before my eyes, and Frances Henri, my own little lace-mender was magically restored to my arms" (p. 241). Frances plays (with astonishing equanimity) two roles which cannot be integrated. In this way, she remains a child, testing her limits, but never able to make a full commitment to herself. Her relationship with Crimsworth can never mature since both of them are forced into static, ultimately paralyzing postures.

It would seem that Brontë could not yet confront her own confusion about the dependence created by "romantic love," nor could she accept as viable any alternative for women to marriage:

> Look at the rigid and formal race of old maids—the race whom all despise; they have fed themselves, from youth upwards, on maxims of resignations and endurance. Many of them get ossified with the dry diet; self-control is so continually their thought, so perpetually their object, that at last it absorbs the softer and more agreeable qualities of their nature; and they die mere models of austerity . . . (p. 207)

The conflict is still the one of her childhood—between self-control and passion, reason and feeling, Wellington and Byron. Her experience with Heger had confirmed her fear that the two were never to be, for her, easily compatible: yet she could not help but feel that, for a woman particularly, a life without love was more frightening than a life given up as a victim to love's service. As in her childhood, the sexual power of Byron was more compelling than the sober virtues of Wellington. It was not until *Jane Eyre,* her next novel, that she would begin to explore the ways in which the conflicting demands of passion and personal integrity could be recognized and answered.

Only in their relationships with Yorke Hunsden do Frances and William seem to overcome at all the bifurcations of their personalities. Interacting with him, they allow the unresolved, more genuine aspects of themselves to emerge. Hunsden evokes their anger and hostility. Opposing their views, he makes them assert themselves. Asserting themselves, they cannot hide their confusions behind their customary complacency. In their interplay with Hunsden, they betray the possibilities that exist beyond the roles which they play with one another.

Hunsden himself is gifted with no particular insight. In fact, if he is more interesting than the other two, it is because he is even less completely defined, more mysterious. He is similar to them in ways that all three are similar to Brontë, but single aspects of his character are never assimilated into a personality "system." Still, it is his inconsistencies which suggest the more complex potential of personality: the deeper levels of Crimsworth's and Frances's motivation, as well as Brontë's own psychological probing moving beneath the story's surface, disturbing its calm but never affecting its form.

Although Hunsden is more aggressive than Crimsworth, more assured of his position, he is also insecure—as William recognizes:

> . . . his general bearing intimated complete, sovereign satisfaction with himself; yet at times, an indescribable shade passed like an eclipse over his countenance and seemed to me like the sign of a sudden and strong inward doubt of himself, his words and actions—an energetic discontent at his life or his social position, his future prospects or his mental attainment—I know not which . . . (p. 23)

As with Crimsworth, insecurity is linked to effeminacy. In Hunsden's case, it shows itself in his handwriting "small and rather neat: neither masculine or exactly feminine" (p. 183), and, more importantly, in his features:

> Character had set a stamp upon each; expression recast them at her pleasure, and strange metamorphoses she wrought, giving him now the mien of a morose bull and anon that of an arch and mischievious girl; more frequently, the two semblances were blent, and a queer composite countenance they made. (p. 29)

The sexual division is neither developed nor resolved in Hunsden, perhaps because he serves more as a foil for William and Frances than as a character in his own right. Still, to the extent that he is androgynous he is vulnerable. Because he is vulnerable, he is defensive, although in *him* defensiveness does not take the form of withdrawal as it does in William.

Brontë draws upon the relationship between Zamorna and Percy in her conception of the ambiguous interaction between Hunsden and Crimsworth. Feelings fluctuate—often with incredible suddenness—between love and hate. From one perspective, the relationship can be characterized as a struggle for power involving two loving antagonists, imprisoned in mutual fascination. But in its progress can also be traced the romantic quest for the "other": the brother-friend, who is necessary to complete the self, but who, because of the element of opposition he represents, is extremely threatening. The two patterns of behavior are not mutually exclusive. The first implies the second. Together they represent the ambivalent interaction of siblings, lovers, parents, and children. The contradictory needs for union and separation are commandingly expressed in Crimsworth's and Hunsden's interdependence and compulsive assertions of pride, in their fierce protection of their vulnerable egos, in their readiness to experience themselves as threatened and in the capacity of each to cruelly attack and manipulate the other. Because the two men do not share a socially defined relationship, the reactions of the moment define the nature of the role which each will adopt. The flexibility afforded by the ability of each to occupy surrogate positions of crucial importance to the other is both anxiety-producing and liberating. Each stimulated by the other seems capable of growth and change.

Because Hunsden is Crimsworth's senior by several years and his superior in social and economic status, he naturally assumes the roles of father and elder brother. As the first he nurtures and punishes. He and William speak for the first time—the circumstance is noteworthy—as they are standing before the portrait of William's mother. Hunsden clearly admires her face, but criticizes it for being "too sensitive" (p. 19). This is a quality which he faults Crimsworth for sharing. Much later in the novel, he demonstrates his sympathy with William's needs and feelings, by purchasing and sending him this same portrait. The note which accompanies it is astonishing in its cruelty as it is in its self-revelation:

> There is a sort of stupid pleasure in giving a child sweets, a fool his bells, a dog a bone. You are repaid by seeing the child besmear his face with sugar; by witnessing how the fool's ecstasy makes a greater fool of him than ever; by watching the dog's nature come out over his bone. In giving William Crimsworth his mother's picture, I give him sweets, bells, and bone all in one; what grieves me is, that I cannot behold the result . . . (p. 200)

He sets himself up as patriarchal father in contradistinction to Crimsworth's mother. He denies in himself those "female qualities" of empathy and sensitivity which caused him to purchase the portrait in the first place, and through his sadistic rejection of the validity of William's feelings he asserts his power and superiority over the younger man. He acts out the same pattern repeatedly: finding ways of being kind to Crimsworth, demonstrating his concern, but always expecting and finally demanding those words of gratitude which will secure their relative positions.

> I, by the sovereign efficacy of my recommendation, got you the place where you are now living in clover, and yet not a word of gratitude, or even acknowledgment, have you ever offered in return . . . (p. 183)

It is just to avoid concretizing their positions, to avoid accepting a lesser status, that Crimsworth responds to Hunsden's "tone of despotism" with "gentleman-like irony" (p. 31). He cannot accept his dependence, but neither can he confront and overcome it.

Crimsworth recognizes that Hunsden, like a sibling rival, can afford to be generous only when his superior position is assured.

Thinking it likely that Crimsworth is about to make a disastrous match, Hunsden is all concerned restraint but, as William points out:

> I am morally certain that if he had found me installed in a handsome parlour, lounging on a soft couch, with a pretty, wealthy wife at my side, he would have hated me— . . . (p. 192)

And when Hunsden does finally meet Frances and recognizes how happy Crimsworth is likely to be with her—the dimension which Crimsworth's life will have which his own will lack—his response is a marvelous, wordless expression of joy and jealousy; anger and sympathy:

> . . . he swayed me to and fro; so I grappled him round the waist. It was dark; the street lonely and lampless. We had then a tug for it; and after we had both rolled on the pavement, and with difficulty picked ourselves up, we agreed to walk on more soberly. (p. 228)

Their "tug" is neither violent nor affectionate. It underscores their ambivalence and their inability to communicate with one another. Hunsden finally claims the advantage: "Your lace-mender is too good for you, but not good enough for me; neither physically nor morally does she come up to my ideal of a woman" (p. 233). His statement is not persuasive. His ideal woman is only a shadow beside the reality of Crimsworth's wife. Still, now as always, Hunsden reserves the right to question and judge and his judgment alone stands between Crimsworth and total complacency; between growth and paralysis. While Crimsworth is finally able to leave behind the hypochondria connected with childhood, deprivation, and insecurity, and while he has successfully rejected both uncles and brother, he must continue to struggle with the pressures of those lost and repressed relationships as they are presented in his "friendship" with Hunsden. It is here also that his femininity remains potential.

The opinionated mill owner serves a similar catalytic function for Frances. In her interchanges with him she is sparked to growth—not making a game of opposition, as she does with Crimsworth; taking her disagreements seriously, defending them passionately. With Hunsden she can afford to speak for herself, to become angry and hostile. She can be more of a person, as can

Crimsworth, because there is nothing at risk. She can—by asserting her intelligence, her self-confidence, her emotional independence, become "masculine." Through Hunsden, she finds the path to her androgynous self and she is neither threatened nor made to feel guilty. Of course, her relationship with Hunsden does not thrive as a result of the space it allows her in which to test her personality. In fact, she can claim this space only because there is an absence of "relationship" between them; an absence, therefore, of the familiar dependence and the necessity of playing sexually defined roles. For Frances and Crimsworth, Hundsen is a gadfly. He tantalizes them with momentary visions of their own possibility. He annoys them and upsets them, but they are dependent upon him—as he is upon them. Each imposes upon the other those questions which should emerge from the self if the self is aware, integrated, troubled enough to ask them. Not one of them, however, is ready to undertake such questioning independently. Only Brontë has begun to probe in this way and the partiality of her understanding is reflected in the fragmentation of her three central personae.

Appropriately, Hunsden hovers above the next generation, represented by Victor Crimsworth, with the same appealing, yet frustrating power, encouraging the child's "spirit," supporting his desire for a degree of freedom and independence which his parents perceive as antisocial and dangerous. His effect upon the boy is treated with predictable ambiguity. But it is clear that where Frances and Crimsworth would repress Victor's strong urge to self-assertion, would make of him a model of loving obedience, Hunsden would push him to experimentation and deny him the easy conventional solutions which he has also denied the boy's parents.

Brontë does seem to support Frances's and Crimsworth's suspicion and resentment of Hunsden's influence upon the child, as well as their bemused wonder at the persistence of the friendship's importance in their own lives. Again the writer is unsuccessful in detaching herself from her fiction, and the reader is able to perceive one of the reasons for the unresolved ambivalence. It is that the Hunsden within herself has pushed Brontë to begin, in *The Professor,* a radical line of investigation which must give her future work a new focus. One cannot miss the eruptions in the strange, unreal surface of this novel any more than one can overlook the flaws which mar the absurdly bright patina of Frances's and Crimsworth's relationship. Brontë has begun to reject, perhaps only half-consciously, an exclusively biological definition of femininity. To some extent, she begins to see femininity as an existential condition, determined by psychological and social forces. To be powerless, without social, economic, or legal status; to be unconfident, dependent, insecure, and vulnerable—is to be female. So much is clear. But the implications of this perception are too far-reaching to be adequately confronted by her at this critical point in her development. Her vision as she writes *The Professor* is enlarged but still limited. Insofar as Crimsworth and Hunsden demonstrate qualities and inhabit positions that feminize them, they are perceived as weak, incompetent, worthy of pity. Hunsden, in his apparent inability to marry or openly commit himself, remains a vulnerable and somewhat androgynous figure. Crimsworth becomes a "man" when he becomes successful, when he achieves power and status; when his sympathy and sensitivity are transformed into the means of *binding* Frances to him. Our occasional awareness of Frances's "masculine" qualities awakens our curiosity, concern, and approbation but, in Charlotte Brontë's world, there is yet no way that these can be assimilated or made primary in her heroine's life.

As an artist and as a woman Brontë was caught in a painful bind. She was not, like Emily, a mystic who saw the world in transcendent androgynous terms. She did not, like Emily, function on a mythic level of perception any more than she placed herself with Branwell in a mythic universe of values. She demanded of herself a greater political and social awareness. She could not yet be a feminist because she could not imagine how the destructive social and psychological roles common to the middle-class mythology of romantic love could be changed. But neither could she simply accept. The awareness which so flaws *The Professor*—an awareness which is incomplete and confused—marks the stirrings of a feminist consciousness and with it a new sense of the possibilities of fiction.

CHAPTER THREE

Jane Eyre: *The Creation of a Feminist Myth*

*I*N *The Professor*, Charlotte Brontë asks the question, "What is female?" Her answer is, "powerlessness." Probing further, she discovers that the male alone may rid himself of "effeminacy" by achieving social status. The woman is caught in a double bind. Her femininity and therefore her powerlessness are largely inescapable. She can, in the manner of Frances Henri, develop her intellectual and personal capacities. Still, her potential "as a woman" will be realized only within the strictures of a conventional marriage which maintains her in a position of infantile dependence and subordination. Androgyny, therefore, is presented as a developmental stage. Males, like Hunsden, who do not fully resolve their gender ambiguity in order to achieve a clear sexual identification, are experienced, in the context of the novel, as regressive. On the other hand, "masculine" qualities while attractive, even liberating, in the female become unseemly and threatening when they are dominant (e.g., Mlle. Reuter). The alternative, paradoxically presented as desirable, is the fragmented personality which functions without continuity in its public and private roles.

To the sequential question: "Who is female?" Charlotte Brontë, accepting women's inferior status as inevitable, would have answered: "Sometimes men, but always women." The answer could not have satisfied her. She must have recognized the partiality of the vision in the flawed nature of her first novel: in the discontinuity of its characterizations. She must have known that she had only begun to understand the complexities of the social and psychological problems she was attempting to treat.

Brontë undertook the writing of *Jane Eyre* in August, 1846, immediately after she completed *The Professor*. Her approach to the new work suggests how great a distance she traveled rapidly. This was, of course, a critical period in her life. Her last letter to Heger had been sent. Branwell had left Thorpe Green in disgrace and was living at home in a state of shock and dissipation. Charlotte was with her father in a boarding house in Manchester, nursing him back to health after his cataract surgery. These events, the surrounding circumstances, the very process of writing her first novel, had all prepared her for the creation of a second work which would not only mark a significant change in her own career but would be a milestone in the development of English fiction.

The critical decision involved her commitment to a new kind of heroine, one who would be neither more nor less than herself:

> She once told her sisters that they were wrong—even morally wrong—in making their heroines beautiful as a matter of course. They replied that it was impossible to make a heroine interesting on any other terms. Her answer was, "I will prove to you that you are wrong; I will show you a heroine as plain and as small as myself, who shall be as interesting as any of yours."[1]

She came of age as a writer, as a feminist and as a human being ready to explore herself when she insisted that it was *morally* desirable to establish her heroine on the same terms as the traditional hero—by virtue of her interiority: her qualities of mind, character, and personality. From this vantage point Brontë could question and pose alternatives to a romantic mythology which exaggerated sex roles defined and supported by social structures. This was the "realism" she had groped for but could not find as she wrote *The Professor*.

Paradoxically, in freeing Jane Eyre from the conventional trappings of femininity and granting her liberty to feel and express her feelings, to think and express her thoughts, in asserting her "humanness," Charlotte Brontë created the first "anti-heroine": one who defied the conventions of both fiction and society. Orphaned, poor, and plain, faced with the pressures of making her own way in a world which measured the likelihood of

---

1. Gaskell, pp. 215–16.

her success by the degree of her marriageability (her familial connections, her economic status, and, above all, her beauty), Jane tests the limits of social, moral, and psychological possibility, discovering the kinds of power which are in fact available to a woman. Of course, the fantasy elements of the juvenile stories are not eliminated altogether. Brontë did not write of what was, but of what could be. She had not surrendered her dreams and aspirations to the uncompromising and bitter facts of her own life, nor could she undervalue the pressures of her own needs. All of these she shared with her heroine. But she insisted that the wish—and the possibility of its realization—be consonant with the truths of Jane's own situation and personality: that the integrity of that personality be maintained. The old mythology was inadequate to this new task. The self could not abandon its search for a fulfillment capable of delivering it from the anxieties of reality while retaining that reality's essential qualities.[2] It is this interweaving of wish and fact that gives *Jane Eyre* its aura of romance. Psychological realism is responsible for its depth and resonance.

The novel is a perfect fusion of experience and invention. The trauma of Cowan Bridge is there, the dreary years spent as a governess, the thwarted passion for M. Heger. And there are more subtle truths: the ambivalence of Charlotte's relationship with Branwell and with her father, her sense of isolation and alienation, the intensity of her imaginative functioning and yearning sexuality; a religious aspiration that transcended traditional belief. All are expressed in a fictive form which, like the metaphors and symbols of dream, make reality luminous. All are filtered through Jane's consciousness and described in her voice. And the consciousness and the voice, like Jane Eyre herself, are valid if elevated representations of their author.

> The essential difference between novel and romance lies in the conception of characterization. The romancer does not attempt to create "real people" so much as stylized figures which expand into psychological archetypes. It is in the romance that we find Jung's Libido, Anima, and Shadow reflected in a hero, heroine and villain respectively. That is why the romance so often radiates a glow of subjective intensity that the novel

2. This is the focus of the "quest-romance" as Northrop Frye defines it in the *Anatomy of Criticism* (Princeton: Princeton University Press, 1957), p. 193.

lacks, and why a suggestion of allegory is constantly creeping in around its fringes.[3]

The form and structure of *Jane Eyre* approximate the form and structure of romance which Northrop Frye describes. There can be little question that Jane is herself portrayed by Brontë as a "real person," but the novel is so much the story of the heroine's psychological development that people and situations seem often to be generated as alternative value systems that she must explore as aspects of her growth. This allegorical quality is underlined by the novel's repetitive structure. As in fairy tale or the quest-romance, characters, situations, and symbols must be rehearsed again and again, the heroine experiencing with each new revolution an increment of pressure and intensity, until the ultimate resolution of conflict is achieved.

We are all familiar with tales of the "dispossessed princess" which focus the conflicts and aspirations of the prepubescent and adolescent female. In these stories (e.g., *Cinderella*), ambivalent attitudes towards members of the family are distanced. Those feelings of rejection, anger, hostility, and thwarted love which are too painful to confront directly, are typically projected onto the wicked stepmother and her cruel children. Guilt translates the blood relationship into one which is necessarily unnatural. The father-protector (the good king) who cannot, in the scenario of the family romance, act in his daughter's behalf, in opposition to the mother, is conveniently absent or dead. The princess must pass through a number of trials—choose among alternative possibilities—which test and prove her moral worth. Ultimately her lover—the "other self" essential to her completion—recognizes the royalty hidden beneath the dust of poverty. He acknowledges their kinship and, through marriage, bestows upon her the family, wealth, and status which are the external signs and guarantees of her true value.

This common fairy tale provides a benign alternative to the Byronic myth. It is responsive to the female dream; not simply an expression of narcissistic male fantasy. Charlotte Brontë adopts the dream form, following the basic pattern of the tale. But she finds that the resolution is not consonant with *her* dream, which is more feminist in impulse.

3. Frye, p. 304.

At the beginning of the novel Jane does indeed appear in the guise of the "dispossessed princess": orphaned (her uncle-protector dead), living in a condition of alienation and dependence with Mrs. Reed and her three children, none of whom accept the responsibilities of familial relationship. It is the Brontë family seen through the distorting lens of sibling rivalry, projected in fantasy. It is an image of Charlotte's jealousy of the companionship of Emily and Anne; her deep ambivalence toward Branwell. And, not least of all, there is her resentment of the parent who has never loved her enough: the mother who died; the father who withdrew. Jane's class and sex define her as victim and she experiences herself as unworthy. She is "humbled by the consciousness of . . . physical inferiority to Eliza, John and Georgiana Reed."[4] Her habitual mood is one of "humiliation, self-doubt, forlorn depression" (p. 14). She has been made unsocial by the status of "outsider" thrust upon her and she is, in turn, punished for her absence of sociability. She learns from the servants that to be plain is to be unloved and rejected even by those who do not occupy a social position superior to her own:

> Bessie . . . sighed and said, "Poor Miss Jane is to be pitied, too, Abbot." "Yes," responded Abbot, "if she were a nice, pretty child, one might compassionate her forlornness; but one really cannot care for such a little toad as that." (p. 26)

But it is from John Reed, the violent, spoiled, bullying son that she learns most painfully what it means to be poor and dependent in a world which respects wealth and position. It is from John that she learns the meaning of powerlessness, the meaning of being a female in a patriarchal society.

His superiority is assumed by his mother, his sisters, the servants, himself. He is incapable of love or affection, concerned only with the appropriation and wielding of power. Because Jane is defenseless, he uses her to inflate his ego. Because she is terrified and "habitually obedient," he preys upon her weakness. His physical presence is loathsome, his appearance "disgusting and ugly." His is the outer form of sadism and excess:

---

4. *Jane Eyre*, ed. Jane Jack and Margaret Smith (Oxford: The Clarendon Press, 1969), p. 3. All subsequent references are to this edition and will be given within the text.

[He was] large and stout for his age, with a dingy and un-
wholesome skin: thick lineaments in a spacious visage, heavy
limbs and large extremities. He gorged himself habitually at
table, which made him bilious, and gave him a dim and
bleared eye and flabby cheeks. (p. 6)

Jane can only escape from him and the other miseries of her
life by withdrawing into fantasy and illusion. She is entranced by
Bessie's tales of love and adventure, by the ballads she sings.
But, like Charlotte Brontë "making out," she enjoys most of all
creating her own stories as she looks at Bewick's *History of British Birds*. She finds in the romantic images of nature, projections
of her own emotional life, seeming symbols of herself.

> . . . the rock standing up alone in a sea of billow and spray
> . . . the broken boat stranded on a desolate coast . . . the
> cold and ghastly moon glancing through bars of cloud at a
> wreck just sinking . . . the quite solitary church-yard with its
> inscribed headstone; its gate, its two trees, its low horizon,
> girdled by a broken wall, and its newly-risen crescent, attest-
> ing the the hour of even-tide . . . (p. 5)

They are images of isolation and despair, of death and infinity.
They are images of the sublime and suggest the kinship of human
feeling with a larger mysterious world that exists beyond the self,
accessible and yet threatening because it cannot be ordered or
contained. This universe of imaginative possibility enthralls Jane
because it offers her a landscape of the mind rather than a canvas
of social interaction. She learns its dangers as well as its potential
for liberation, however, when she surrenders for the first time to
the unconditioned demands of the ego. It is a lesson which haunts
her into maturity.

The incident, which reverberates through the novel, origi-
nates in Jane's unexpected defense against John Reed's casually
cruel physical attack upon her. Her justifiable anger, her pure assertion of self, is interpreted as unjustifiable passion. *His* unjustifiable cruelty is thought to be an appropriate assertion of his role
of "master." Her punishment for allowing herself to be released
into passion is imprisonment in the "red-room" where the principle of irrationality is given concrete form. The cold magnificence
of the bedchamber, its profound silence, the "sense of dreary
consecration" that marks its association with her uncle's death,

the muffled windows, the great looking glass, the "vacant majesty" everywhere, the crimson draperies, hangings, carpets, and coverings; the pinkish walls—all the color of blood, of fire, of passion—contribute to the fearsome sublimity of the scene. It is a terrifying womb-world from which she is born into a new state of being. Within it she is overwhelmed by the feelings and fantasies of the spirit-self. Catching sight of herself in the mirror she does, in fact, think that she has become an inhabitant of that other universe. She feels herself to be totally alienated from the living, thrust alone into a world of the dead and the supernatural.[5] She loses her sense of the boundaries of her identity. She feels the terror of total self-abandonment:

> My heart beat thick, my head grew hot; a sound filled my ears, which I deemed the rushing of wings: something seemed near me; I was oppressed, suffocated: endurance broke down—I uttered a wild, involuntary cry—I rushed to the door and shook the lock in desperate effort.[6] (p. 15)

Forced to remain, she is overwhelmed by feelings of impotence. Her fainting fit marks the end of the submission of her childhood and the beginning of a new stage of growth.

Jane awakens to the knowledge that she must test the strength of her private self against the constraints of the social world. Her ordeal has aroused in her a burning sense of injustice and the realization that although she is badly treated, she is not necessarily guilty: to be a victim is not necessarily to be unworthy:

> "Unjust!—unjust!" said my reason, forced by the agonizing stimulus into precocious though transitory power, and Resolve, equally wrought up, instigated some strange expedient to achieve escape from insupportable oppression—. . .
> (p. 13)

---

5. Lucile Dooley points out that the moving, gleaming light which Jane sees and interprets as a portent of some supernatural vision, is a typical symptom of adolescent hysteria: "taken literally from an experience of her own at Roe Head School and it is said that her health failed from the time of that shock, and she was finally compelled to go home" (Dooley, p. 242).

6. It is important to note that, in her letters to Ellen Nussey, Charlotte uses the word "imagination" as a euphemism for sexual fantasy. This suggests a connection between the imaginative frenzy of the red-room scene and later experiences of fantasized sexual violation. The sexual implications of "wings" and flight throughout the writing further corroborate the association.

Her new capacity for moral judgment and her nascent sense of self are supported, when she recovers, by the compassion shown to her by Bessie and the apothecary. From Bessie's nurturing she forms a positive image of maternity and it is this which, while fragile, allows her to condemn the bad mother, Mrs. Reed.

Each act of liberation, each assertion of self, brings with it an awareness of possibility. She understands the nature of John's cowardice and sees that her aunt's guilt makes her vulnerable. And while the angry reproach she offers Mrs. Reed is followed by "the pangs of remorse and the chill of reaction" (p. 40), she is, in fact, largely freed from her blind fear of authority. She knows now that a display of powerlessness invites scorn and she learns, therefore, that she too holds the secret of power: that its exercise is within her intellectual and psychological control.

Jane's knowledge that the responsible creation of an authority *within* makes it possible to judge the claims of the authority *without* prepares her to meet the difficulties of the next trial. Like Christian in *The Pilgrim's Progress,* she finds that a temptation overcome is not overcome forever. A capacity achieved must be tested against more formidable obstacles. It is the obsessive movement of dream: the spiraling cycle of allegory. Having vanquished John Reed and demonstrated her superiority to his petty tyrannies, Jane must confront a more substantial representative of the patriarchal system in the Rev. Mr. Brocklehurst.

She first meets the head of Lowood School in Mrs. Reed's breakfast room:

> I looked up at—a black pillar!—such, at least, appeared to me,
> at first sight, the straight, narrow, sable-clad shape standing
> erect on the rug: the grim face at the top was like a carved
> mask, placed above the shaft by way of capital. (p. 33)

The extraordinary phallic imagery makes of Brocklehurst a symbol of male sexuality and associates that sexuality with sadism and death. The association is appropriate. John Reed's crude snobbishness and bullying become, through Brocklehurst's misuse of power, institutionalized oppression motivated by class and sexual bias. The girls at Lowood School cannot and will never be able to assume functions traditionally thought suitable for middle- and upper-class women. They are not marketable commodities, valuable possessions, symbols (like Brocklehurst's wife and daughters) of their owner's wealth and status, themselves adornments and decorations. They are not proper heroines of romance. Poverty deprives them of their sexuality, their individuality, and hence of their humanity. Brocklehurst is an effective agent of this deprivation, insisting that their hair be cut off ("we are not to conform to nature" [p. 73]) and that they all be clothed in the same dreary, childish attire.

Because Brocklehurst is a more threatening expression of male authority than John Reed, because he is sophisticated in the wielding of power, he cannot—like the boy—employ that sadism in its own guise. Instead, he cloaks his greed, selfishness, and vanity in the hypocritical vestments of religious principles, disguising fear and guilt with love of God. And his ultimate crime, murder by neglect, is automatically justified by his claim that the desirable destiny of the charity students must be the same as that which would be appropriate to saints and martyrs.

From the time that Jane first meets him, it is clear that she has not discovered the power of her will only to surrender it to join, through self-sacrifice, the hypocritically defined ranks of the Presbyterian "elect." In some ways it is easier for her to defend herself against his authority, despite the social, sexual, and religious sanctions he brings with him, than it was for her to oppose her cousin. In the allegorical mode, interior conflict is acted out in successive scenes of struggle which yield victories symbolizing psychic growth. At the Reeds, Jane was isolated. Now, because all the students are victims, all are her companions and allies. Because she has achieved power over herself, she has earned the supplemental power she needs to triumph over a more sophisticated threat to her ego. Typically, the earlier victory (John Reed) determines the nature of the succeeding trial (Brocklehurst) and is the best preparation for it.

When Jane arrives at Lowood she is emotionally starved; spiritually and intellectually hungry. Her life has been one of extreme deprivation and her only reinforcement has come from the mercurial Bessie. Living predominantly in the world of her imagination, she has barely begun her social development. Childlike, withdrawn, she responds with most immediacy to the frustration of her physical needs. She is pressingly aware of the cold, the inadequate clothing, and, most of all, the skimpy and spoiled food: the burned porridge, rancid fat, rusty meat. But after Miss Tem-

ple has cleared her of the charges made against her by Brocklehurst, has given her the chance to construct a new identity, her
focus changes. She can apply herself to her work, define herself
as a student, aspire instead of grieve:

> That night, on going to bed, I forgot to prepare in imagination
> the Barmecide supper of hot roast potatoes, or white bread and
> new milk, with which I was wont to amuse my inward crav-
> ings: I feasted instead on the spectacle of ideal drawings . . .
> all the work of my own hands . . . I examined too, in thought,
> the possibility of my ever being able to translate currently a
> certain little French story book which Madam Pierrot had that
> day shown me. (p. 87)

Whereas she had previously accepted the Reeds' values ("I was
not heroic enough to purchase liberty at the price of caste" [p.
24]), and therefore their evaluation of her, she can now observe
happily:

> Well has Solomon said: —"Better is a dinner of herbs where
> love is, than a stalled ox and hatred therewith."
>
> I would not now have exchanged Lowood with all its priva-
> tions, for Gateshead and its daily luxuries. (p. 87)

Indeed, Lowood does, paradoxically, provide Jane with a supportive environment.[7] It is important for her development that the
school is exclusively female and that the students share her social
and economic background. She is no longer an outsider, necessarily inferior. Miss Temple and Helen Burns provide her with
role models, friendship, a new universe of values and the opportunity to excel. Maria Temple (her name suggests the importance
of her position, the degree of her idealization) not only stands between Brocklehurst and Jane, deflecting his power thrusts. But as
the superintendent of the school, she offers an alternative view of
authority. Appropriately, it is from her that Jane receives the first
bit of food that is more than the most minimal nutriment: a seed

---

7. The original of Lowood School was, of course, the Clergy Daughters
School at Cowan Bridge opened in January 1824, and founded by the Rev.
William Carus Wilson, the model for Mr. Brocklehurst. Charlotte Brontë was at
the school for a year at most, when she was eight years old. It was during this
period that she saw her two sisters, Maria (the model for Helen Burns) and Elizabeth, sicken and die. Her own experience there was profoundly unhappy. She
never forgot it and assured W. S. Williams in 1849 that "the Lowood part . . .
is true" (Wise and Symington, II, 313).

cake. Just, calm, and humane, Miss Temple is a maternal figure, an intelligent guide, a warm companion. She stimulates independence and respect for learning, pride in identity: a corrective to the oppression of male dominance. She also inspires love.

For Jane, this is the most crucial gift of all. Living at the Reeds, Jane had recognized the depth of her own need to love, but her doll had been the only possible recipient of her feelings. At Lowood she learns the depth of her need to *be* loved. When Helen Burns observes:

> If all the world hated you, and believed you wicked, while your own conscience approved you, and absolved you from guilt, you would not be without friends.

Jane replies:

> No; I know I should think well of myself; but that is not enough: if others don't love me, I would rather die than live—I cannot bear to be solitary and hated, Helen. Look here; to gain some real affection from you, or Miss Temple, or any other whom I truly love, I would willingly submit to have the bone of my arm broken, or to let a bull toss me, or to stand behind a kicking horse, and let it dash its hoof at my chest. (p. 80)

Her deprivation of love has been too great and has lasted too long. Jane, like Charlotte Brontë herself, must *be* loved in order to know herself lovable and she cannot accept love without imagining its cost, without expecting, even embracing, the necessity of sacrifice. She cannot perceive the world in moral terms as Helen does. She feels it, knows it, through her emotions. Sensitivity, vulnerability, and disappointment have tinged that knowledge with masochism and dependence.

Oddly enough, although Helen seems to stand at the furthest possible pole from Jane, they have both simply chosen opposite ways of achieving the same goal. Helen accepts the lesson of *Rasselas* (which she is reading when Jane first meets her): that the practice of virtue, rather than happiness, is the desired end of life. Helen makes a strength of humility. She accepts the Calvinist language of morality and religion—Brocklehurst's language—and with it she builds the prison of her life. It is the reverse side of the "red-room" experience. Helen's alternatives are only enslavement through self-denial or enslavement in abandonment. To be devoured in the fire of passion or to "burn" on the altar of

abnegation and repression. Helen is the "good girl" who identifies herself completely with authority. Masochistically oppressed, she participates in the power of the oppressor by accepting
his punishment and assuming his blame.

Jane does not share Helen's temperament and experiences
"impotent anger" on her friend's behalf.[8] But Jane's absence of
comprehension does not make her admire Helen less. She accepts
her friend's moral superiority as she accepts her intellectual superiority. She sees her as a martyr, noble and inspiring, and a martyr indeed she is for she is one of those whose death marks a
period of regeneration at Lowood.

Still, despite Jane's admiration and love—despite the fact that
she learns from Helen lessons of patience, fidelity, serenity, and
the importance of self-discipline—there is also the recognition
that Helen has compromised. Jane sees that her friend has ideals
which release her from the conflict which would accompany confrontation. In Helen's utterances there is "an alloy of inexpressible sadness" (p. 81) and in the words she speaks before she dies,
she reveals the degree to which she undervalues herself because
she is without an adequate sense that she is loved: because she
has been rejected by the one person who ought to cherish her the
most:

> I am very happy, Jane; and when you hear that I am dead you
> must be sure and not grieve. . . . We all must die one day,
> and the illness which is removing me is not painful; it is gentle
> and gradual: my mind is at rest. I leave no one to regret me
> much: I have only a father; and he is lately married, and will
> not miss me. By dying young I shall escape great sufferings. I
> had not qualities or talents to make my way very well in the
> world: I should have been continually at fault. (p. 96)

Helen's reasons for accepting death so easily—perhaps for embracing, even welcoming it—prove justified. She is not mourned
by her family: "Her grave . . . in Brocklebridge churchyard
. . . for fifteen years after death . . . was only covered by a
grassy mound" (p. 97). It is then, after fifteen years, that Jane

8. Elizabeth Gaskell in discussing Charlotte's feelings about the teacher at
Cowan Bridge School who provided the model for Miss Scatcherd, says: "Her
heart, to the latest day on which we met, still beat with unavailing indignation at
the worrying and the cruelty to which her gentle, patient, dying sister had been
subjected by this woman" (Gaskell, p. 44).

places there a marble tablet "inscribed with her name—and the word 'Resurgam' " (p. 97). Thus Jane "bears witness" (as Brontë has done in telling Maria's story). It is the fragile relief of the survivor.[9]

From Miss Temple and Helen Burns, Jane learns to value duty and self-control and by the time she is ready to leave Lowood, she can say, "I appeared a disciplined and subdued character" (p. 99). The word "appeared" is crucial. The childhood trauma of Gateshead had plunged Jane into the awesome depths of passionate response. The fear of irrational experience remains although it is tempered by the ordered life at Lowood. Jane has confronted her commanding need for love and respect and she accepts with some trepidation her consequent condition of dependence: the potential power of passion. She can only attempt to guard herself against extremes of behavior which must result in the loss of selfhood.

This phase of her development is ended and her ties with Lowood severed by Maria Temple's marriage and departure. It is then that Jane begins to long for a new experience. Like Charlotte, who wrote to Ellen of her "wish for wings," Jane has a nameless need: an unacknowledged yearning for sexual fulfillment. It is this which qualifies and makes more poignant the constructive and realistic compromise which Jane reaches with herself:

> I desired liberty; for liberty I gasped; for liberty I uttered a prayer; it seemed scattered on the wind then faintly blowing. I abandoned it, and framed a humbler supplication; for change, stimulus: that petition, too, seemed swept off into vague space; "Then," I cried, half desperate, "Grant me at least a new servitude!" (p. 101)

She consciously rejects the perspective of romance, but her impassioned language belies the common sense of her plea.

Jane's arrival at Thornfield initiates the next stage of the allegorical journey of development. Although her new environment is pleasant enough (she is warmly treated as Adele Varen's governess and Mrs. Fairfax's companion) Jane is lonely and becalmed. She withdraws again into the world of the imagination in

9. This might well be an expression—indirect, perhaps even unconscious—of Charlotte's feeling that Patrick Brontë was, by his negligence, responsible for the death of Maria.

which fears, aspiration and conflict find form. From the moment of his appearance, Rochester seems to be part of this interior world: an object of need; a cause of anxiety. He comes in response to Jane's restlessness which disappears with his presence. He is linked to the childhood world of "fancies bright and dark," to distant memories of nursery stories. Both the great dog who heralds his coming and the horse he rides out of the stillness of evening against the muted colors of the darkening sunset, seem masks of the "Gytrash," the ill-omened spectral beast who, in Bessie's tales, haunted solitary ways and accosted belated travelers.

Rochester, in turn, associates Jane immediately with an imaginative and romantic world:

> No wonder you have rather the look of another world. I marvelled where you had got that sort of face. When you came on me in Hay Lane last night, I thought unaccountably of fairy tales, and had half a mind to demand whether you had bewitched my horse: I am not sure yet. (p. 149)

He enjoys this sense of her, insists upon it: repeatedly describing her as "elfin," a "nonnette," "a fairy," "his good genii," "a dream or shade," a "strange . . . almost unearthly thing." The fact that she is without family or friends, without social ties, makes her an appropriate dweller within the remote "fairy tale castle" which is his home.

Rochester also lives as an "outsider." Circumstances have made him one and like other Byronic heroes—like Charlotte's beloved Zamorna—he embraces this definition of himself. He knows that "Nature meant to me to be, on the whole, a good man" (p. 166), but he was wronged by fate, weakened—like Branwell—by his education ("suppose you were no longer a girl well-reared and disciplined, but a wild boy, indulged from childhood upwards" [p. 273]). First made desperate and then degenerate by the misery of his enforced marriage, orphaned, the last of his family, he is isolated. Surviving his father and older brother, but still suffering the effects of their cruel and selfish treatment, he rejects external authority, defying the world's judgment and man's opinion, claiming his right to establish for himself the moral laws by which he will live, echoing Milton's Satan in his claim that he has the right to pleasure since he cannot find happiness.

Rochester's economic position, class, and sexual status allow him to act as if he were not, in fact, responsible to society. His imagination defines for him a rebel's role. Energy and will enable him to inhabit it. Jane, on the other hand, seems able to function without society's consideration because she is beneath society's notice. Her education at Lowood was appropriate to an intelligent and moral human being who could bring nothing to the marriage market and did not need, therefore, to be trained as a lady. Her aspirations and her perspective are therefore more human, less sex-typed, than those conventionally held.

> Women are supposed to be very calm generally: but women feel just as men feel; they need exercise for their faculties, and a field for their efforts as much as their brothers do; they suffer from too rigid a restraint, too absolute a stagnation, precisely as men would suffer; and it is narrow-minded in their more privileged fellow-creatures to say that they ought to confine themselves to making puddings and knitting stockings, to playing on the piano and embroidering bags. It is thoughtless to condemn them, or laugh at them, if they seek to do more or learn more than custom has pronounced necessary for their sex. (p. 133)

Having little to lose, she can afford to be spontaneous and open. In her interaction with Rochester, both are liberated from the superficial gestures and restraining, repressive behavior associated with traditional sex roles. Jane feels herself to be freed by Rochester's rude openness: his disregard for "civilities." They communicate on a new level, revealing themselves emotionally and intellectually. They share a profound sympathy of mind and spirit. It is in part from this that their sexual passion derives and passion it is—portrayed with a vividness not found before in the English novel. It is an emotion that pleads for physical expression; the obverse of character revealed through physical features. Rochester's massive head, his "granite-hewn features," jetty eyebrows, "great, dark eyes," his abundant hair: these attract Jane. It is his will, his superb self-confidence, his power and authority and the mysterious promise of emotional intensity by which she is compelled. It is his "masculinity" which arouses her "femininity."

Jane has escaped some forms of social conditioning and can identify and condemn the more obvious forms of social inequality. Still, the circumstances of her life have created in her a psychological need for the kind of symbiotic relationship which is essential to the stability of middle-class patriarchy, and is supported and justified by the romantic myth. Once she is aware that Rochester's urge to dominate her does not rest on class snobbery, her guard is lowered:

> What, you are my paid subordinate, are you? Oh, yes, I had forgotten the salary! Well, then, on that mercenary ground, will you agree to let me hector a little?

> No, sir, not on that ground: but on the ground that you did forget it, and that you care whether or not a dependent is comfortable in his dependency, I agree heartily. (p. 164)

Her pride will not allow her to be humbled by her economic and social situation. Here her history has made her sensitive. But she is not aware of the dangers—potentially more destructive—of psychosexual dependence.

Her vulnerability leads her into the romantic trap. She bows before the strength of Rochester's personality. It has always been her tendency. Rochester has told her, "I am old enough to be your father," and he does, indeed, become the loving father whom she has never known. She treasures this paternal aspect of his feelings and when she is separated from him, she mourns the loss of *that* most deeply.

> I shall never more know the sweet homage given to beauty, youth and grace—for never to anyone else shall I seem to possess these charms. He was fond and proud of me—it is what no man besides will ever be. (p. 459)

She is "mastered" by his "energy, decision and will"; stimulated by his experience of life. Infatuated, she desires to live through him, to give herself to the exploration of his mysterious, tortured personality. She wishes to "look into the abyss at her leisure, explore its secrets and analyze its nature" (p. 235). She wants to save him from himself, from the fate he fears:

> To live, for me Jane, is to stand on a crater-crust which may crack and spue fire any day. (p. 271)

And she:

> I cannot deny that I grieved for his grief, whatever that was, and would have given much to assuage it. (p. 181)

She retains the belief she had shared with Helen Burns that love must be merged with self-sacrifice. She is grateful for his love and tells him: "I'd give my life to save you" (p. 255).

Like Christian, who beholds from a distant shore the outlines of the Eternal City, Jane feels herself to be at the verge of happiness but, like Christian, she has not yet understood the nature of her quest: has not resolved those internal conflicts which block fulfillment. Anxiety is submerged in the bright hopefulness of day. Ambivalence is repressed. But both are released in the psychic images of night.

> Till morning dawned I was tossed on a buoyant but unquiet sea, where billows of trouble rolled under surges of joy. I thought sometimes I saw beyond its wild waters a shore, sweet as the hills of Beulah; and now and then a freshening gale, wakened by hope, bore my spirit triumphantly towards the bourne: but I could not reach it, even in fancy,—a counteracting breeze blew off land, and continually drove me back. Sense would resist delirium: judgment would warn passion. (p. 188)

Jane is not aware of the extent to which her autonomy is threatened by her love for Rochester. She understands that social differences might separate them. But despite the fact that she calls him "master" and accepts obedience as his due, she believes that they meet as equals. Fortunately her self-confidence is strengthened before she is enlightened. The crucial opportunity for growth is offered when she receives a summons to her Aunt Reed's death-bed. She leaves Rochester, aware both of his love for her and his apparent intention to marry Blanche Ingram. What might seem to be an awkward digression, useful only in creating further suspense, has in fact all of the artistic symmetry and psychological validity of earlier struggles.

In the Ingrams—the overbearing mother, the proud, unfeeling Blanche, the insipid younger daughter and effete son, Jane has confronted another version of the Reed family (the technique of fairy tale need hardly be mentioned again). That she can meet their snobbish rejection with cool self-confidence is, perhaps, an indication of repression, but it is also a measure of her maturity. The depth of that maturity is tested by her return to the substance of which the Ingrams are but the shadow: to that trauma which is buried nine years in her past.

> The same hostile roof now again rose before me: my prospects
> were doubtful yet; and I had yet an aching heart. I still felt as a
> wanderer on the face of the earth: but I experienced firmer trust
> in myself and my own powers, and less withering dread of
> oppression. The gaping wound of my wrongs, too, was now
> quite healed; and the flame of resentment extinguished.
> (p. 285)

Like the fairy tale princess and with the simplicity of wish fulfillment fantasy, Jane has been completely vindicated. By a process
of inversion, rivalries are resolved. The family which had excluded her—the family which she had resented—has itself disin-
tegrated—morally and economically. Her prime oppressor, John
Reed, first "sunk and degraded," is now dead. Georgiana and
Eliza are both frustrated and miserable, imprisoned in mutual
suspicion and dislike. Georgiana, with all of her vanity and para-
sitic selfishness, demonstrates the emptiness of upper-class values. Eliza, about to enter a religious order, reveals the meaning-
lessness of discipline practiced for its own sake; the sterility of
religion based upon hatred instead of love.[10] Jane quickly wins
the admiration and trust of her two cousins, proving her superiority to them. She graciously forgives her aunt who proves her own
unadulterated wickedness by dying unrepentant. Jane returns to
Thornfield convinced of the validity of her own values, confirmed in her faith and love, bound to her recognition that personal integrity is crucial to the integrity of her personality. She is
ready for her ordeal. At Thornfield Jane responds to Rochester's
devious game-playing with a degree of courage and depth of feeling which is completely ennobling and feminist in impulse.

> Do you think, because I am poor, obscure, plain, and little, I
> am soulless and heartless?—You think wrong!—I have as
> much soul as you,—and full as much heart! And if God had
> gifted me with some beauty and much wealth, I should have
> made it as hard for you to leave me, as it is now for me to leave
> you. I am not talking to you now through the medium of cus-
> tom, conventionalities, nor even of mortal flesh:—it is my
> spirit that addresses your spirit; just as if both had passed
> through the grave, and we stood at God's feet equal,—as we
> are! (p. 318)

10. She invites comparison with Helen Burns and St. John Rivers, and is
found to occupy a curious middle ground between them.

Rochester replies, "My bride is here . . . because my equal is here, and my likeness" (p. 319), but after their betrothal, his behavior suggests that his bride can be neither his equal nor his likeness. All that drew him to Jane has become irrelevant. She is now his object, his possession, an extension of himself: a demonstration of his taste, a badge of his position, proof of his masculinity. He wants to clothe her in rich silks and magnificent satins: to cover her with jewels. He finds nobility stamped on her brow and "will make the world acknowledge you a beauty, too" (p. 326). Jane is degraded by his changed tone ("You are dreaming, Sir—or you are sneering. For God's sake, don't be ironical" [p. 326]). To be transformed by his snobbery—placed on a pedestal by his insecurity—is to be denied her selfhood and it is for herself that she wishes to be loved.[11]

Rochester would use her to erase his past. Taking her to Europe, he will "revisit it healed and cleansed, with a very angel as my comforter" (p. 326). Appropriating her innocence, he believes he can avoid confronting the implications of his own experience. And as Jane feels her independence sifting away, her identity being negated, she tries to regain control. She wants to be his friend and companion, she insists that rudeness is preferable to flattery, she asks to earn her keep by maintaining herself as Adele's governess. She has begun to understand the meaning of economic dependence, the connotations of class inferiority and the subtle implications that both have for sexual relationships.

> He smiled; and I thought his smile was such as a Sultan might, in a blissful and fond moment, bestow on a slave his gold and gems had enriched: I crushed his hand, which was ever hunting mine, vigorously, and thrust it back to him red with the passionate pressure . . ." (p. 339)[12]

As Rochester's sexuality becomes more open, Jane begins to withdraw, alternately "vexing and teasing," keeping him at a distance. It is her only defense against self-abandonment. Her

11. The implications of Rochester's treatment of Jane parallel in an interesting way Byron's destructive treatment of Caroline Lamb: "It was Byron's misfortune that he felt impelled to despoil his mistress of those very qualities which had in his romantic imagination made her attractive—the freshness and naiveté of her personality" (Marchand, I, 341).

12. Here we are reminded of Crimsworth's sense of himself as a sultan—a feeling of power inspired in him by the seductive Mlle. Reuter.

fear of sexuality is not the effect of repulsion. Quite the contrary. It is part of her recognition of the depth of her passion: of her capacity for surrender and submergence. She wants to keep both herself and Rochester from "the edge of the gulf" (p. 344) which they have both glimpsed with horror in Rochester's mad wife, Berthe, who stands in the novel at the nexus of romance and allegory.[13] Crucial to the plot as the focus of Gothic horror and suspense, she is the secret of Rochester's destroyed youth, responsible for his bitter disillusionment, the cause of his separation from Jane and, ultimately, the agent of Rochester's physical destruction. But her fascination and power derive from still deeper sources. She is the monstrous embodiment of psychosexual conflicts which are intrinsic to the romantic predicament—paralleled and unconscious in both Jane and Rochester.

Although Berthe is specifically identified with Rochester's past, imprisoned on the third floor of Thornfield Hall, itself "a shrine of memory" (p. 128), she emerges for the reader through enlarging stages of Jane's perception. She comes initially in answer to Jane's same vague sexual longings for freedom and expression which later seem to summon Rochester. Descending from the attic where she delights in the vast prospect of the countryside, Jane hears Berthe's laugh for the first time: "distinct, formal, mirthless." "Tragic" and "preternatural" the laugh is strangely joyless: a sound that denotes neither feeling nor personality. It is heard often when Jane retreats to the attic window

---

13. Adrienne Rich moves in a somewhat similar interpretive direction in her provocative essay, *"Jane Eyre:* The Temptations of a Motherless Woman," *Ms,* II (October 1973).

It is interesting to note that despite Berthe's symbolic status in the novel, the events surrounding Rochester's first marriage were apparently suggested to Charlotte Brontë while she was teaching at the Roe Head School:

> It was about this time that an event happened in the neighborhood of Leeds, which excited a good deal of interest. A young lady, who held a situation of governess in a very respectable family, had been wooed and married by a gentleman, holding some subordinate position in a commercial firm to which the young lady's employer belonged. A year after her marriage, during which time she had given birth to a child, it was discovered that he whom she called husband had another wife. The report now says, that this first wife was deranged, and that he had made this an excuse to himself for his subsequent marriage. But, at any rate the condition of the wife who was no wife—of the innocent mother of the illegitimate child—excited the deepest commiseration; and the case was spoken of far and wide and at Roe Head among other places. (Gaskell p. 91)

wishing for active involvement, for "a stake in life," for a constructive use of her energies.

As Jane is drawn closer to Rochester, focusing upon him the desires and aspirations which before were undefined yearnings, she has a concrete sense of Berthe's presence—and the danger it represents. The night on which she first admits to herself the centrality of Rochester to her own happiness ("Suppose he should be absent, spring, summer and autumn: how joyless sunshine and fine days will seem!" [p. 182]) is the same night that Berthe sets Rochester's bed aflame. On the evening that Jane vows to her "master" that she will be faithful to him, despite society's opinion, Berthe violently attacks her brother, Richard Mason, who ultimately prevents Rochester and Jane's marriage. Considered together, the events suggest that Berthe expresses a repressed but clearly negative component of Jane's attitude towards her own sexuality and toward her lover as well. This is further borne out by the fact that, as Jane sits in the chamber nursing the bleeding Mason, imprisoned there, in a sense, by her vow of fidelity, the association emerges in her mind between Berthe, the "mystery that broke out, now in fire and now in blood, at the deadest hours of the night" (p. 264) and the dread images of the red-room—reverberating with death, passion, hidden fears of the loss of self. Similar anxieties reveal themselves when Jane and Berthe meet just prior to Jane's wedding day. Then Jane awakens suddenly from a recurrent nightmare in which she sees herself carrying a child:[14]

> I dreamt that Thornfield Hall was a dreary ruin . . . wrapped up in a shawl, I still carried the unknown little child: I might not lay it down anywhere, however tired were my arms— however much its weight impeded my progress, I must retain it. I heard the gallop of a horse at a distance on the road: I was sure it was you; and you were departing for many years, and for a distant country. I climbed the thin wall with frantic perilous haste, eager to catch one glimpse of you from the top: the stones rolled from under my feet, the ivy branches I grasped gave way, the child clung round my neck in terror, and almost strangled me: at last I gained the summit. I saw you like a

14. This was similar to a recurrent dream of Charlotte's own: one in which she carries a weeping, suffering child who will not be comforted (Dooley, p. 242).

> speck on a white track, lessening every moment. The blast
> blew so strong I could not stand. I sat down on the narrow
> ledge; I hushed the scared infant in my lap: you turned an angle
> of the road; I bent forward to take a last look; the wall crum-
> bled; I was shaken; the child rolled from my knee; I lost my bal-
> ance, fell and woke. (pp. 356–67)

But the scene to which she wakens is more terrifying than the one
imagined in her dreams. She sees ''a woman, tall and large, with
thick and dark hair hanging long down her back.'' The woman
places Jane's wedding veil upon her head and looks at herself in
the mirror.

> It was a discolored face—it was a savage face . . . the lips
> were swelled and dark; the brow furrowed; the black eye-
> brows wildly raised over the bloodshot eyes. (p. 358)

Berthe tears the wedding veil in two then leans over Jane's bed in
an attitude that suggests a fantasy of sexual violation.

> Just at my bedside, the figure stopped: the fiery eye glared
> upon me—she thrust up her candle close to my face, and extin-
> guished it under my eyes. I was aware that her lurid visage
> flamed over mine, and I lost consciousness: for the second time
> in my life—only the second time—I became insensible from
> terror. (pp. 358–59)

Loss of consciousness was experienced once before: in the red-
room. The causes were the same then as they are now: impotence
and terror rising from the blurring of the boundaries of the self,
an intense fear of submergence—negation. Here the association
with the vampire figure makes the sexual implication explicit.

Berthe has from the beginning functioned as a warning
against the consequences of Jane's desire for emotional release,
her longing to cast aside conventional restraints. In the horror of
her presence, Berthe expresses Jane's fear of marriage as violation, her sense of ''Mrs. Rochester'' as alien, ''a being not yet
born'' (p. 349). She is the menacing form of Jane's resistance to
male authority, her fear of that sexual surrender which will seal
her complete dependence in passion. Berthe's joyless laugh is a
metaphor for sensuality without mind, feeling without control.
She is a jealous, vengeful mother who prohibits marriage to the
beloved father. An androgynous figure, she is also the violent
lover who destroys the integrity of the self; who offers the corrup-

tion of sexual knowledge and power—essentially male in its opposition to purity and innocence.

The dream which precedes the apparition expresses Jane's fear of dependence, sexual initiation, and the maturity associated with childbearing. In it, Jane is presented simultaneously as child and mother. She is the child who, dependent upon Rochester, will be betrayed. She is the woman who wishes for independence and maturity, but fears the infant whose conception and birth imply the loss of a part of herself.[15]

As Berthe's importance as an alter ego for Jane is central in the novel, her importance in Rochester's psychosexual development is crucial as well. It must be remembered that from the beginning of their relationship Rochester insists that Jane is elfin, other-worldly, childlike: a "little sunny-faced girl with . . . dimpled cheeks and rosy lips" (p. 325). Appropriately, he makes their love story into an imaginative tale for Adele. Her governess, he says, is a fairy who will bestow upon him the power of flight allowing them both to leave the earth behind and take up their blissful if somewhat fey inhabitance on the moon (p. 337). Thus he denies to Jane her sexuality, her humanness, her social and moral nature. He betrays the fact that he wants to find in her the very opposite of that aggressive sexuality, that uncontrollable passionate will that has its form in Berthe: bestial, athletic, monstrously and paradoxically virile.

If their expression is striking, Rochester's sexual anxieties themselves are not atypical. The fear of the female is common, among civilized as well as primitive men.[16] Since it is a crucial

15. Gregory Zilboorg comments on the common female fear of intercourse: a fear that "contents of her body will be destroyed, stolen or sucked out" and he adds that these "fears . . . are in some way deeply connected with her physical fear of man and of child bearing" (p. 106). The vampire figure appropriately embodies this fear.

16. Freud observes:

Perhaps this fear is founded on the difference of woman from man, on her eternally inexplicable, mysterious and strange nature, which thus seems hostile. Man fears that his strength will be taken from him by woman, dreads becoming infected with her femininity and then proving himself a weakling. The effect of coitus in discharging tensions and inducing flaccidity may be a prototype of what these fears represent; and realization of the influence gained by the woman over a man as a result of sexual relations, and the favours she extorts by this means may all conduce to justify the growth of the fears. (Freud, "The Taboo of Virginity," trans. J. Riviere, pp. 223–24.)

product and cause of Victorian repression, we are not surprised that Berthe is a vampire: one of those who haunted the Victorian imagination. Jane identifies her in this way in describing the nighttime visitation and Berthe does, in fact, suck Mason's blood ("She sucked the blood: she said she'd drain my heart" [p. 267].) as she tries to suck her husband's. She would deprive him, Rochester knows, of his energy, his vitality, his manhood.[17]

Always intrinsically connected to man's insecurity concerning his own sexuality, the fear of women is particularly pronounced in the psychology of the Byronic hero whose need to prove his masculinity by sexual conquest drives him to extremes of behavior. He fears impotence and he loathes the aggression he must summon in himself as a defense against the sexual threat he imagines. In short, he fears with unusual acuteness both powerlessness and power. The hostility, therefore, born of his anxiety, is projected onto the "love object." It is not enough, therefore, for Rochester to reject Berthe. He must protect himself as well against everything in Jane that suggests an affinity with his first wife. He must deny that aspect of her sexuality which is perceived as aggressive and "masculine." He must bifurcate her personality. But because he fears as well the power of his own virility, he incorporates into himself that aspect of feminity which is unthreatening: the capacity for intense and absolute love. In this way Jane is not only divided. She is negated: denied function and space. She becomes quite simply an extension of him. His narcissism is the romantic resolution of sexual conflict. In this, he is truly the Byronic hero.

The discovery of the existence of Rochester's first wife at the very moment that the marriage vows are being exchanged has an extraordinary psychological validity. It is an expression of the ambivalence which Jane and Rochester both experience. In preparing for his wedding, Rochester has revealed a need to dominate strong enough to effectively negate the identity of the woman he loves and therefore fears. And Jane, who feels increasingly that her marriage will not be a union of equals but a submersion of self in the ego of another, is as apprehensive of her wedding ("There was no putting off the day that advanced—the

17. In Rochester's relation to Berthe we have a more striking and psychologically convincing version of the sexual ambivalence expressed in Crimsworth's hypochondria.

bridal day'' [p. 347]), as she is apprehensive of her husband to be: ''the dread, but adored, type of my unknown future day'' (p. 361).

It is appropriate that Richard Mason, acting in behalf of Jane's uncle should be the one to stop the wedding ceremony. When Jane had first recognized the role which Rochester would impose upon her as his wife, she had written to her uncle to identify herself and to inquire about her legacy. Economic and social status seem after all to be minimal conditions of sexual equality. These would at least lend support to the sense of self which makes love possible in a patriarchal world.

From this point of view, Jane's decision to leave Rochester, her decision not to live with him as his mistress, is not simply a moral decision. She does not leave him because she finds him guilty or distasteful. In fact, she forgives him rather easily because she sees in him ''deep remorse'', ''true pity,'' ''manly energy,'' and, not least of all, ''unchanged love'' (p. 381). She will not live with him as his mistress because he will think of her then as he thinks now of the others with whom he has had brief, disillusioning affairs:

> It was a groveling fashion of existence: I should never wish to return to it. Hiring a mistress is the next worse thing to buying a slave: both are often by nature, and always by position, inferior; and to live familiarly with inferiors is degrading. I now hate the recollection of the time I passed with Celine, Giacinta and Clara. (p. 398)

To become one of these women now seems to be her only alternative. In fact, this has always been potentially her situation. With the threat that Berthe represents subconsciously present, Rochester must have attempted, despite his love, to turn Jane into a plaything, a sexual object, a dependent, a slave—as soon as she agreed to marry him. It was her absence of status, her powerlessness, which allowed Rochester to see Jane initially as an appropriate bride, completely vulnerable to him. It is this which she now, on some level, begins to understand. The depth of her love, the profundity of her need, is the measure of her obligation to leave him.

> Not a human being that ever lived could wish to be loved better than I was loved; and him who thus loved me I absolutely

> worshipped: and I must renounce love and idol. One drear
> word comprised my intolerable duty—"Depart!" (pp.
> 402–13)

Brontë had written to Ellen Nussey from Roe Head in 1837:

> Why are we to be divided? Surely it must be because we are in
> danger of loving each other too well—of losing sight of the
> *creator* in idolatry of the *creature*. [18]

Jane Eyre had learned that in idolatry one must also lose sight of
the self and it was to herself that she owed her "intolerable
duty"—to depart. This is the point at which the old romance
failed and the stasis of the old mythology was denied. This is
where a new resolution had to be discovered. Here morality and
psychology meet for the first time in a feminist context. [19]

III

In deciding to leave Rochester, Jane takes the first crucial step
toward independence. She has discovered that there is, after all,
something more important to her than pleasing those whom she
loves, or giving satisfaction to those who love her. Despite the
pain of her conflict, she has acted decisively to preserve her own
integrity. At the moment of her decision, Jane returns to the critical scene of her childhood. She is alone in her room as she was
alone then—powerless before external circumstances and internal
pressures. The limits of the rational world are lost in the bound-
less universe of imagination:

> That night I never thought to sleep: but a slumber fell on me as
> soon as I lay down in bed. I was transported in thought to the
> scenes of childhood: I dreamt I lay in the red-room at Gates-

18. Quoted in Gaskell, p. 100.
19. Winifred Gerin attributes this departure from the romantic formula to
Charlotte Brontë's own moral victory in her relationship with Heger: "Not until
Charlotte had herself fallen in love, suffered temptation, sought and found the
courage to resist it, endured the heartbreak of fleeing from it, was the Byronic
image superseded in her heart, the Byronic morality outdistanced by a pattern of
conduct whose disciplines she set herself to follow to the end" (*Charlotte
Brontë*, p. 19). But Ms. Gerin does not take into account the fact that Charlotte's love was not, after all, returned: that she had to suffer the humiliation of
her emotional dependence and had to find within herself the strength to overcome her sense of inadequacy.

head; that the night was dark, and my mind impressed with strange fears. The light that long ago had struck me into syncope, recalled in this vision, seemed glidingly to mount the wall, and tremblingly to pause in the centre of the obscured ceiling. I lifted up my head to look: the roof resolved to clouds, high and dim; the gleam was such as the moon imparts to vapours she is about to sever. I watched her come—watched with the strangest anticipation; as though some word of doom were to be written on her disk. She broke forth as never moon yet burst from cloud: a hand first penetrated the sable folds and waved them away; then, not a moon, but a white human form shown in the azure, inclining a glorious brow earthward. It gazed and gazed on me. It spoke, to my spirit: immeasureably distant was the tone, yet so near, it whispered in my heart—

"My daughter, flee temptation!"

"Mother, I will." (p. 407)

The terrifying supernatural experience of the red-room is confronted and resolved at last. The strange powers of the nonhuman world seem now but sympathetic extensions of the compelling, equally mysterious forces of the personality. The authority which Jane has sought is female: the moon, maternal nature, the mother within herself—a cosmic and personal principle of order and control.

The trauma at Gateshead had first been neutralized in the experience at Lowood and now, as part of the more profound conflict of Thornfield, is finally resolved. But the antithetical claims which emerged from Jane's relationship with Rochester have still to be reconciled: the needs of the self and the demands of the "other": passion and discipline, egotism and denial. The dialectic proceeds. The first antithesis to Jane's emotionality had been represented by Helen Burns. The second is offered in the more developed and sophisticated form of St. John Rivers. The allegorical movement of self-discovery, present throughout the novel, is intensified here and its Christian structure is emphasized as Jane moves once again into a level of experience that is social and moral rather than personally and sexually defined.

At Lowood Jane was drawn out of the private fantasy world into which she had been thrust by deprivation. Now, after rejecting the romantic idolatry which parallels her childhood experience on another level, she must consciously relocate herself in a complex hierarchy of values: redefining her relationship to God, to nature, to a heterogeneous society previously unknown. She must create a personality independent enough to be separate within the unity of love, secure enough sexually to temper the passion that cloaks self-abnegation. Hers is a radical trial and is expressed through Christian parable.

Fleeing temptation, Jane is set down at Whitcross which "is no town, nor even a hamlet; it is but a stone pillar set up where four roads meet" (p. 412). She is at a beginning and must discover her own way. Like Bunyan's pilgrim, Christian, she is bereft of friends and family: homeless and penniless. She must be purged of all human vanity, enduring the humiliation of body and spirit. At first she finds comfort in the maternal nature which had always before offered her solace:

> Nature seemed to me benign and good: I thought she loved me, outcast that I was; and I, who from man could anticipate only mistrust, rejection, insult, clung to her with filial fondness. To-night, at least, I would be her guest—as I was her child: my mother would lodge me without money and without price. (p. 413)

But although she, like all men and women, is related to the natural world, she is not truly a part of it:

> What a golden desert this spreading moor! Everywhere sunshine. I wished I could live in it and on it. I saw a lizard run over the crag; I saw a bee busy among the sweet bilberries. I would fain at the moment have become bee or lizard, that I might have found fitting nutriment, permanent shelter here. But I was a human being, and had a human being's wants: I must not linger where there was nothing to supply them. (p. 415)

God, the Father, had given and secured her life. The only mother she can look to in her present trouble is the mother within. She had discovered her presence on the evening of the departure from Thornfield. Now she must test her power:

> Life, however, was yet in my possession; with all its requirements, and pains, and responsibilities. The burden must be carried; the want provided for; the suffering endured: the responsibility fulfilled. I set out. (p. 415)

At Lowood, hunger seemed in part to be experienced as a need for love. Now the mature Jane confronts similar but more pressing deprivations—starvation and death from exposure. Both are spiritual as well as physical trials. She must again discover and assert the self that can endure. Despite privation (reduced to eating pig's food, brought to a state of beggary) Jane is able to retain a degree of pride appropriate to a character strengthened by the resolve of independent choice and action. And that pride is also softened by new sympathy for those who must, as she, endure the humbling miseries of existence.

Finally, at the point of death, Jane follows a light which leads her to Marsh End, a sanctuary of civilization poised at the edge of the wild, open moors. Looking through the window into the scrupulously clean and pleasant kitchen, she sees an elderly female servant and "two young, graceful women—ladies in every point" (p. 424), one with a dog's head resting on her knee, one with a kitten curled in her lap.[20] Busily involved in their translation of German, they are indeed images of "delicacy and cultivation." First denied entrance by the servant, Hannah, Jane is finally admitted by St. John Rivers, the brother of Diana and Mary. Her ordeal is ended. She sleeps for three days and three nights, waking only to eat and drink of the food and water of life. Her sleep renews her spirit as it restores her body and is reminiscent of the crisis that followed her ordeal in the red-room. Her first act after awakening is her forgiveness of Hannah for denying her shelter. She cautions this impotent surrogate for the wicked parent that "Some of the best people that ever lived have been as destitute as I am; and if you are a Christian, you ought not to consider poverty a crime" (p. 437). Her clasping of Hannah's hand marks her entrance into the Christian community and her acceptance of social interrelatedness.

Jane had before found comfort and definition in the female environment at Lowood. Now, after completely identifying with Rochester, it is crucial for her to discover herself anew in the images of women. Through her friendship with Diana and Mary Rivers, she becomes stronger, more confident, more focused. In them, free as they are of dependence upon men, strong in their devotion to one another, she finds the form of a new promise of fulfillment. She shares with them their love of nature. She admires and respects their superior learning, their fine minds. She listens to them talk as she had once listened to Maria Temple and

20. Marsh End seems to be an idealized version of Haworth: Diana Rivers modeled on Emily Brontë; Mary on Anne; their servant, Hannah, on Tabby.

Helen Burns, as Charlotte had listened to Emily and Anne. She responds to the authority in Diana—with her it is natural to be passive, "feminine," "to bend where my conscience and self-respect permitted, to an active will" (p. 439). But there is still equality among them. No longer functioning within the authoritarian context of the master-student relationship she had with Rochester, she finds instead that there can be intellectual reciprocity: a sharing of knowledge and gifts, delight in the interaction of personalities. The strength and confidence which she derives from their friendship allow her to accept the job which St. John offers her as teacher in the village school. Assuming this role, she begins to overcome her feelings of social humiliation:

> I felt desolate to a degree. I felt—yes, idiot that I am—I felt degraded. I doubted I had taken a step which sank instead of raising me in the scale of social existence. I was weakly dismayed at the ignorance, the poverty, the coarseness of all I heard and saw round me. But let me not hate and despise myself too much for these feelings: I know them to be wrong—that is a great step gained; I shall strive to overcome them.
> (p. 459)

And she does largely overcome them (although Jane Eyre, as Charlotte Brontë herself, could not be accused of excessive egalitarian tendencies). She discovers in many of her poor and unlearned students a degree of "natural politeness" and "innate self-respect" which wins her good will and admiration. She takes pride in her accomplishment, in her ability to teach and befriend her students, to be self-sufficient and useful. And her success earns her a position in the little community so that it is enjoyable for her "to live amidst general regard, though it be but the regard of working-people" (p. 468).

The tone of *noblesse oblige* which informs these words provides us with some understanding of the direction which Charlotte Brontë's myth must take. Feminist it might well be, but it is not a feminism which can preach or envision radical social change. Jane, in leaving Rochester, must, it is true, discover her own capacities and strengths. She must learn the pleasures of independence and self-sufficiency. But only economic independence and social position will give her the status essential to the recognition which is the better part of equality.

When St. John informs her of her sizable inheritance and of the fact that he and his sisters are her real cousins, Jane realizes immediately the way in which her life will now be changed. "It was a grand boon doubtless; and independence would be glorious—yes, I felt that—*that* thought swelled my heart" (p. 488). She recognizes also that by sharing her wealth with Diana and Mary she can free them as she herself is now freed, from the dreary servitude of work. She will have with them "a home and connections" and she will be liberated from the necessity of marrying where there is no love.

Discovering her kinship with the Riverses, Jane does, of course follow in the tradition of the heroes and heroines of quest-romance. Social recognition validates internal worth. The implication is that class membership is its very condition. A "lady" is born, not made, even though the secret of her birth might remain hidden. The Riverses are the last of the series of families to which Jane has found herself intimately or distantly connected. In structure they resemble the Reeds and the Ingrams.[21] All have two daughters (Jane stands outside as a stepsister) and a son. The fathers are dead, the mothers living (Hannah is a kindly, unthreatening, surrogate-mother for the Rivers children as Tabby was for the Brontës). But all the earlier families are "bad" or "false." As indications of the incompleteness of Jane's development, they have signaled successive stages of her "trial": a continuing inability to confront a self that has been "earned." It is with her "real" family that Jane shares her birthright, joyously seizing "the delicious pleasure of which I have caught a glimpse—that of repaying, in part, a mighty obligation, and winning to myself lifelong friends" (p. 494). Here is the multi-layered magic of fairy tale. Jane is transformed from stepsister to benefactress. This is the role which Charlotte was to play with her sisters; which she would have wished to play with Branwell, had he been less threatening.

Significantly, it is St. John who pushes her to further recognition of possibility; to further discoveries of herself. He must be the agent of her liberation. If Rochester represents one aspect of Jane's personality, St. John represents the other. On one level, it is the conflict between Byron and the duke of Wellington artic-

21. The Brocklehurst family can be included here as well. The only difference is that both the Rev. Brocklehurst and his wife are still alive.

ulated with psychological subtlety. St. John Rivers is an older and, more importantly, a masculine version of Helen Burns. Without innocence, or naiveté, he is purposeful, directed, threatening. In both of them the spiritual impulse is carried to an extreme: a form of sublimation which can be liberating and creative, but can also destroy.

St. John's Grecian appearance identifies him with the classical virtues of reason and control so admired in *Rasselas*. He is fair and pale, his light is repressed and "burns" as Helen's did, within. While the fire of the red-room and the fire of the wild, impassioned Berthe threaten destruction to others, St. John's fire is, as Jane sees, self-consuming.

> . . . that heart is already laid on a sacred altar: the fire is arranged round it. It will soon be no more than a sacrifice consumed. (p. 469)

In him, Charlotte Brontë has drawn a stunning portrait of the martyr—unsoftened by the childish idealism or female vulnerability which made Helen sympathetic. Defining self-denial as its own virtue, St. John wishes to sacrifice his life to others although he is, by his own admission, a "cold, hard man."

He subscribes, as Helen did, to a Calvinism that is bitter and stern, full of the promise of guilt and punishment. But he identifies himself with the punishing authority of that religion, casting himself as avenging angel rather than as victim. He has found in the missionary's calling a way of channeling his ambitions as soldier, statesman, orator: "a lover of renown, a luster after power" (p. 462), and he brings to his "profession" the hardness and despotism that befit a man of the world. His sadistic arrogance is the male version of Helen's masochism.

Charlotte Brontë describes St. John as "a cold, cumbrous, column" (p. 502). She had used a similar image for Brocklehurst who was "a black pillar . . . a straight, narrow, sable-clad shape."[22] The identification of male sexuality and power on one hand and that same sexuality with rigidity—even death—on the other, is hardly accidental.[23] The extent to which St. John pur-

22. It might be recalled that in *The Professor*, Crimsworth is transformed by Mlle. Reuter's servility, into a "rigid pillar of stone."

23. It would seem that Brontë was ambivalent about many of the parallels which she suggests between St. John and Brocklehurst. Despite strongly negative aspects of St. John's characterization, Brontë chooses to praise him as a martyr whose way, while flawed and not Jane's own, is still worthy of respect.

chases his religious calling at the cost of sexual passion is illustrated in his abortive relationship with Rosamond Oliver, the charming girl whom he rejects precisely because he is attracted to her. And the extent to which his religious fervor is the result of sexual fear and repression is revealed in his more subtle and complex relationship with Jane.

He is attracted to Jane initially because of her courage in adversity. Knowing her past, he is familiar with the strength of her moral fiber. In her attention to her students he sees that she is diligent, orderly, and energetic as well as intelligent. He recognizes in her desire to share her inheritance, a gift for sacrifice, and he feels in her response to him an appropriate recognition of his power. For these reasons, he concludes that she would make him a useful helpmate. But there is an enormous contradiction in his attitude toward her. He does not want to see her as a woman. He would, in fact, have her deny her sexual nature, her feelings, her body—subordinate that which is most vital in her self to his own spiritual quest. Her passivity and masochism respond to him:

> As for me, I daily wished more to please him: but to do so, I felt daily more and more that I must disown half my nature, stifle my faculties, wrest my tastes from their original bent, force myself to the adoption of pursuits for which I had no natural vocation. He wanted to train me to an elevation I could never reach: it racked me hourly to aspire to the standard he uplifted. (p. 509)

The great problem arises from his insistence that she must join him in his missionary labors, not as a friend, not as a "sister," but as a wife: "A sister might any day be taken from me. I want a wife: a soul helpmeet I can influence efficiently in life and retain absolutely till death" (p. 518). He wants to control her completely. For Jane the temptation is strong. Commitment to the work, even to the death which she sees as the inevitable outcome of her existence: this would focus her life and obscure her love for Rochester by employing her physical and intellectual energies. She is willing to defy society and sacrifice her life to participate in that larger mission in which she can only partially believe. It is possible to compromise worldly interests and spiritual doubts, but she cannot sacrifice her sexuality. And there is no question that her sexuality is at issue.

St. John's manipulative power, the loftiness of his aspirations, the largeness of his will—all evoke a response based upon her habitual tendency to submit to a dominating spirit, her need for approval and respect.

> By degrees he acquired a certain influence over me that took away my liberty of mind: his praise and notice were more restraining than his indifference. (p. 508)

The attraction Jane feels is not unrelated to the idolatry of her love for Rochester. It is that aspect of sexuality which is power-oriented, potentially sadomasochistic:

> . . . Though I have only sisterly affection for him now, yet, if forced to be his wife, I can imagine the possibility of conceiving an inevitable, strange, torturing kind of love for him: because he is so talented; and there is often a certain heroic grandeur in his look, manner and conversation. (p. 531)

Jane recognizes that St. John would buy her body with the coin of spirituality, hypocritically posing as God's agent. "Do you think God will be satisfied with half an oblation?" he asks her. "Will he accept a mutilated sacrifice? It is the cause of God I advocate: it is under His standard I enlist you" (p. 519). St. John must make a religious duty of sexual need. He explicitly denies his own and therefore her sexuality, fearing the passion which would make him mortal and vulnerable. As she comes to understand St. John, Jane is so distressed by his twisted, sadistic (albeit unconscious) misrepresentation of his own feeling and by his misunderstanding of hers that she angrily and openly opposes him. When he says: "Undoubtedly enough of love would follow upon marriage to render the union right even in your eyes," she replies: "I scorn your idea of love . . . I scorn the counterfeit sentiment you offer: yes, St. John, and I scorn you when you offer it" (p. 522). It is the extraordinary contempt of a virginal young woman for the Victorian concept of sex as duty, for the Victorian denial of the dignity of human passion. But there still remains in Jane the other side of that Victorian repression: the overwhelming desire to submit to a power that will envelope her, possess her, negate her.

> I was tempted to cease struggling with him—to rush down the torrent of his will into the gulf of his existence, and there lose my own. (p. 534)

Well might she say, "I was almost as hard beset by him now as I had been once before, in a different way, by another" (p. 534).

In the final scene between Jane and St. John, the language of spiritual transfiguration is interlaced with the language and imagery of sexuality. The images of the red-room are recalled as well as the dreams that preceded Jane's decision at Thornfield:

> I stood motionless under my hierophant's touch. My refusals were forgotten—my fears overcome—my wrestlings paralyzed. The Impossible—i.e. my marriage with St. John—was fast becoming the Possible. All was changing utterly, with a sudden sweep. Religion called—Angels beckoned—God commanded—life rolled together like a scroll—death's gates opening, shewed eternity beyond: it seemed, that for safety and bliss there, all here might be sacrificed in a second. The dim room was full of visions.

> The one candle was dying out: the room was full of moonlight. My heart beat fast and thick: I heard its throb. Suddenly it stood still to an inexpressible feeling that thrilled it through, and passed at once to my head and extremities. The feeling was not like an electric shock; but it was quite as sharp, as strange, as startling: it acted on my senses as if their utmost activity hitherto had been but torpor; from which they were now summoned, and forced to wake. (pp. 534–35)

Two other profound psychic experiences had occasioned the fear of loss and violation sufficiently terrifying to induce unconsciousness. This third time, much strengthened, Jane is impelled to self-assertive action. Now she is released by orgasmic convulsion into spiritual resolution and sexual redefinition. The response is summoned by the sexual component of St. John's power, but it yields awareness and self-discovery instead of dread annihilation. Much of the dangerous appeal of Rochester's sexuality had derived from a similar charisma of power (a charisma not completely lacking, as masculine force, even in Brocklehurst and John Reed). That appeal is experienced here fully—and finally, absolutely rejected. (Not least of all, the brother-lover is implicitly rejected, literally "sacrificed," as we later learn, in favor of the lover-husband.) Now Jane is free to explore the potential that remains. When she hears Rochester's voice calling to her, she responds as surely to the need it expresses as she responds to the need in herself which she must acknowledge. Rather than accepting the sublimation of desire in a patriarchal religious value system, she finds spiritual meaning in human experience. She rejects sexual passion that derives its force from masochistic self-denial and insists that duty and obligation must be placed within the context of a generous and reciprocal human love.

In rejecting St. John, Jane comes to terms with her need for an external authority. She completes the move toward independence begun in the red-room and continued in her departure from Thornfield. In rejecting St. John's repressive sexuality she rejects the perverse sadomasochism it implies, and she attempts to distinguish the sexuality of love from the sexuality of power: the love born of equality from the love subject to idolatry.

This is the last of the symbolic "separations." At every previous point of parting (from Bessie, Helen, Maria Temple, Rochester) Jane's "self," apparently severed and divided, has become stronger and more integrated than before. The separation from St. John marks the ultimate resolution of her spiritual and sexual being, but the transformation of the Edward Rochester to whom she returns is the crucial condition of the actualization of that being and therefore of the viability of the new romantic myth which the novel has articulated.

In her return to Thornfield, Jane is as little motivated by moral considerations as she had been before in her departure. She is driven by premonition and passion rather than principle or judgment.

> Could I but see him! Surely, in that case, I should not be so mad as to run to him? I cannot tell—I am not certain. And if I did—what then? God bless him! What then? Who would be hurt by my once more tasting the life his glance can give me? (pp. 541–42)

She finds Thornfield in ruins: destroyed by the mystery of fire and blood which had been secreted within it for so long: set aflame by Berthe, who was killed while attempting to escape from her husband. The house is the very image of its former master who, Samson-like, maddened by loneliness, desperate and trapped within the futility of his rebellion, had pulled his home down about himself, blinded and crippled his body, deprived himself of that which he had most valued and most feared: the power and pride of his "masculinity." The ambivalence of the Byronic hero towards his own sexuality is nowhere better expressed than in Rochester's attempted rescue of his mad wife, described to Jane by one of the townspeople:

> I witnessed, and several more witnessed Mr. Rochester ascend
> through the skylight to the roof; we heard him call "Berthe!"
> We saw him approach her; and then, ma'am, she yelled, and
> gave a spring, and the next minute she lay smashed on the
> pavement. (p. 548)

The saviour appears to the victim as avenger and rescue itself
becomes a kind of murder. Rochester's heroism, not unlike
Byron's own, is realized in self-destruction.

Jane seeking Rochester at Ferndean reminds us paradoxically—yet justly—of the Prince who comes to awaken the sleep-
ing Beauty with a kiss. Their roles are now reversed. All is dark
and overgrown, the decaying house buried in the gloomy, tangled
forest as Rochester's spirit is hidden in his broken body. Watching him emerge, Jane thinks "of some wronged and fettered
wild-beast or bird, dangerous to approach in his sullen woe . . .
the caged eagle, whose gold-ringed eyes cruelty has extinguished" (p. 552). That she had in past times reminded him of a
small, helpless bird trapped in a nest metaphorizes our sense of
their role reversal.

Brontë has afflicted her hero with the Christian punishment
appropriate to one who has "committed adultery in his heart"
and "put aside his wife."[24] It is the punishment prophesied earlier by Jane in the first agony of her discovery of Rochester's
wife.

> You shall, yourself, pluck out your right eye; yourself cut off
> your right hand: your heart shall be the victim; and you, the
> priest, to transfix it. (p. 379)[25]

And the punishment is appropriate in far more subtle ways as
well: in ways which speak to the social, psychological, and sexual disease of which "romantic love" is a symptom. In the cost
to Rochester of the resolution of Jane's conflict, the severity of
social and psychological pressures are most painfully demonstrated. Just as Henry Hastings's disintegration was essential to
Elizabeth's discovery of her own abilities and as Charlotte's personal and artistic growth were predicated upon both Branwell's

24. One recalls the apparently guilty fantasy of blindness which Brontë reported to Heger in one of her letters.
25. (See Matt. 5:27–32.) Rochester's left eye remains blind. We are told
on p. 552 that he loses his left hand, but on p. 557, Jane contradicts herself and
says it was his right hand that was destroyed.

moral and physical collapse and Patrick Brontë's increasing dependence,[26] so too can Jane's development be maintained only at the cost of Rochester's romantic self-image. Rochester's mutilation is, in the terms of this nascent feminist myth, the necessary counterpart of Jane's independence: the terrible condition of a relationship of equality.[27]

But what, in fact, is the nature of this "equality?" Jane's flight from the orgasmic knowledge of St. John's sexual power and Rochester's last catastrophic struggle with his vampire-bride are not the bases of a mature sexuality which is an extension of social liberation. They are rather preludes to the desexualization which is the unhappy compromise necessary when psychosexual need is unsupported by social reality or political self-consciousness. The mystery of fire and blood is not solved. It is simply eradicated. Jane's sense of Rochester, as she looks at him on the morning after her return, is crucial:

> His countenance reminded one of a lamp quenched, waiting to be relit—and alas! it was not himself that could kindle the lustre of animated expression: he was dependent on another for that office. (p. 562)

26. Charlotte's description of Jane's reading and writing for Rochester recalls her description in a letter to Heger of her own execution of similar services for her father.

27. Carolyn Heilbrun notes that "Jane Eyre's demand for autonomy or some measure of freedom echoes politically in the cries of all powerless individuals whether the victims of industrialization, racial discrimination or political disenfranchisement. So we today begin to see that Rochester undergoes, not sexual mutilation as the Freudians claim, but the inevitable sufferings necessary when those in power are forced to release some of their power to those who previously had none." (*Toward A Recognition of Androgyny* [New York: Alfred A. Knopf, 1973], p. 59.)

Heilbrun's perspective would be acceptable if Brontë had, in fact, been able to place the problem of her heroine within a political framework. It is just her inability to do this which creates the ambiguities of the novel's concluding section.

Most notable among those critics who have applied a Freudian perspective to the novel and have insisted upon Rochester's symbolic emasculation are: Armour Craig, "The Unpoetic Compromise: On the Relation Between Private Vision and Social Order in Nineteenth Century English Fiction," in *English Institute Essays* (New York: Columbia University Press, 1965); Earl Knies, *The Art of Charlotte Brontë* (Athens: Ohio University Press, 1969); Richard Chase, "The Brontës: A Centennial Observance," *Kenyon Review*, 9 (Autumn 1947), pp. 486–506; M. H. Scargill, "All Passion Spent: A Reevaluation of *Jane Eyre*," *University of Toronto Quarterly*, 9 (1949); Morton S. Day, "Central Concepts of *Jane Eyre*," *Personalist*, 40, 1.

He is devitalized; the fire of his passion burnt to ash; the quick of his nature paralyzed. He is not the bereaved lover, expectantly awaiting his mistress's return. His is a comatose soul, unable to cry out for rebirth. It is not a lover he requires, but a mother who can offer him again the gift of life. And it is this function which Jane will gratefully assume.

> I love you better now, when I can really be useful to you, than
> I did in your state of proud independence, when you disdained
> every part but that of the giver and protector. (p. 570)

Brontë, dividing her time between the writing of her novel and the nursing of her weak and sightless father, could well have spoken these words with Jane. They belong to the virginal daughter who has been magically transformed—without the mediation of sexual contact—into the noble figure of the nurturing mother. Once the magical transformation has taken place, the dependence defined, the partial restoration of Rochester's vision cannot reverse the pattern of relationship any more easily than the removal of Patrick Brontë's cataracts could completely reestablish the old patriarchal order.

Jane's money and social status, even her confidence and self-knowledge, would not have offered her sufficient protection against the psychosexual power of Rochester, her "master"; would not have defended her against the arrogance and pride supported by society through its laws, its structures, its attitudes, its mythology. Nor would her new position, her developed self, have protected Rochester from the fears and actual dangers associated with the "masculine" role assigned to him. So strong are these external forces that the reduction of Rochester's virility and the removal of them both from contact with society are necessary to maintain the integrity of the emergent female self. Rochester is brought into the "female" word of love and morality, out of the "masculine" universe of power: out of society, into Jane's sphere of psychic functioning. His transformation heralds the death of the Byronic hero whose many charms were the imaginative instruments of a sexually repressive and oppressive society. But the society into which his maimed Victorian spirit is reborn, is still more repressive and more closed. Brontë's myth reflects those social limitations even as it attempts to define a new feminist freedom. Rochester is, in this sense, a pivotal figure;

marking the transition from the romantic to the modern hero, heralding the paralyzing alienation which will be chronicled by Dickens, by Thackeray, by George Eliot, and Lawrence: by Melville, by Mann, by Kafka, and Dostoevsky. His mangled body projects his psychic scars. His absence of vitality derives from a psychic illness which will become, in many of his successors, spiritual death.

Rochester is the representative and victim of forces over which Jane has triumphed in order to redefine herself. But the self which emerges from the sequential struggles it endures cannot be tested again by former adversaries. The allegorical quest follows a necessary and irreversible path. In its victories, the ego absorbs those components of reality which it has successfully confronted, negating their existence as objective form. The aggressive, even sadistic "masculinity" of John Reed, and Brocklehurst, of St. John and the younger Rochester are all contained within the humbled and broken hero whom Jane ultimately nourishes and sustains. This is, of course, the fantasy element of Brontë's feminist myth. It would not be for almost fifty years that social change and aroused political consciousness would make it possible to test an awareness and achievement like Jane Eyre's against realistic pressures. In England it would not be until the twentieth century and the fiction of D. H. Lawrence that the descendants of the maimed Rochester and the liberated Jane would be able to face each other in the full complexity of their social, sexual, and psychological conflicts.[28] In our own time we struggle still to break through the irrational identification of phallic potency with political, social, and economic domination.

There is, in the naive resolution of *Jane Eyre,* an idealization of Jane and Rochester's life together which is part of the logic of the psychosexual romance. The last chapter begins with an extraordinary statement that places Jane at the center of the relationship. "Reader, I married him," she says and continues:

> I have now been married ten years. I know what it is to live entirely for and with what I love best on earth. I hold myself supremely blest—blest beyond what language can express; be-

---

28. One thinks, for example, of Gerald and Gudrun in *Women in Love,* of Ursula and Skrebensky in *The Rainbow,* and Clifford and Constance in *Lady Chatterley's Lover.* It ought to be noted that Lawrence's perspective was hardly feminist.

cause I am my husband's life as fully as he is mine. No woman
was ever nearer to her mate than I am: absolutely more bone of
his bone, and flesh of his flesh. I know no weariness of my
Edward's society: he knows none of mine, any more than we
do of the pulsation of the heart that beats in our separate bo-
soms; consequently, we are ever together. To be together is for
us to be at once as free as in solitude, as gay as in company.
We talk, I believe, all day long: to talk to each other is but an
animated and audible thinking. All my confidence is bestowed
on him; all his confidence is devoted to me: we are precisely
suited in character; perfect concord is the result. (p. 576)

But the truth of this relationship is an interior truth, as remote
from social reality as are Gateshead, Lowood, Thornfield, Marsh
End, and Ferndean—themselves all landscapes of psychological
development. It is the truth of Charlotte Brontë's dream that we
have here: the truth of her fantasy. To the extent that it dramatizes
the conflict of larger social and psychological forces, it offers
also the larger truth of myth. But what is extraordinary is that this
novel, born of repression and frustration, of limited experience
and less hope, should have offered an insight into psychosexual
relationships that was visionary in its own time and remains active in ours.

On the facing page: Haworth Parsonage and graveyard in the time of the Brontës / *By Permission of the Brontë Society*

Branwell Brontë's portrait of his sisters, c. 1825. *From left:* Anne, Emily, and Charlotte. The painted-out space in the center of the painting is thought to have once contained a self-portrait of Branwell / *National Portrait Gallery, London*

On the facing page, above: Branwell Brontë's portrait of Emily
National Portrait Gallery, London
Below: The Reverend Patrick Brontë / *The Mansell Collection*

Plaster relief. Head of Branwell Brontë by Branwell's friend,
Leyland / *The Mansell Collection*

A Fragment August the y 1829

One Cold dreary ~~stormy~~ night in the month of December
the Marquis Marchioness of Wellesly & ~~all~~ their children ~~who were~~ who were
all grown up were sitting ~~now~~ in the private parlour round a
blazing cheerful fire they appeared quite comfortable in all
outward things & yet they kept sighing & fieting & yawning
as if some great trouble oppressed at last Lady Wellesly
rose up from her seat and going to the window she drew
aside the splendid curtain & looked out into the dark
stormy night ● after gazing for some time she returned
to the fire saying in a despairing tone "when will little
Authur come?. I wonder what he is like now" exclaimed
Lord Wellesly "O Authur Authur do come" said the
Honourable & Reverend ~~the~~ Docter Wellesly I dont
know what I shall do if he does not come soon" returned
Lord Cowley "its quite miserable without him answered
Lord Maryborough "when we last saw him he was a
pretty little baby said the Marquis of Wellesly sweet
little creature ejaculated the Marchioness just at
this moment the door opened & a tall handsome
young man appeared they all started up joyfuly ex-
claiming thats Authur & runing towards ~~him~~ him
almost smothered him with kisses & caresses while he
in return did the same ~~thing~~ to them after the exuberance
of their joy had a little subsided they all gathered round
the fire once more but now perfectly happy as little
Authur was there ~~~~ after a ~~short~~ time the Marquis
of Wellesly said now my dear son tell us that you have
done & suffered since I placed you in the arms of
your orderly man to be conveyed on board the ship which
was to take you to Eaton college yes do Authur exclaimed the rest Arthur consented & began as follows
                    C Bronte August the 8 1829

George Smith, the director of Smith, Elder, and Company, Charlotte Brontë's publisher and the model for Graham Bretton in *Villette By permission of the Brontë Society*

Arthur Bell Nicholls, Charlotte's husband, c. 1854 *The Mansell Collection*

CHAPTER FOUR

Shirley: *Feminism and Power*

FOR REASONS which I will shortly sketch, Charlotte Brontë turned away from the quasi-allegorical mode of *Jane Eyre* and attempted to write what she conceived as a social and political novel. She would, of course, not abandon the psychological conundrums she had explored in that violent and radical new myth of heterosexual relationship, but she would now emphasize the pressures of the workaday world. She would discipline herself, as she had announced she would try to do in *The Professor,* to the dictates of "realism."

> Something real, cool and solid lies before you; something unromantic as Monday morning, when all who have work wake with the consciousness that they must ride and betake themselves thereto.[1]

Several factors contributed to the change of perspective. Although *Jane Eyre* had received enthusiastic reviews, its unknown author had been accused by many of impropriety and "coarseness."[2] The attacks on the novel's open sexuality and expression of "unseemly" feeling, might well have caused Brontë to regret her self-revelation and sent her scurrying for the comfort of authorial distance. Her respect for the ironic and omniscient posture of Thackeray, whom she considered to be the greatest of all

1. Charlotte Brontë, *Shirley, A Tale* (London: Oxford University Press, 1969), p. 1. All subsequent references are to this edition and will be included within the text.
2. For a thorough summation of the critical reception accorded the Brontës' novels, see Winnifreth, Chapter 7.

living writers, would have further reinforced this impulse. She also took seriously the sobering advice of George Henry Lewes who had qualified his praise of *Jane Eyre* with concern about its melodramatic nature. He referred her to Jane Austen. She abjured the model:

> I had not seen *Pride and Prejudice* till I read that sentence of yours, and then I got the book. And what did I find? An accurate daguerreotyped portrait of a commonplace face . . . with neat borders and delicate flowers; but no glance of a bright, vivid physiognomy, . . . no fresh air, no blue hill, no bonny beck. I should hardly like to live with her ladies and gentlemen, in their elegant but confined houses.[3]

But her response to Lewes suggests that she did not weigh his judgment lightly:

> I mean to observe your warning about being careful how I undertake new works; my stock of materials is not abundant, but very slender; and besides, neither my experience, my acquirements, nor my powers are sufficiently varied to justify my ever becoming a frequent writer . . .
>
> If I ever *do* write another book, I think I will have nothing of what you call "melodrama;" I *think* so, but I am not sure. I *think,* too, I will endeavour to follow the counsel which shines out of Miss Austen's "mild eyes," "to finish more and be more subdued;" but neither am I sure of that. When authors write best, or, at least, when they write most fluently, an influence seems to waken in them, which becomes their master—which will have its own way—putting out of view all behests but its own, dictating certain words, and insisting on their being used, whether vehement or measured in their nature; new-moulding characters, giving unthought-of turns to incidents, rejecting carefully elaborated old ideas, and suddenly creating and adopting new ones.[4]

Her awareness of the conflict which might exist between a desired goal and the demands of her genius suggests a new depth of self-knowledge and a more conscious definition of purpose. Reading her correspondence—particularly her letters to her editor and friend, W. S. Williams—one feels the growing intellectual confidence which allows her to advance ideas without timidity or

3. January 12, 1848. Wise and Symington, II, 179–80.
4. Ibid.

apology. She had been vastly successful as a writer. There was the sense of doors opening to welcome her into a world which had previously been inaccessible. Her position at Haworth was central—literary agent for her less successful sisters, nurse to her father, Branwell's righteous judge. All contributed to feelings of worth and responsibility. But there remained, after all, the parochial nature of her experience, the intense and even morbid self-involvement that characterized her psychological life. She must have been thinking of these when she courageously wrote to Lewes of her "slender stock of materials" and of the commanding urgency of her particular genius. She must have had in mind the conflict between the personal demands of her reticent nature and the wrenching disquiet of her growing social awakening when she observed in *Shirley:*

> It is good for women, especially, to be endowed with a soft blindness: to have mild, dim eyes, that never penetrate below the surface of things—that take all for what it seems. Thousands, knowing this, keep their eye-lids drooped, on system; but the most downcast glance has its loophole, through which it can, on occasion, take its sentinel-survey of life. (p. 271)

Like many women whose vulnerability and dependence spawn an exquisite sensitivity to the responses and attitudes of others, Brontë had been "accustomed to silent soul-reading." Professional and intellectual self-confidence gave her a voice—allowed her to abstract and judge. But persistent feelings of personal inadequacy (the habitual stance of a lifetime) made it difficult for her to translate criticism into concepts of antiauthoritarian action relevant to her characters. This clash between intellect and emotion was at least partially responsible for the eccentric nature of her novel: as ambitious as any written during the Victorian period; fascinating in its flaws, frustrating in its inability to offer resolutions, thrilling in its capacity for posing the most meaningful kinds of problems.

There is always present in *Shirley*'s probing analysis of society a haunting cry of personal alienation. One feels that *this* is the cry that marked the novel's birth, that the fiction was conceived out of Brontë's sense, probably quite vague at first, that her misery was part of a larger, complex pain; that the meshes in which she felt herself to be imprisoned represented only a tiny segment of an enormous web in which innumerable others were trapped. At the heart of her view was profound pessimism.

> There are hundreds of human beings who trample on acts of kindness and mock at words of affection. I know this, though I have seen but little of the world. I suppose I have something harsher in my nature than you have, something which every now and then tells me dreary secrets about my race, and I cannot believe the voice of the Optimist, charm he never so wisely.[5]

She had agonizingly experienced personal rebuffs and rejections, bitter disillusionments; but it was not these alone which fostered negative thoughts. The political concerns of her childhood, still primary in her father's life, must have held a place in her own awareness. Her publishers at Smith, Elder kept her supplied with much of the reading material which occupied intellectual London. Her friendship with Mary Taylor had long stimulated her feminist consciousness. The writings of her two new friends, Elizabeth Gaskell and Harriet Martineau, gave that consciousness a more objective focus. The 1840s were years of intellectual and social ferment and Brontë could not have been unaffected by the new free-trade liberalism of the middle class or by the revolutionary socialism which was becoming the faith of increasing numbers of workers. By 1846, with the repeal of the Corn Laws and the beginning of the railway mania, there is all the horror of the modern industrial age. Amelioration would come later.[6]

Her response to these public and private pressures, was to write what was, for her, a different kind of novel. It is set in Yorkshire during the Napoleonic wars. The rebellion of weavers against textile manufacturers (the Luddite uprisings) provided the background. There are two heroines. Caroline Helstone, abandoned as a small child by her mother, has been grudgingly raised by her minister uncle, the brother of her dead father. Caroline is hopelessly in love with Robert Moore, her Belgian cousin who, as a beleaguered mill owner, cannot afford the fripperies of romance. The second heroine, Shirley Keeldar, does not appear until a third of the way through the novel, but occupies a position

5. To W. S. Williams, October 18, 1848. Wise and Symington, II, 267.

6. See Barbara Ward, "Charlotte Brontë and The World of 1846," *Brontë Society Transactions*, XI, 56 (1951), 3–13. The essay is illuminating but underestimates Brontë's grasp of dominant social issues.

of special importance. She is the ''lady'' of the parish manor house, a wealthy orphaned heiress, secretly in love with Robert Moore's brother, Louis, her impoverished former tutor. In the process of conducting her heroines through their romantic trials, Brontë introduces her readers to various aspects of life in this transitional society. She examines the state of the church, England's political struggles, the position of women, attitudes of owners and workers.

When the novel was published in 1849, Lewes wrote in the *Edinburgh Review* that *Shirley* was ''a portfolio of sketches'' lacking in unity. Critics and readers have agreed ever since, persistently confusing the novel's fragmented and unresolved conclusions with its fundamental unity of concept. Having underestimated the power of Brontë's social vision, critics have not been able to see the way in which the breadth of that vision is unsupported by an adequate political consciousness. Blind to the subtlety of the novel's design, they have justified their claim of its absence by a sympathetic depiction of her tragic milieu. It is typical of the undermining sentimentality that has typified Brontë biography and criticism.[7]

For the most part, then, even those who have attempted to approach the novel seriously have been unable to connect the author's ironic treatment of the clergy, her use of the Luddite riots, references to the Napoleonic wars, the jaundiced presentation of marriage, the sympathetic, even agonized analyses of spinster life, and the impassioned pleas for useful work for women. They have not reconciled the strongly antiromantic strain of the novel

7. Among more recent critics who have dismissed or underestimated the novel because of its absence of unity are: Lord David Cecil, *Early Victorian Novelists* (Indianapolis: Bobbs-Merrill, 1935), pp. 117–54; Ivy Holgate, ''The Structure of *Shirley*,'' *Brontë Society Transactions*, 14 (1962), 27–35; Fanny Ratchford, *The Brontës' Web of Childhood*; J. M. S. Tompkins, ''Caroline Helstone's Eyes,'' *Brontë Society Transactions*, 14 (1961), 18–28; Janet Spens, ''Charlotte Brontë,'' in *Essays and Studies by Members of the English Association*, 14 (1929), 54–70; Asa Briggs, ''Private and Social Themes in *Shirley*,'' *Brontë Society Transactions*, 13 (1958), 203–14.

In recent years only Jacob Korg, ''The Problem of Unity in *Shirley*,'' *Nineteenth Century Fiction*, 12 (September 1957); Arnold Shapiro, ''Public Themes and Private Lives: Social Criticism in *Shirley*,'' *Papers on Language and Literature*, 4 (Winter 1968); and most persuasively, Carol Ohman, ''Charlotte Brontë: The Limits of her Feminism,'' in *Female Studies*. 6, The Feminist Press (Old Westbury, N.Y.) 1972, 152–64 have argued for coherent principles of unity within the novel.

and its conventionally "happy ending." They have sought to place the novel's focus, wondering why Brontë chose to use two heroines instead of one. They have rejected as extraneous the Yorke family—modeled on Mary Taylor's "people"—interesting in themselves, apparently irrelevant to the work as a whole.

Masking this misreading, clumsy criticism has then advanced the needless apology of tragic circumstance. At this time, the novelist had herself confessed to James Taylor, another of her publishers:

> I took great pains with *Shirley*. I did not hurry; I tried to do my best, and my own impression was that it was not inferior to the former work; indeed, I had bestowed on it more time, thought and anxiety: but a great part of it was written under the shadow of impending calamity and the last volume, I cannot deny, was composed in the eager, restless endeavor to combat mental sufferings that were scarcely tolerable.[8]

Three deaths in nine months. Three times the writing had been interrupted—three times resumed in an increasing mood of hopelessness and despair: "Too often I feel like once crossing an abyss on a narrow plank—a glance round might quite unnerve. . . ."[9] How small the pretense of art must have seemed to Brontë in comparison with the realities of her situation. Caroline Helstone could be miraculously revived in the chapter, "Valley of the Shadow of Death," but Anne, the youngest of them all, had just been placed in her coffin. Emily and Branwell had been buried several months before. The tone of the novel would naturally have been affected by Brontë's grief and it is altogether likely that she might have modified her heroines' characters, as displayed in the earlier chapters, after the deaths of her sisters.[10]

8. Wise and Symington, III, 154.

9. To W. S. Williams, January 18, 1849. Wise and Symington, II, 301.

10. Winifred Gerin suggests that "as Emily's life ebbed away (Shirley) became increasingly endowed with the characteristics of her sister. Finally there was a change in Caroline's character. Even the color of her eyes and hair came to resemble Anne's in the end" (pp. 389–90).

According to Gaskell, Shirley Keeldar was "what Emily Brontë would have been had she been placed in health and prosperity" (p. 277). Ivy Holgate ("The Structure of *Shirley*") suggests that Shirley began as a portrait of Mary Taylor but that, after Emily's death, Charlotte felt free to incorporate into that portrait elements of her sister's personality:

> Thus in Shirley Keeldar we find the noblest traces that were to be found in Emily Brontë. We also find in the heroine the commercially-minded Mary,

Still, the modifications involved are relatively minor. Ruthlessly shunting the tragedies aside, we are able to find the principle of unity which reconciles what for so long have been seen as disparate themes, dissonant chords.

By the time Brontë sat down to write *Shirley* she had so matured psychologically, artistically, and intellectually that she could place the psychosexual problems which had long concerned her within a larger social context. We have seen how, in both *The Professor* and *Jane Eyre,* she drew parallels between women and statusless men. In *The Professor* she had described as effeminized, men deprived of social or economic power. But their effeminacy was often transitional. Her impotent female, on the other hand, could not be released from the double bind of both her gender and her social situation. In *Jane Eyre,* working with the same recognitions, she resolved the dilemma of her heroine by awarding her social and economic status at the same time that she drastically redefined the role and identity of the male. She could do this only by isolating Jane and Rochester within an asocial, mythic universe.

The time had come for her to confront more directly the nature of female oppression and to consider as analytically as possible the way in which this form of oppression was related to others: to find the connections which could be drawn between women and the poor and socially dispossessed, between women and unemployed laborers, between women and children. She had reached a level of consciousness which allowed her to ask what characteristics ''women'' shared with other groups of powerless ''victims'': in what ways the nature of women's interaction with men and with other women was determined by the complexity of their impotent situation. The theme of her new book would be nothing less then the misuse of power within a patriarchal society, and ''women,'' rather than a particular woman, would stand for her as the appropriate and central symbol of powerlessness. She realized that in the female subculture values have been developed in relative isolation. Because they are different from those of the ''official'' society, they offer a critical perspective of accepted structures and attitudes.

the feminist, the pioneering woman. But Charlotte was at this time by no means at her best; she derived a kind of stimulus of mind from her obsession, but the grafting has not been skillfully done. (pp. 27–35)

It is an extraordinary subject for Charlotte Brontë to have conceived: not less impressive when one remembers that Engels had just published *The Condition of the Working Class in England in 1844*. The differences between their analyses derive from the fact that Engels's political consciousness—infinitely more powerful, of course, than Brontë's own—was formed in response to his sophisticated social awareness. The result was a vision of radical social change completely absent from *Shirley*. Still, Brontë was asking, in her novel, questions as acute as any which were then being asked in England.

II

In the first chapter of *Shirley,* Brontë demonstrates her resoluteness of purpose by launching immediately into an attack on the Church—the church of which Patrick Brontë was minister. By 1812, the year in which her story begins, the Anglican Church—respected arbiter of value, source of divine inspiration and support—has become increasingly indifferent to its people. Its spine broken, the organism must collapse. In the rotted moral fiber of those who should intercede between God and man, the extent and nature of society's disease can be diagnosed.

The symptoms of the disease are found in the false pride, the petty vanities, the egotism of the curates. The trivial concerns of Donne, Malone, and Sweeting imply much: their "love of feasting and drinking," their endless socializing and foolish squabbling; the grudging condescension towards the members of their parishes to whom they are strangers and from whom they are alienated; the preoccupation with females as so many sexual objects with so much dowry value. Significantly, the curates do not number their landladies, upon whom their comforts depend, among the rest of "the fair sex." Because these females have no "human" qualities, they share the same name, always spoken in tones of cruel command. The name is "woman." It designates function: to clean, to cook, in short—to serve.

> "Cut it woman," [said Mr. Malone] and the "woman" cut it accordingly. Had she followed her inclinations, she would have cut the parson also; her Yorkshire soul revolted absolutely from his manner of command. (p. 5)

In two of their rectors—the Reverends Matthew Helstone and
Hiram Yorke—the curates' symptoms become more pronounced,
made virulent by class and status. The nature of the disease is
now identifiable: it is the desire for and the misuse of power.
Brontë had suggested, in her portraits of Brocklehurst and St.
John Rivers, the ministry's potential for self-delusion and cruelty, for sexual sadism linked to sexual repression. Here she
widens her perspective. Yorke and Helstone are not starkly
drawn figures of allegory. Their complexity, particularly
Yorke's, rejects simplistic summation. They are men, not villains. But neither is appropriately a man of the church. Both are
manipulative, arrogant, and worldly. Of Helstone:

> He was not diabolical at all. The evil simply was, he had
> missed his vocation: he should have been a soldier, and cir-
> cumstances had made him a priest. For the rest, he was a con-
> scientious, hard-headed, hard-handed, brave, stern, implaca-
> ble, faithful little man; a man almost without sympathy,
> ungentle, prejudiced, and rigid; but a man true to principle,
> honourable, sagacious and sincere. (p. 34)

And of Yorke:

> The want of veneration . . . made him dead at heart to the
> electric delight of admiring what is admirable; it dried up a
> thousand pure sources of enjoyment; it withered a thousand
> vivid pleasures. He was not irreligious, though a member of no
> sect, but his religion could not be that of one who knows how
> to venerate. He believed in God and heaven, but his God and
> heaven were those of a man in whom awe, imagination and
> tenderness lack.
>   The weakness of his powers of comparison made him in-
> consistent; while he professed some excellent general doctrines
> of mutual toleration and forbearance, he cherished towards
> certain classes a bigoted antipathy; . . . at heart he was a
> proud man: very friendly to his workpeople, very good to all
> who were beneath him, and submitted quietly to be beneath
> him, but haughty as Beelzebub to whomsoever the world
> deemed (for he deemed no man) his superior. (p. 44)

There is little place for the human affections in a world characterized on every level by conflict, competition, and aggression. England is at war with France. National interests divide: Jacobin
against Loyalist; Tory against Whig. It is a world in which re-

ligious sects line up as armies—Dissenters, Methodists, Baptists, Wesleyans, Independents. It is a world in which birth assigns status and material success confirms it. And everywhere, at the head of every faction, leading every battle, filling the ranks of armies, political parties, professional workers, and simple laborers—there are men, only men: each one defining his situation according to his own self-interest: each one attempting to retain whatever bit of social, economic, and sexual power he possesses: each one attempting to garner more.

Thus when the unemployed textile workers rebel against the mill owner, Robert Moore, first smashing the machinery he has purchased to replace them and finally, in desperation, attacking his mill,[11] Helstone who feels no sympathy for them, and Yorke who does, both join against the workers in an expression of class solidarity. Social and economic interests ally them with the Belgian despite their professional responsibilities and national allegiance.

As for Moore himself, he typifies in his attitudes the crass selfishness of the growing middle class:

> All men, taken singly, are more or less selfish, and taken in bodies they are intensely so. The British merchant is no exception to this rule; the mercantile classes illustrate it strikingly. These classes certainly think too exclusively of making money; they are too oblivious of every national consideration but that of extending England's (i.e., their own) commerce. Chivalrous feeling, disinterestedness, pride in honour, is too dead in their hearts. (p. 167)

Robert, too, is guided virtually exclusively by the economic motive softened only slightly by the necessity he feels of paying his father's debts. He sees himself as "a man [who] has been brought up only to make money, and lives to make it, and for nothing else, and scarcely breathes any other air than that of mills and markets" (p. 122). With other mill owners, he is a Whig, "at least as far as opposition to the war-party was concerned, that

11. Asa Briggs suggests that the account of the workers' rebellion against Robert Moore was based upon events which initiated the Luddite movement near Nottingham during the winter of 1811–12. The rebellion represented a protest against machinery and was stimulated by the scarcity of work and the high price of provisions. The model for Robert Moore, according to Briggs, was William Cartwright who bravely defended his mill with four of his workmen and five soldiers. ("Private and Social Scenes in *Shirley*," pp. 208–9.)

being the question which affected his own interest; and only on that question did he profess any British politics at all'' (p. 34). But, with the other mill owners, he also wants stricter government intervention to suppress machine-wrecking and attacks on property. Like Helstone and Yorke, he enjoys the exercise of power, and even welcomes being wronged so that he can avenge himself and demonstrate his courage—his possession of the manly virtues. Emotion is not among them. It is a luxury he can ill afford. He rejects a love-match with Caroline, whose devotion he acknowledges, whose attraction he feels, in favor of a possible union with Shirley, whose fortune would guarantee his future. For the poor he feels no sympathy. "Poverty is necessarily selfish, contracted, groveling, anxious" (p. 60), he observes, with the smug superiority born of class consciousness and separation. When William Farren, one of his unemployed workers, gives voice to his frustration:

> Invention may be all right, but I know it isn't right for poor folks to starve. Them that governs mun find a way to help us: they mun mak' fresh orderations. Ye'll say that's hard to do—so much louder mun we shout out, then, for so much slacker will t'Parliament-men to be set on to a tough job.
> (p. 137)

Moore cannot understand that they share a common problem: "Worry the Parliament-men as much as you please . . . but to worry the mill-owners is absurd; and I, for one, won't stand it" (p. 137). He is neither capable of the kind of social analysis which will demonstrate that he, like Farren, is a victim of the same system: that both are, in fact, powerless; nor does he grasp the fundamental meaning of need and deprivation: that "misery generates hate" (p. 28). His kinship with Farren escapes him. In fact, if he is only slightly less frustrated and miserable than the starving members of the working class, he is not less self-involved. The threat of economic ruin deprives him of humane attitudes. Hungry, all men—Brontë observes—are the same:

> National honour was become a mere empty name, of no value in the eyes of many, because their sight was dim with famine; and for a morsel of meat they would have sold their birthright.
> (p. 27)

It is interesting that Farren, striving to maintain moral principles, should identify himself with Caroline and Shirley:

> Human natur', taking i' th' lump, is nought but selfishness. It is but excessive few, it is but just an exception here and there, now and then, sich as ye two young uns and me, that being in a different sphere, can understand t'one t'other, and be friends wi'out slavishness o'one hand, or pride o' t'other. (p. 325)

In fact, there is both "slavishness" and "pride." They patronize him. He treats them with deference. His class expectations are such that he accepts this as "equality." But still he is right. There are ways in which they are "like." The introduction of machinery has made Farren as extraneous as women to the cash nexus. Cut off from the patriarchal hierarchy he becomes, quite appropriately, a gardener—part of the natural world from which most men are estranged but with which women are still associated. This association gives them their special "intuitive" knowledge, but it is a kind of knowledge which cannot be translated into action or made a meaningful part of history.

To the extent that the laborer remains within the structures of industrialization he becomes economically, socially, and psychologically alienated. He, like women, is made to experience himself as "victim": powerless and oppressed. Increasingly devalued as "things" become more valuable, he is assessed according to his usefulness just as women are desired according to their material wealth and physical attractiveness—their "sexuality." As long as he is enmeshed in a competitive system which rewards him with money, he is alienated from other men, from his work, from the natural world and from himself. So women compete with one another for the status of marriage, seldom realizing that the marriage relationship, based on impersonal considerations, cannot yield "love." The inner quality of the power structure places husband and wife in a situation of conflict which approximates the one that exists between owner and worker. Sexual politics can be defined in terms similar to those of class antagonism. At every point, workers and women are expected to recognize their inferiority and their dependence. Joe Scott speaks for most men when he explains to Caroline and Shirley that "Women is to take their husbands' opinion, both in politics and religion—it's wholesomest for them'' (p. 328). Although he could be speaking also of Robert Moore's expectation of *him*, it is clear that he still sees himself as in a position superior to any woman's, no matter what her class. The androgynous vision of *The Professor* has finally been subject to social and economic analysis.

That Charlotte Brontë perceived her world in much the same way as Engels did[12] (as a power struggle conducted on personal and familial as well as on socioeconomic levels), is repeatedly demonstrated in the male and female attitudes recorded—relationships described—in *Shirley*. Men and women are mysteries to one another: inevitably sealed and separate. Marriage—the most fundamental social relationship—is materially based. The curate, Malone, rejects ''marriage in the vulgar, weak sense, as a mere matter of sentiment'' although he accepts its value when it offers ''an advantageous connection'' (p. 20). And when he observes to Moore that ''you and I will have no gray mares in our stable when we marry,'' Moore responds with typical pragmatism, ''If the gray mare is handsome and tractable, why not?'' (p. 24). So, too, Shirley's uncle, Mr. Sympson, is anxious that she make ''a suitable match'': ''a fine unencumbered estate; real substance; good connections'' (p. 465), since, '' 'Love' is Preposterous stuff! indecorous! unwomanly!'' (p. 467). Shirley correctly observes to Caroline:

> If men could see us as we really are, they would be a little amazed; but the cleverest, the acutest men are often under an illusion about women: they do not read them in a true light: they misapprehend them, both for good and evil: their good woman is a queer thing, half doll, half angel; their bad woman almost always a fiend. (p. 350)

It is the classic distinction between the Virgin Mary and the Whore of Babylon: man projecting his own bifurcated nature onto women: Rochester divided between the elfin Jane and the vampire Berthe.

Helstone's insecurity, his desire for power, his fear of feeling, all express themselves in his cruel, sexual sadism. His vanity

---

12. See *The Origin of the Family, Private Property, and the State* (New York: International Publishers, 1942). It is interesting to note that Engels's relationship with the Irish factory girl, Mary Burns—and her sister, Lizzie—hints of the class and sexual chauvinism attacked in *Shirley* as well as in Engels's own work.

prods him to flirtation: "Yet, at heart, he neither respected nor liked the sex, and such of them as circumstances had brought into intimate relation with him had ever feared rather then loved him" (p. 113). He finds it convenient to see women as "a different, probably a very inferior, order of existence" (p. 50).

> He could not abide sense in women: he liked to see them as silly, as light-headed, as vain, as open to ridicule as possible; because they were then in reality what he held them to be, and wished them to be—inferior: toys to play with, to amuse a vacant hour and to be thrown away. (p. 115)

His former wife, Mary Cave, had found physical death preferable to the spiritual death of her marriage. She had also been loved by Hiram Yorke, who thought her "perfect." But, as Yorke admits to Robert Moore: ". . . The odds are, if Mary loved me and not scorned me; if I had been secure of her affection, certain of her constancy . . . the odds are I should have left her" (p. 537). His is a psychology that Shirley understands. She explains it to Caroline, while they watch the attack on Moore's mill. In this moment of crisis it is clear that there cannot be a real place in the serious world of male affairs for an idealized woman. Where there is no heroism there is no room for inspiration: "These are not the days of chivalry: it is not a tilt at a tournament we are going to behold, but a struggle about money, and food, and life" (p. 340). Idealization has little place in the best of courtships. In marriage, it can find no place at all. Although men pursue women, and women can imagine marriage as the only desirable goal of life, few who are or who have been married speak of that state with anything less than either Helstone's practical bitterness: "A yoke-fellow is a fellow sufferer" (p. 99), or Mrs. Pryor's agonized understanding:

> [Love] is said to be strong—strong as death! Most of the cheats of existence are strong. As to their sweetness, nothing is so transitory: its date is a moment—the twinkling of an eye; the sting remains forever. It may perish with the dawn of eternity, but it tortures through time into its deepest night. (p. 378)

Only one "family" appears in the novel: Hiram Yorke and his six children. Most critics have cited the inclusion of the Yorkes—based on the family of Mary Taylor—as the prime example of *Shirley*'s absence of unity: a demonstration of Brontë's inability to combine fact and fiction in a satisfactory whole. The inclusion is crucial, however, even if the integration is not wholly successful. Through the Yorkes, Brontë raises a number of sophisticated questions which are central in her consideration of the nature and effects of the patriarchal structure.

On the face of it, the Yorkes are a good, "successful" family; Yorke himself a loving and proud father. He stimulates the minds of his children as he cares for their bodies: appreciating their intelligences, recognizing their gifts, respecting their freedom. He, in turn, earns *their* respect and affection by virtue of his character, his personality, and, not least of all, his position in the community and in his home. The boys share their father's self-possession. Despite personal differences and moments of discord, the three are guaranteed, by virtue of sexual privilege, a strong stake in the future, secure positions and the promise of success.

For Rose and Jessy—as blithe, as imaginative, as strong as their brothers—the future is less certain. Raised in equality by their father, they are not treated with equality by others:

> There are plenty of people . . . who take notice of the boys. All my uncles and aunts seem to think their nephews better than their nieces; and when gentlemen come here to dine, it is always Matthew, and Mark, and Martin that are talked to and never Rose and me. (p. 155)

Although they share their brothers' aspirations and attitudes, their prospects are inferior. Their mother acts, ironically, as society's representative: interpreting for them its sexist will: urging upon them suspicion and repression ("discretion and reserve is a girl's best wisdom" [p. 155]): attempting to restrain their spirits, limit their sense of possibility, reduce them as she has been reduced.

A strong-minded woman, intelligent and able, circumstances have turned her sour and cynical. Since she cannot move happily in the demanding, rigidly defined insularity of her life, she will, at least, move efficiently—making a martyrdom of her domesticity and a model of her martyrdom. Defined only as a wife and mother—all her prodigious energies focused here—she is possessive of her husband ("if she could have had her will, she would not have permitted him to have any friend in the world beside herself" [p. 147]) and dictatorial with her children:

> I would advise all young ladies . . . to study the characters of
> such children as they chance to meet with before they marry
> and have any of their own; to consider well how they would
> like the responsibility of guiding the careless, the labour of
> persuading the stubborn, the constant burden and task of train-
> ing the best. (p. 401)

She depresses where she ought to cheer, angers where she ought
to comfort, stimulates rebellion instead of love.[13] Powerless in a
larger world, she behaves in a way which renders her powerless
in her home as well. There too, her husband rules:

> Mrs. Yorke often complained that her children were mutinous.
> It was strange that with all her strictness, with all her "strong-
> mindedness"; she could gain no command over them. A look
> from their father had more influence with them than a lecture
> from her. (p. 405)

Although she is chiefly bent on forcing her daughters into her
own mold (their independence threatens the foundations of her
life) her example becomes the primary motive in their rejection of
the traditional role defined for them. Rose refuses—as will
Jessy—to bury her talents in domestic tasks:

> If my Master had given me ten talents, my duty is to trade with
> them, and make them ten talents more. Not in the dust of
> household drawers shall the coin be interred. I will *not* deposit
> it in a broken-spouted teapot, and shut it up in a china-closet
> among tea things. I will *not* commit it to your worktable to be
> smothered in piles of woolen hose. I will *not* prison it in the
> linen-press to find shrouds among the sheets; and least of all,
> Mother . . . least of all, will I hide it in a tureen of cold pota-
> toes, to be ranged with bread, butter, pastry and ham on the
> shelves of the larder. (p. 399)

She is only twelve and will submit to her apprenticeship for four
more years, learning those household arts which are useful for all
to know. Then she is resolved to travel, to "see the outside of our
own round planet at least" (p. 398). She believes that it is "better

13. Winifred Gerin writes: "Mrs. Taylor, née Ann Tickell, seems to have
united in her person all the disagreeable qualities of Mrs. Gummidge, Mrs. Wil-
fer, and Mrs. Vardon; she was cordially disliked by Charlotte and not particularly loved by her daughters, whose life she oppressed with her gloom and tyranny." (*Charlotte Brontë*, p. 71)

to try all things and find all empty than to try nothing and leave
your life a blank'' (p. 399).

Brontë's depiction of Jessy's eventual death on a foreign
shore, while moving, *is* perhaps extraneous. But her inclusion of
the Yorke family and her suggestion of the girls' emigration are
not. In the characterization of Mrs. Yorke still another chain of
reactions to sexism is revealed. In the functioning of the family—
one of the "best" in Yorkshire—some of the undermining effects
of patriarchy are described. And in Rose and Jessy, who represent the glorious success of enlightened education, who are the
most authentic achievements of their father's confused liberalism, the cruel moral of the novel is drawn. For feminism that is
wholly committed and uncompromised there can be no place in
England. For the woman who, like Rose, has "a fine, generous
soul, a noble intellect profoundly cultivated, a heart as true as
steel" (p. 156), a woman who would use her talents and her
mind, who will accept neither dependence nor oppression, who
defines herself in terms of freedom and possibility, for a woman
refusing alienation, a new home must be built on alien soil.

III

Charlotte Brontë loved and respected Mary Taylor. She was
much influenced by her ideas; inspired by her fervor. But Mary's
form of feminism was different from her own. Brontë's vision
was less whole than Taylor's: less clear, less radical, more troubled—as her personality was less free. Where Mary's childhood
had prepared her for rebellion, Charlotte's had made her long for
survival. She was bound by her own insecurity. Feelings of inadequacy projected outward became forebodings of doom. If, after
her Brussels experience, she could not make herself leave the
stultifying security of Haworth, how could she conceive of emi-
grating to a strange country? For Brontë, the dilemma of women
was as inescapable as hunger. Both, as we have seen were related
to the larger problem of exploitation, defined politically, economically, socially, culturally, sexually. To such problems Charlotte Brontë, who was not a revolutionary, could offer no large
solutions. She could conceive only of compromise. To work out
the terms of that compromise, to define the nature and limits of
the power which women could claim, she placed two heroines at
the center of her story: two women who, by virtue of their per-

sonal, social, and economic differences would suggest alternative personal styles and possibilities. Of the two, Caroline Helstone occupies the more conventional position. Left penniless by her father, a cruel, sadistic man who died when she was a child, abandoned by her mother, she is completely dependent upon the benevolence of Matthew Helstone, the uncle with whom she lives. Helstone is not unkind to her. He is simply unconcerned. She is of no greater value to him than is any other woman and because he cannot flirt with her, she is of less interest. She has been educated according to her uncle's standards (''stick to the needle—learn skirt-making, and gown-making, and pie-crust making, and you'll be a clever woman some day'' [p. 96]). She has learned to sew a little, draw a little, speak a little French. She reads the books she finds in Helstone's library. In short, she has been prepared for nothing and can do nothing. She must wait passively for ''events'' to offer her an appropriate occupation, i.e., marriage. Mistreated by her father, rejected by her mother, ignored by her uncle, she is insecure and repressed: ''slow to make fresh acquaintance, she was always held back by the idea that people could not want her, that she could not amuse them'' (p. 205). Caroline is merely pretty, intelligent, gentle, serious, and good. Only a woman. Without fortune, she is without prospects. She has ''fallen in love'' with her cousin, Robert Moore, one of the few men who have treated her with kindness. But she doesn't really know him. He will not, as Shirley points out, allow himself to *be* known:

> You can't fix your eyes on him but his presently flash on you. He is never off his guard; he won't give you an advantage; even when he does not look at you, his thoughts seem to be busy amongst your own thoughts, tracing your words .·. . at his ease. (p. 273)

Caroline looks to Robert as her superior in everything and he obligingly treats her with condescension; patronizing his ''little democrat,'' enjoying the fact that with him, she is like a ''happy, docile child'' (p. 93).

Despite the fact that the rules of courtship do not allow her to initiate action,[14] Caroline tries, quite movingly, to be open with

14. Charlotte Brontë had written to Ellen Nussey:
Ten years ago I should have laughed heartily at your account of the blunder you made in mistaking the bachelor doctor of Burlington for a married

Robert, allowing him to know her feelings for him, risking the rejection which is ultimately his response. When he tells her, with intended kindness, "If I could guide that benignant heart, I believe I should counsel it to exclude one who does not profess to have any higher aim in life than that of patching up his broken fortune" (pp. 122–23), he leaves her without hope. Having nothing to divert her mind, she dwells endlessly on the small details of their relationship, punishing herself for surrendering her pride: remembering, for example, that it was she who first asked *him* for the lock of hair which she now wears upon her heart:

> It was my doing, and one of those silly deeds it distresses the heart and sets the face on fire to think of—one of those small but sharp recollections that return, lacerating your self respect like tiny penknives and forcing from your lips, as you sit alone, sudden, insane-sounding interjections. (p. 227)

Her preoccupation with trivia would be absurd, her dependency pathetic, if her bitterness were less real; if Charlotte Brontë's sense of her as a victim of power were less persuasive: if her position as a woman were not convincingly presented as universal in its implications:

> A lover masculine so disappointed can speak and urge explanation: a lover feminine can say nothing; if she did, the result would be shame and anguish, inward remorse for self-treachery . . . Take the matter as you find it; ask no questions, utter no remonstrances; it is your best wisdom. You expected bread, and you have got a stone; break your teeth on it, and don't shriek because the nerves are martyrized; do not doubt that your mental stomach—if you have such a thing—is strong as an ostrich's: the stone will digest. You held out your hand for an egg, and Fate put into it a scorpion. Show no consterna-

---

man. I should have certainly thought you scrupulous over much—and wondered how you could possibly regret being civil to a decent individual merely because he happened to be single instead of double. Now, however, I can perceive that your scruples are founded on common-sense. I know that if women wish to escape the stigma of husband-seeking, they must act and look like marble or clay—cold—expressionless, bloodless—for every appearance of feeling of joy—sorrow—friendliness, antipathy, admiration—disgust are alike construed by the world into an attempt to hook in a husband—never mind, Nell—well meaning women have their own conscience to comfort them after all. (April 2, 1845. Wise and Symington, II, 30)

tion; close your fingers firmly upon the gift; let it sting through your palm. Never mind; in time, after your hand and arm have swelled and quivered long with torture, the squeezed scorpion will die, and you will have learned the great lesson, how to endure without a sob. For the whole remnant of your life, if you survive the test—some, it is said, die under it—you will be stronger, wiser, less sensitive. (p. 103)

So is the pride of martyrdom born. So is the masochist made: "Robert had done her no wrong; he had told her no lie; it was she that was to blame, if anyone was" (p. 104). To defend oneself against rejection requires self-confidence. A life of self-abnegation and insecurity produces acceptance. One had to face the truth. It was what Charlotte Brontë had done, as she wrote to Ellen Nussey:

> Not that it is a crime to marry—or a crime to wish to be married—but it is an imbecility which I reject with contempt—for women who have neither fortune nor beauty—to make marriage the principle object of their wishes and hopes and the aim of all their actions—not to be able to convince themselves that they are unattractive and that they had better be quiet and think of other things than wedlock—[15]

But of what can one think? For Caroline life becomes an endless expanse of time which must be filled. She tries to adjust to the idea of leading a spinster's life by coming to know Miss Ainley and Miss Mann, by learning what "old maids" do, the way in which they get through every day. She attempts to confront herself, as Brontë had already done:

> It seems that even a "lone woman" can be happy, as well as cherished wives and proud mothers—I am glad of that—I speculate much on the existence of unmarried and never-to-be married women nowadays, and I have already got to the point of considering that there is no more respectable character on this earth than an unmarried woman who makes her own way through life quietly, perseveringly,—without support of husband or brother, and, who, having attained the age of forty-five or upwards—retains in her possession a well-regulated mind—a disposition to enjoy simple pleasures—fortitude to support inevitable pains, sympathy with the sufferings of oth-

15. April 1, 1843. Wise and Symington, I, 296.

ers, and willingness to relieve want as far as her means ex-
tend.[16]

But what Caroline perceives is that the generosity of the spinster
does not relieve her loneliness, nor does it earn her a genuine
place, "a stake," in society. She is used and manipulated as she
has always been used and manipulated. The selfish and materialistic people around her calculatedly allow her desperation to be
channeled into altruism, and the altruism turns bitter with the recognition of abuse.

Caroline lives a life which is, as Rose Yorke describes it, "a
black trance like the toad's buried in marble . . . a long slow
death" (p. 398). It is a life such as Brontë herself lived after she
returned from Brussels:

> I can hardly tell you how time gets on here at Haworth—There
> is no event whatever to mark its progress—one day resembles
> another—and all have heavy lifeless physiognomies—Sunday,
> baking day and Saturday are the only ones that bear the slight-
> est distinctive mark—meantime life wears away—I shall soon
> be thirty—and I have done nothing yet—sometimes I get mel-
> ancholy—at the prospects before and behind me—yet it is
> wrong and foolish to repine—and undoubtedly my duty directs
> me to stay at home for the present—There was a time when
> Haworth was a very pleasant place to me—it is not so now—I
> feel as if we were all buried here—I long to travel—to work, to
> live a life of action.[17]

Caroline's voice is indistinguishable from Charlotte's when she
cries out:

> Men of England, look at your poor girls, many of them fading
> around you, dropping off in consumption or decline; or, what
> is worse, degenerating to sour old maids—envious, backbit-
> ing, wretched, because life is a desert to them; or, what is
> worst of all, reduced to strive, by scarce modest coquetry and
> debasing artifice, to gain that position and consideration by
> marriage, which to celibacy is denied. Fathers . . . seek for
> them an interest and an occupation which shall raise them
> above the flirt, the manoeuverer, the mischief-making tale-
> bearer. Keep your girls' minds narrow and fettered, they will
> still be a plague and a care, sometimes a disgrace to you. Cul-

16. To Miss Wooler, January 30, 1846. Wise and Symington, II, 77.
17. To Ellen Nussey, March 24, 1845. Wise and Symington, II, 28.

tivate them—give them some scope and work—they will be
your gayest companions in health, your tenderest nurses in
sickness, your most faithful prop in age. (p. 392)

For if, as Caroline observes, labor alone cannot bring happiness,
"it can give varieties of pain, and prevent us from breaking our
hearts with a single tyrant master-torture" (p. 226).

It is the "stagnant state of things," living on frustrated hope
and inactivity, which makes young women ill, which makes
"their minds and views shrink to wondrous narrowness" (p.
391). It is their distance from the realities of their society, their
inability to bind themselves *in fact* to the complexity of human
experience, which makes them long for escape and leads them
into the airless, endless, dead-end of the romantic myth. By encouraging acceptance, it chains them to the futility of their condition.

Brontë had learned the value of work through the lonely
agony of her bereaved life. She knew, as she wrote to Williams,
that only her career had given her a hope and motive adequate to
sustain her.[18] The passion of Caroline's plea reflects the certainty
of Brontë's knowledge. But there were also questions and doubts
which arose from the novelist's awareness of the complexity of
social problems and the division within women themselves.

> I often wish to say something about the "condition of women"
> question, but it is one respect in which so much "cant" has
> been talked that one feels a sort of repugnance to approach it. It
> is true enough that the present market for female labour is quite
> overstocked, but where or how could another be opened?
> Many say that the professions now filled only by men should
> be opened to women also; but are not their present occupants
> and candidates more than numerous enough to answer every
> demand? Is there any room for female lawyers, female doc-

18. Freud wrote in *Civilization and Its Discontents* (p. 27):
It is not possible, within the limits of a short survey, to discuss adequately
the significance of work for the economics of the libido. No other technique for the conduct of life attaches the individual so firmly to reality as
laying emphasis on work; for his work at least gives him a secure place in a
portion of reality, in the human community. The possibility it offers of
displacing a large amount of libidinal components, whether narcissistic,
aggressive or even erotic, on to professional work and on to the human
relations connected with it lends it a value by no means second to what it
enjoys as something indispensable to the preservation and justification of
existence in society.

tors, female engravers, for more female artists, more author-
esses? One can see where the evil lies, but who can point out
the remedy? When a woman has a little family to rear and edu-
cate and a household to conduct, her hands are full, her vocation is evident; when her destiny isolates her, I suppose she
must do what she can, live as she can, complain as little, bear
as much, work as well as possible.[19]

There is in her observation a greater awareness than that of John
Stuart Mill of the dimension of the economic revolution which
would have to take place if women were to be "allowed" to
work. But this is not her major concern. Despite her cynicism
about love and marriage, Brontë still distinguished, as Caroline
does, between women who had to work and those more fortunate
souls who were able to fulfill themselves in domestic duties. Hers
was a moderate feminism which accepted the fact that women's
natures were fundamentally different from men's; that although
women craved social and psychological equality, they would not
wish—except in extraordinary circumstances—to enter those oc-
cupational and political bastions traditionally arrogated by men to
themselves. It was just this distinction which drew from Mary
Taylor an angrily outspoken reproach:[20]

I have seen some extracts from *Shirley* in which you talk of
women working. And this first duty, this great necessity you
seem to think that some women may indulge in—if they give
up marriage and don't make themselves too disagreeable to the
other sex. You are a coward and a traitor. A woman who
works is by that alone better than one who does not, and a
woman who does not happen to be rich and who *still* earns no
money and does not wish to do so, is guilty of a great fault—
almost a crime—a dereliction of duty which leads rapidly and
almost certainly to all manner of degradation. It is very wrong
of you to *plead* for toleration of workers on the ground of their
being in peculiar circumstances and few in number or singular

19. To W. S. Williams, May 12, 1848. Wise and Symington, II, 215–16.

20. Years after Charlotte's death, Mary wrote a treatise called *The First
Duty of Women,* a compendium of a series of articles which she had first contributed to the *Victorian Magazine* in the years 1865–70, when she was living at
High Royd. In this work she insisted that it was woman's duty to earn money
and she pitilessly examined such problems as the redundancy of women, female
earnings, idleness, marriage and poverty (Holgate, p. 33).

in disposition. Work or degradation is the lot of all except the very small number born to wealth.[21]

Female compliance with the sexist structure was denied by Mary Taylor's radicalism. Charlotte Brontë recognized it as a social and psychological constant: undesirable perhaps, but apparently inevitable. The fabric of society would not be slashed more readily by women than by men. The oppressed conspired willingly with the oppressors. Had she not seen it demonstrated repeatedly in Ellen Nussey's futile attachments? Had she not noted it in Mary Taylor's unfortunate attraction to Branwell? Had she not discovered the reality stamped upon her own heart? She knew that if women are trapped on one side by the attitudes of a patriarchal society, they are trapped also by the attitudes which they have themselves internalized: by their overwhelming need for recognition and love, by their search and desire for a "master." With few exceptions (Rose and Jessy Yorke typified these), only those who are rejected and desperate would cry out for social and political change. The others would bend to the system, modifying it only in their fantasies.

It was, apparently, in order to explore the validity of this insight that Brontë conceived Shirley Keeldar, her "other" heroine, whose external circumstances and personal qualities suggest alternative possibilities for a woman's acquisition and use of power and thus for her realization of self. A wealthy young heiress, Shirley adds to the conventional female virtues of beauty, charm, and intelligence the more useful attributes of status and education, the altogether desirable condition of freedom. Orphaned, in full control of her money, she is dependent on no one for the shape of her life. Good health and self-confidence, optimism, humor, courage, and creativity: all seem to promise that her future must be extraordinary, a model of possibility. But she is, after all, a woman—and this qualifies the rest.

Whenever she wishes to be effective in the "real" world—the world of business, of politics, of "serious" conversation, Shirley assumes a "role"':

> Business! Really, the word makes me conscious I am indeed
> no longer a girl, but quite a woman and something more. I am

21. Wellington, New Zealand, April 25, 1850. Wise and Symington, III, 104–5.

an esquire! Shirley Keeldar, Esquire, ought to be my style and
title. They gave me a man's name, I hold a man's position; it is
enough to inspire me with a touch of manhood. (p. 202)

The sense of inadequacy is her birthright, given her by her
parents with the name intended for the son whom they wanted but
never had. To express the unique self molded by her rare good
fortune, to have it perceived and responded to, Shirley must
"play" the conventional male: fragmenting her identity, denying
herself. Experience has taught her that gender negates social and
economic position. Therefore, she must try to be "something
more" than a woman. But the redefinition is only a game. "Captain Keeldar" is a collection of postures, gestures, and words: a
child who, at the sufferance of adults, plays at being one of them.
The game might spark mischief, spirit, and glee but it will not
earn respect. In males like Helstone, female political fervor
arouses not anger but patronizing amusement: "We are independent—we think for ourselves! . . . We are a little Jacobin, . . .
a little freethinker, in good earnest" (p. 198).

Shirley sees men too clearly to allow them to feel comfortable
with her. Her queer, significant smile reveals that she is not endowed with the "soft blindness" that is endearing in a woman.
But she knows that if there is a purpose to be achieved, she can
accomplish it only by playing coquette: manipulating the men she
needs so that they think they are manipulating her.

Her position as mistress of the manor house allows her to
tease the curates, to berate the workers, to lecture the villagers, to
ignore anyone who displeases her. But when there is serious business afoot, business involving money and power, "They won't
trust me . . . that is always the way when it comes to the point"
(p. 313). When her mill must be defended against the laborers, it
is the men who secretly plot to defend it, although the power is
really hers to claim. She is a pawn, allowing herself to be used.
And in fact she is not fit to function amid the harsher realities of
the social system which awards her, by virtue of her class and
money, the place of oppressor: which defines her by virtue of her
sex, as victim. Identifying herself (as "Captain Keeldar") with
the values of the system which has blessed her, she cannot begin
to assume the responsibility of acting upon those impulses which
transcend class allegiance, impulses which cause her "to admire

the great, reverence the good, and be joyous with the genial'' (p. 220).[22] Her sympathies move her to charity, but her charity is fundamentally pragmatic:

> I must give more, or, I tell you, my brother's blood will some day be crying to Heaven against me. For, after all, if political incendiaries come here to kindle conflagration in the neighbourhood and my property is attacked, I shall defend it like a tigress—I know I shall. Let me listen to Mercy as long as she is near me . . . (p. 264)

"When it comes to the point" Shirley's position does not isolate her less than other women in her relationships with men. Her wealth and status don't make her their equal. They make her more valuable; a prize worth winning: a trophy worth exhibiting. And since men approach her with motives similar to those with which they approach all other women, they naturally attribute to her, motives typical of all courting females. She talks business and politics with Robert Moore, lends him money, shows concern for his welfare. That she is offering friendship never occurs to him. His pragmatic proposal of marriage is the response he deems appropriate to her apparent infatuation. At first she is humiliated and outraged:

> You have made a strange proposal—strange from *you;* and if you knew how strangely you worded it, and looked it, you would be startled at yourself. You spoke like a brigand who demanded my purse, rather than like a lover who asked my heart. (p. 529)

But finally, when Robert, shocked into recognition, asks her to forgive him, she replies, "I could, if there was not myself to forgive, too—but to mislead a sagacious man so far I must have done wrong" (p. 532). The necessity of role-playing is paralyzing. Even the most well-meaning attempt to function spontane-

22. The confusion of social values is one which Brontë seemed to have shared with her heroine. The patronizing tone of this comment of Shirley seemed to be as unconscious on the author's part as it is on her own: "There is nothing the lower orders like better than a little downright good-humored rating. Flattery they scorn very much; honest abuse they enjoy. They call it speaking plainly, and take a sincere delight in being the objects thereof" (p. 354). This does not, of course, undercut the validity of the novel's perspective. It rather accounts for the probing, questioning quality which makes the fiction so convincing.

ously within power-oriented structures results in behavior which must destroy the integrity of the individual.

So despite her gifts of mind and fortune, despite the fact that she is stable and self-sufficient, Shirley is also thrown back upon herself, lonely in many of the same ways as Caroline. And the two young women find in their relationship with one another the possibilities of a kind of friendship which is rare indeed in their society. Between men, who must guard their own power, there can be common causes (e.g., Helstone and Moore) and manipulative interaction. Some men are like Yorke, focused on their families, with "few intimates." Others, like Robert Moore, are isolated in their suspicions, able only to relate to the few who, like Joe Scott, openly acknowledge their own superiority.

Between most women competing relentlessly with one another for husbands, relationships are superficially polite but equally blocked and frustrated. It is, of course, the intelligence and decency of Caroline and Shirley, their mutual awareness and shared concerns, which make their friendship possible. It is also because Shirley's position, inhabited with full confidence, is supported by Caroline's deference, that their friendship can thrive. While both girls feel comfortable occupying the relative positions with which they are familiar, the absence of strain within the acknowledged hierarchy derives from the fact that, on another level, both are as women, outsiders and equals. Caroline experiences enormous relief at the absence of those feelings of inadequacy which always accompany her interactions with men whom she respects:

> If the company of fools irritates, as you say, the society of clever men leaves its own peculiar pain also. Where the goodness or talent of your friend is beyond and above all doubt, your own worthiness to be his associate often becomes a matter of question. (p. 211)

With Shirley she feels none of the pain that accompanies "love": the pain of enforced passivity, of insecurity, of humiliation: the pain of being denied open, unashamed communication, the spontaneous expression of feeling:

> Shirley, I never had a sister—you never had a sister; but it flashes on me at this moment how sisters feel toward each other—affection twined with their life, which no shocks of

feeling can uproot, which little quarrels only trample an instant
that it may spring more freshly when the pressure is removed—affection that no passion can ultimately outrival, with
which even love itself cannot do no more than compete in force
and truth—Love hurts us so, Shirley—it is so tormenting, so
racking, and it burns away our strength with its flame; in affection is no pain and no fire, only sustenance and balm. I am supported and soothed when you—that is, *you only*—are near,
Shirley. (p. 261)

Shirley and Caroline seek in their friendship the kind of support
that Jane had sought and found first with Helen Burns and Maria
Temple, later with Diana and Mary Rivers; that Charlotte had
found, in her maturity, with Emily and Anne.

Not insignificantly, they can share with one another their puz-
zlement about men's "otherness," their hardness, their apparent
incapacity for love and fidelity. They wonder whether it is "necessary to be new and unfamiliar to them, in order to seem agree-
able or estimable in their eyes" (p. 212); whether it is not true
that "we each find an exception in the one we love, till we *are*
married" (p. 213). Both are painfully aware of male inadequacies, frightened by the psychological dangers posed by marriage.
Both recognize that most men have none of their own intuitive
love of nature, and might cut them off from a world which is nurturing. And yet, both are trapped by forces within, by their own
feelings of inferiority, by their adoption, largely unconscious, of
the values of their society and the fantasies which support them.
They can be made whole only if they are elevated by the recognition of "the other"; if they are allowed to partake of *his* status
and position, if they are in fact "mastered." Shirley must admit
that "nothing ever charms me more than when I meet my superior" (p. 215). Caroline continues to pine, secretly, for the love
of Robert Moore. Both find the prospect of sacrifice appealing,
and Caroline understands that the greatest pain derives from
being deprived of the opportunity for self-denial. When Shirley
observes—with the touch of masochism that is familiar—"One
could have loved Cowper, if it were only for the sake of having
the privilege of comforting him" (p. 224), Caroline responds
from the depth of her own experience: "You might have sought
Cowper with the intention of loving him; and you would have
looked at him, pitied him, and left him, forced away by a sense of

the impossible, the incongruous . . ." (p. 224). Ironically, Shirley asks, "Who told you that? Did Moore?" She reveals that she has as little faith as the men she despises, in a woman's capacity for intelligent perception and serious thought. It is because she has inadequate confidence in herself.

Shirley's ambivalence is reflected in her religious attitudes as well. She feels, as did Jane Eyre, the need for a female mythology, a religion which is not the product of the male imagination, not an extension of the patriarchal structure. And, like Jane, Shirley finds her spiritual affinity in nature. She urges Caroline not to worship God in Helstone's church and offers her, instead of the minister's sermon, her own celebration of "my mother Eve," who dwells still in Nature, an "undying, mighty being." She reminds her resistant, somewhat frightened friend that Eve was the mother of Titans, the daughter of Jehovah, equal to Adam, his son: "The first woman was heaven-born. Vast was the heart whence gushed the well-spring of the blood of nations; and grand the undegenerate head where rested the consort-crown of creation" (p. 319). But although Shirley longs for a maternal deity with whom she can identify, by whom she wil be inspired and ennobled, the myth of creation which she had written for her tutor—Louis Moore—Robert's brother, reveals conflicting prejudices and needs. This is the story of the union of Humanity (the second Eve) and Genius, a son of God who, discovering a portion of himself in the beautiful, solitary, orphaned girl, reclaims it "to foster and aid that it shall not perish hopeless" (p. 484). This story belies the equality claimed by Shirley for the first mother and father. It offers, instead, in its vision of subsequent generations, a deeply personal mythology which justifies inequality and female dependence by reestablishing the patriarchal hierarchy. The attitude it reveals has reverberations in many of Shirley's relationships, including the one which she maintains with Caroline.

Despite Charlotte Brontë's attempt, unique in her own time, to discover in the friendship between women an alternative to the alienation and hostilities that existed between the sexes, her probing exploration yielded the image of a relationship which was, while well-intentioned, deeply flawed: truncated and frustrated by personal ambivalence. It is an image of her own relationships: painful enough to recognize; more painful still for her to admit. It is understandable that the insight she offers should not be clearly emphasized. In its incomplete expression, it seems in fact only half conscious. The evidence that supports it is partial, obscure. The girls' thoughts are not wholly presented. The process of their relationship is fragmented. Still, the implication is there: when women are not drawn together by the indissoluble ties which bound Charlotte to Anne and Emily, ties strengthened for Charlotte by her growing ascendancy, sexual competition and social differences prove more divisive than the unifying influence of shared concerns. Jane's idealized friendship with Diana and Mary Rivers, her good "sisters," the romantic dream of friendship as a union of the self with the "other": this could only be realized where conventional social, cultural, economic, and sexual distinctions were abolished: familial responsibilities ignored or made subordinate. Only with a radically new flexibility could there be the kind of redefinition of traditional structures and roles which made it possible for Mary Taylor and her cousin, Ellen, to forge a different type of friendship in New Zealand.

> Our keeping shop astonishes everybody here; I believe they think we do it for fun. Some think we shall make nothing of it, or that we shall get tired; and all laugh at us. Before I left home I used to be afraid of being laughed at, but now it has very little effect upon me.

> Mary and I are settled together now: I can't do without Mary and she couldn't get on by herself. I built the house we live in, and we made the plan ourselves, so it suits us. We take it in turns to serve in the shop, and keep the accounts, and do the housework—I mean, Mary takes the shop for a week, and I the kitchen, and then we change.[23]

> Besides nonsense, we talk over other things that I never could talk about before she came. Some of them had got to look so strange, I used to think some times I had dreamt them. Charlotte's books were of this kind. Politics were another thing where I had all the interest to myself, and a number of opinions of my own I had got so used to keep to myself that at last I thought one side of my head filled with crazy stuff.[24]

In the more conventional friendship of Caroline and Shirley, there could only be moments of escape from the strains of reality.

23. Ellen Taylor, Wellington, New Zealand, August 1850. Wise and Symington, III, 134.
24. Mary Taylor to Ellen Nussey, Wellington, New Zealand, August 15, 1850. Wise and Symington, III, 136.

There could be no support for the confrontation of those strains, no stimulus to change. Brontë had no models she could use to define .their relationship differently. Whatever her initial intention, experience guided her hand. The fact that these women do not develop any more than the other characters who people the novel, suggests the extent to which all are trapped in a "system" which some don't know how, and others don't care to fight. Both remain isolated in their vulnerability: protective even with one another of those aspects of their thought and feeling which are most important and therefore most painful to them.

Robert Moore casts the longest shadow over their relationship. Caroline will not speak freely to Shirley of her feelings for him. She takes if for granted that Shirley knows them, but she takes it for granted also (she is an uncompromising realist) that Shirley will accept the inevitable proposal when he offers it. More curiously (and this is probably a failure on Brontë's part) Shirley makes no attempt to share with Caroline the fact that she is not Caroline's competitor. This can be attributed to the secretiveness of her personality: her tendency to be withdrawn and introspective about the matters that most affect her, and this secretiveness is a response to fear.[25]

> I may be communicative, yet know where to stop. In showing my treasure I may withhold a gem or two—a curious, unbought, graven stone, an amulet of whose mystic glitter I rarely permit even myself a glimpse. (p. 447)

Her "treasure," of course, is Louis Moore. To reveal the nature of her concern for Robert might be to reveal the secret of her interest in his brother. But even after that interest becomes clear, after she and Louis have agreed to marry, she does not—as Caroline explains to Robert—"condescend" to openness:

25. This aspect of Shirley's personality does indeed seem to be based upon Emily Brontë's fierce sense of privacy. Emily never shared Charlotte's agony of isolation. In fact, she derived from the solitude of Haworth the nutriment necessary for her existence. In her birthday letter of July 30, 1845, she wrote:

> I am quite contented for myself: not as idle as formerly, altogether as hearty, and having learnt to make the most of the present and long for the future with the fidgetiness that I cannot do all I wish; seldom or never troubled with nothing to do, and merely desiring that everybody could be as comfortable as myself and as undesponding, and then we should have a very tolerable world of it. (Wise and Symington, II, 51.)

> There was no confession—no confidence in the matter; to these things she cannot condescend; but I am sure that man's happiness is dear to her as her own life. (p. 601)

"Condescend" is the key word. Shirley's status is the condition of whatever freedom she does in fact have. Without it, she is "just a woman." And so she separates herself in a confusion of prejudice which is also a partial denial of feeling. She and Caroline never discuss Caroline's passionate desire to work: her ambivalent wish to be a governess. Caroline recognizes the "inappropriateness" of the subject—focusing as it would the disparity between their situations. Shirley does nothing to make the subject seem more appropriate nor does she discuss with Caroline her own growing conviction that Mrs. Pryor is, in fact, Caroline's mother. After the secret has been disclosed she does not explore with her friend its extraordinary implications. Typically, Shirley generously offers to whisk Caroline away on a holiday trip but doesn't help her confront the pressing realities of her life. And when Caroline falls ill she neither postpones nor interrupts her own vacation. She cares—but not too much. The result is that they touch one another only superficially. Caroline finds that the respect and fondness she feels for her friend will not make her less "painfully circumstanced." Shirley remains aloof, mistress of herself, victim of her pride.

If the conflict between the rights and privileges of her social position and those of her sex are largely instrumental in short-circuiting her friendship with Caroline, it is almost cataclysmic in undermining her relationship with Louis. The ambiguity of Shirley's situation is centered here, in her choice of a mate. The love relationship is conceived on one level in terms still reminiscent of the "Jane" poem placed by Brontë in *The Professor*. Louis Moore stands for Shirley in the familiarly interconnected roles of father-teacher-lover.[26] Shirley has said that she "will accept no hand which cannot hold me in check" (p. 546). It is a "master" she wants:

> One in whose presence I shall feel obliged and disposed to be good. One whose control my impatient temper must acknowledge. A man whose approbation can reward—whose dis-

---

26. The critical, if unconvincing, threat of hydrophobia takes the place of the catalytic illness and Shirley's uncle assumes the role of the lover's enemy.

> pleasure punish me. A man I shall feel it impossible not to love, and very possible to fear. (p. 547)

As a pupil, she had easily accepted Louis's dominance, bowed before the power of his intellect and sensitivity, been reinforced by his praise and encouragement. But the psychosexual component of this relationship is complicated by the fact that Brontë adds to it the unusual circumstance of Shirley's superior social and economic position. The romantic myth is tested once again and now the force of sexism is measured against that of class elitism. The situation is fascinating even if its outcome is disappointing.

The conflicting claims of their relative positions trap both in their pride. Shirley's psychological need for domination stifles the normal spontaneity of her response. Louis, a paper tiger at best, wants to claim the power over her which is common to one of his sex and requisite to his self-image. He cannot do it without seeming to compromise his self-respect: without appearing to be a "fortune-hunter." Their interchanges are patterned alternations of invitation and rejection:

> "Take a wife that has paid you court to save your modesty, and thrust herself upon you to spare your scruples."
> "Only show me where."
> "Any stout widow that has had a few husbands already, and can manage these things."
> "She must not be rich, then. Oh, these riches!"
> "Never would you have gathered the produce of the gold-bearing garden. You have not courage to confront the sleepless dragon! You have not craft to borrow the aid of Atlas!"
> "You look hot and haughty."
> "And you far haughtier. Yours is the monstrous pride which counterfeits humility."
> "I am a dependent: I know my place."
> "I am a woman: I know mine."
> "I am poor: I must be proud."
> "I have received ordinances and own obligations stringent as yours." (p. 614)

The resolution cannot be effected, as in *Jane Eyre,* by a magical transformation. Neither will it be the result of direct confrontation and redefinition. Society remains for Charlotte Brontë an unchangeable condition of personal life. Shirley and Louis can

only regress to an earlier stage of their relationship in order to acknowledge and accept one another's love:

> "My pupil," I said.
> "My master," was the low answer. (p. 618)

The regression determines the form that marks their future development. Louis Moore had, before his betrothal, represented—albeit tentatively—an alternate mode of male behavior. Poor,
though of a "good" family, identified with nature (it is significant, that Louis alone shares with Shirley the devotion of her
great dog, Tartar), an artist and intellectual, Louis stands outside
of the patriarchal structure in an attitude of defiance. But he is no
more able to find an appropriate way to express his defiance than
can Jessy and Rose Yorke. Like them, he plans to emigrate
across the Atlantic to claim Freedom and Liberty—and a docile
Indian maid. He finds it more convenient, however, to remain in
England, sharing with Shirley the "burden" of her money and
property, the duties and obligations of wealth and position:

> Never was wooer of wealthy bride so thoroughly absolved
> from the subaltern part, so inevitably compelled to assume a
> paramount character. (p. 636)

In abdicating her position, Shirley yields to her ambivalent nature, defined in the "system" which she has conceived: "Louis
would never have learned to rule if she had not ceased to govern;
the incapacity of the sovereign had developed the powers of the
premier" (p. 636).

Although Louis is neatly assimilated into the ruling class,
Shirley finds her own adjustment to simple femininity more difficult. If Brontë compromises her heroine with all she represents
far too easily, considering the complexity of the novel's perspective, she does not completely underestimate the cost of the sacrifice. The image of Shirley, awaiting her wedding day is striking,
although it implies a truth which Brontë cannot directly confront.

> Pantheress!—beautiful forest-born—wily, tameless, peerless
> nature! She gnaws her chain; I see the white teeth working at
> the steel! She has dreams of her wild woods, and pinings after
> virgin freedom. (p. 627)

Shirley's longing remains. It has assumed a reality of its own. It
denies the unsuitability of the conventional structure to which

Brontë is committed: a social structure reflected in the conventional literary form.

When Louis complains of his unhappiness at being forced to wait indefinitely for the fulfillment of his hopes, Shirley responds a bit ominously, "O yes, you *are* happy, you don't know how happy you are: any change will be for the worse" (p. 629). Because no resolution seems possible, this attempt at resolution is profoundly unsatisfying. It expresses the author's confusion no less than her heroine's. Shirley's marriage ironically seals the personal fate that Brontë had predicted for her in another context:

> She does not know her dreams are rare—her feelings peculiar: she does not know, has never known, and will die without knowing, the full value of that spring whose bright, fresh bubbling in her heart keeps it green. (p. 387)

In the almost parodic comic ending, Brontë seems to suggest the sad inevitability of female oppression. Since Shirley represented, in the novel, the single medium through which feminist values might be asserted, her marriage marks her as society's ritual victim. The regressive movement, the weary tones of compromise and futile sacrifice are echoed and reechoed on personal, political, and social levels. The novel—so wise in its comprehension and definition of problems—seems to exhaust itself in resignation. There is no political consciousness capable of unifying the diverse elements. Instead, there is withdrawal from conflict: a dispersal of energy, a movement from social vision to private perspective: a descent from artistic vitality to personal confusion and disillusionment.

Caroline's story moves in a direction parallel to Shirley's. The apparent differences of their situations are submerged by the larger similarities of the female condition. Caroline's profound depression—her response to Robert's rejection—can only be relieved by the development of another symbiotic relationship. ("The deep, secret anxious yearning to discover and know her mother strengthened daily [p. 187].") Ultimately, that discovery saves her from death. But Mrs. Pryor, embittered by the misery of her marriage to a sadistic "gentleman," made cynical by the humiliation of her years as a governness, can only offer Caroline the nurturing love necessary to a dependent child. She cannot provide the supportive, imaginative optimism which would move her daughter to independent maturity. Mother and daughter live together in passive domesticity waiting for Robert to reappear and shelter them both within the benevolence of his enlightened paternalism.

Having been humbled by Shirley's rejection, Robert has, in his absence, learned more readily the lessons of poverty contained in the slums of Birmingham and London, which he has visited. He confides to Hiram Yorke upon his return:

> Something there is to look to . . . beyond a man's personal interest, beyond the advancement of well-laid schemes, beyond even the discharge of dishonouring debts. To respect himself a man must believe he renders justice to his fellow-men. Unless I am more considerate to ignorance, more forbearing to suffering, than I have hitherto been, I shall scorn myself as grossly unjust. (p. 538)

Robert is prepared to see with more justice the needs of the workers and to identify with their humanity but it is not clear that he can yet, or will ever be able to identify with their cause, diametrically opposed as it seems to be to his own. He can also be purified by personal suffering. Shot by a religious fanatic, made helpless in his illness, Robert comes to appreciate his home, his work and Caroline's fidelity and love. But because it is a madman who shoots him, he can maintain his opposition to the "ringleaders" who corrupt the people instead of recognizing the more profound corruption of which all are victims, for which all are responsible. Because Shirley lends him more money, because the war is soon ended and the Orders in Council repealed, none of the larger social issues need be confronted.

Through Robert, Brontë seems to suggest that the individual must change before there can be any hope for social progress, but because she does not equate individual with social interest she does not really suggest how social redefinition can result from personal enlightenment.[27] In fact there is little in this fictive

27. Asa Briggs suggests that Charlotte Brontë's vision extended beyond her own time: extended as far as it could, since she was, "able to state the issues as seen both by employer and workers, to measure the social distance between them, and to point to the healing influence of time and experience, the kind of experience that affected Moore" (p. 214–15). Briggs suggests that Brontë anticipated the thesis of Sir William Beverage, who in 1944 published *Full Employment in a Free Society,* in which he says: "To look for individual employers for maintenance of demand and full employment is absurd. These things are not

world that does ultimately change and there is less optimism at the end of the novel than there was at the beginning. Although the heroines find husbands, they seem diminished rather than fulfilled by their marriages. Shirley's potential is thwarted. Caroline's questions are silenced. Legal contracts replace communication.[28] The ideal of friendship has been undermined along with the ideal of equality. Because Shirley and Caroline are unable to act autonomously in relating to their husbands (and Caroline is also dependent in her relationship to Mrs. Pryor), both ultimately are defined and define themselves as daughters. Authority, once internalized, can be more easily questioned than it can be overthrown.

In the last chapters of the novel, Shirley and Caroline recede into the background, deprived of energy and vitality. With them perish psychological, moral, and imaginative alternatives. Nature itself is doomed. The final vision is Robert's. He and Louis will live out the capitalist patriarchal fantasy. They will divide Briarfield Parish between them. Louis will become a major political as well as economic influence. The country will be industrialized, the land despoiled:

> I can double the value of their mill-property; I can line yonder barren Hollow with lines of cottages, and rows of cottage-gardens . . . the copse shall be firewood ere five years elapse; the beautiful wild ravine shall be a smooth descent; the green natural terrace shall be a paved street; there shall be cottages in the dark ravine, and cottages on the lonely slopes; the rough pebbled track shall be an even, firm, broad, black, sooty road, bedded with cinders from my mill. (p. 642)

To Caroline the vision is "horrible" and Robert pats her on the head, promising her sugar plums in the form of a wonderful

---

within the power of employers. They must therefore be undertaken by the State, under the supervision and pressure of democracy, applied to the Parliament" (p. 215–16). One can agree with Brigg's general presentation of Brontë's position, but it is clear that she did not anticipate the necessity of government control.

28. Charlotte was, with her editors, somewhat disappointed in her failure to delineate well the characters of her heroes ("When I write about women I am sure of my ground—in the other case, I am not so sure." To James Taylor, Wise and Symington, II, 312.) But it is most likely that given her perspective, she could not envision heroes worthy of Caroline and Shirley. The Byronic hero, who was more truly the child of her imagination, could have no appropriate place in this society.

Sunday-school that she can run all by herself a day-school that she and Shirley can manage, and work for all the poor. Of these embellishments we hear no more, but an ironic commentary is offered on the substance of Robert's dream:

> I suppose Robert Moore's prophecies were, partially at least, fulfilled. The other day I passed up the Hollow, which tradition says was once green, and lone, and wild; and there I saw the manufacturer's daydreams embodied in substantial stone and brick and ashes—the cinder-black highway, the cottages and the cottage gardens; there I saw a mighty mill, and a chimney, ambitious as the Tower of Babel. (p. 644)

At the novel's end, the "present" of the story has become the past: a better time, nostalgically recalled by an old woman who knows that there are no ladies now like Shirley who "had een that pierced a body through" (p. 44). The Hollow, once "a lonesome spot and bonnie," is much altered. The last "fairish that ever was seen on this countryside" appeared there fifty years ago. New curates replace the old: they are better, more efficient. Any hope of successful struggle has passed. The momentary glimmering of light is extinguished. It can only be recaptured in tales told by women to children and to one another.

Villette: *The Romantic Experience as Psychoanalysis*

Men begin to regard the position of woman in another light than they used to do; and a few men, whose sympathies are fine and whose sense of justice is strong, think and speak of it with a candour that commands my admiration. They say, how-ever—and to an extent, truly—that the amelioration of our condition depends on ourselves. Certainly there are evils which our own efforts will best reach; but as certainly there are other evils—deep-rooted in the foundations of the social system—which no efforts of ours can touch; of which we can-not complain; of which it is adviseable not too often to think. [1]

*I*N THE CREATION OF *Shirley*, Brontë had attempted to write a large-scale social novel, detailed with "realism." She had emerged from her scrutiny of the manifestations of power with the pessimism that infuses her letter to Gaskell. She had journeyed a long distance to return once again to herself. Intellec-tual exploration confirmed the knowledge long since gleaned from experience. She had found neither a solution, an overriding perspective, nor a positive course of action. It could not benefit her now to probe further into those obscure problems "of which we cannot complain; of which it is adviseable not too often to think." Instead, she had to confront directly—and at last—the one irreducible fact of her life: her loneliness. Its specter had haunted her throughout her girlhood. It had become an agonizing reality after she returned from Brussels to wait through two long years for the letters from Heger, which never came. And then,

1. To Elizabeth Gaskell, August 27, 1850. Wise and Symington, III, 150.

with the deaths of Branwell, Emily, and Anne, it seemed to be a nightmare from which she could not and never would awaken.

Haworth, her once beloved home, was now almost intolerable to her:

> . . . the deficiency of every stimulus is so complete . . . the deadly silence, solitude, desolation were awful—the craving for companionship—the hopelessness of relief—were what I should dread to feel again.[2]

> For my part, I am free to walk on the moors; but when I go out there alone everything reminds me of the times when others were with me, and then the moors seem a wilderness, featureless, solitary, saddening. My sister Emily had a particular love for them, and there is not a knoll of heather, not a branch of fern, not a young bilberry leaf, not a fluttering lark or linnet, but reminds me of her. The distant prospects were Anne's delight, and when I look round she is in the blue tints, the pale mists, the waves and shadows of the horizon. In the hill-country silence their poetry comes by lines and stanzas into my mind; once I loved it; now I dare not read it, and am driven often to wish I could taste one draught of oblivion, and forget much that, while mind remains, I never shall forget.[3]

Her only comfort was in the memory of the past and that was accompanied by a pain so deep that she could not think of what she had possessed but only of what she had lost.

> The two human beings who understood me, and whom I understood, are gone. I have some that love me yet, and whom I love without expecting, or having a right to expect, that they shall perfectly understand me.[4]

Charlotte and her father were united by bonds of mutual grief and dependence. But the satisfaction Brontë derived from the performance of duty was tempered by the ambivalence of sacrifice, by their fundamental incompatibility, and by her still constant, overwhelming sense of inadequacy ("Papa has now me only—the weakest, puniest, least promising of his six children."[5]). Friendship with Elizabeth Gaskell and Harriet Martineau confirmed her confidence as a writer but offered her little of the emotional sup-

2. To Ellen Nussey, October 23, 1850. Wise and Symington, III, 173–74.
3. To James Taylor, May 22, 1850. Wise and Symington, III, 111–12.
4. To W. S. Williams, September 21, 1849. Wise and Symington, III, 24.
5. To W. S. Williams, June 4, 1849. Wise and Symington, II, 338.

port for which her spirit yearned.[6] If any solace was to be offered her, any promise of change held out, it was by three men who occupied central positions at her publishing firm, Smith, Elder, and Co. William Smith Williams, a sensitive critic of literature and the graphic arts had first read and recognized the potential power of *The Professor*. With him Charlotte carried on a continuing personal correspondence which stimulated her mind and provided an emotional outlet during these terrible years of loss. To him she confided her troubled thoughts and anguished feelings, always receiving sympathy and kindness in return. In James Taylor, the firm's manager, and in George Smith, her publisher, she found two erratic suitors whose attentions were bewildering and ultimately disappointing.

James Taylor was astonishingly like Branwell in appearance, small and redheaded, forceful and domineering.

> . . . the resemblance to Branwell struck me forcibly. It is marked. He is not ugly, but very peculiar; the lines in his face show an inflexibility, and I must add, a hardness of character which do not attract.[7]

Charlotte thought him to be "of the Helstone order of men—rigid, despotic and self-willed." She was suspicious of his kindness, but could not help admitting that "he is horribly intelligent, quick, searching, sagacious and with a memory of relentless tenacity."[8] With his physical resemblance to her brother, and the similarity of his personality to the heroes who had moved so commandingly through her girlhood writings, Taylor alternately attracted and repelled her. There was no question about the nature of his interest. Apparently it was his jealous antagonism toward

---

6. Charlotte Brontë wrote to W. S. Williams (November 24, 1849. Wise and Symington, III, 45.):

> The note you sent yesterday was from Harriet Martineau; its contents were more than gratifying. I ought to be thankful, and I trust I am for such testimonies of sympathy from the first order of minds. When Mrs. Gaskell tells me she shall keep my works as a treasure for her daughters, and when Harriet Martineau testifies affectionate approbation, I feel the sting taken from the strictures of another class of critics. My resolution of seclusion withholds me from communicating further with these ladies at present, but I now know how they are inclined to me—I know how my writings have affected their wise and pure minds. The knowledge is present support and, perhaps, may be future armour.

7. To Ellen Nussey, April 9, 1851. Wise and Symington, III, 220.
8. Wise and Symington, III, 53.

George Smith which made his youthful superior decide to exile him to their Indian agency, where he remained for five years. Before his departure, he came to Haworth, apparently to make an offer of marriage. The response he received—surprising even to Brontë herself—was adequate discouragement.

> . . . each moment he came near me—and that I could see his eyes fastened on me—my veins ran ice. Now that he is away I feel far more gently towards him—it is only close by that I grow rigid—stiffening with a strange mixture of apprehension and anger—which nothing softens but his retreat and a perfect subduing of his manner. I did not want to be proud nor intend to be proud—but I was forced to be so.[9]

He was abashed. The correspondence that followed was fitful and only tended to increase her frustration and ambivalence.

George Smith was another matter. He had befriended her from the beginning and the happiest moments she experienced after Anne's and Emily's deaths were spent in his company. There were visits to London—even a journey to Edinburgh—when she stayed with him and his mother, attending the theatre and concerts, meeting the reigning writers and intellectuals of her time, learning the secrets of the city which never ceased to excite her. That Brontë seriously considered George Smith a prospective suitor there can be little doubt. That his behavior toward her created such a sense of possibility must be true as well. The fact is that he never proposed and that it is not clear whether she would have accepted him if he had. She was older than he, his inferior in fortune, delicate in health. He was, despite his charm and kindness, insensitive in some ways, perhaps in some respects shallow. The only clue to Brontë's own feelings survives in the representation of him in *Villette* as Graham Bretton, a portrait which fascinates in its ambiguity. It was this portrait and that of his mother (as Louisa Bretton) which ultimately confirmed the rift between them and made a reality of the separation which Brontë had apparently already accepted as inevitable.[10]

In *Villette*, Charlotte Brontë sought to confront not only the meaning of her Brussels experience (this aspect of the novel has been generally recognized) but the implications of the life she

9. To Ellen Nussey, April 9, 1851. Wise and Symington, III, 222.

10. For a complete account of Charlotte Brontë's relationship with George Smith see Gerin, *Charlotte Brontë*, pp. 486–512.

was living then—and the quality of the life she had still to endure. As she revealed to Ellen Nussey, a couple of months before *Villette*'s completion:

> I am silent because I have literally nothing to say. I might indeed repeat over and over again that my life is a pale blank and often a very weary burden, and that the future sometimes appals me; but what end could be answered by such repetition except to weary you and ennervate myself?
>
> The evils that now and then wring a groan from my heart, lie in my position, not that I am a *single* woman and likely to remain a *single* woman, but because I am a *lonely* woman and likely to be lonely. But it cannot be helped and therefore *imperatively must be borne,* and borne with as few words about it as may be.[11]

Her experience with Heger, the personal meaning of Emily's and Anne's deaths, her separation from Branwell, the thwarted relationships with Taylor and Smith, all suggested that she had been singled out for a fate which she had always found too painful to assign to her heroines. She had touched upon it in "Henry Hastings"—the distance of the romance made it possible. But after she had begun in earnest to explore her own identity and her situation as a woman she had persistently grasped at some form of optimism, however muted. This was no longer possible. The aborted resolution of *Shirley* betrayed her doubts. Loneliness—bleak and absolute—was her present companion, her future destiny. To learn how she could make it bearable, she had to look within.

To W. S. Williams, Charlotte had written:

> Labour must be the cure, not sympathy—labour is the only radical cure for rooted sorrow— The society of a calm, serenely cheerful companion—such as Ellen—soothes pain like a soft opiate—but I find it does not probe or heal the wound— sharper, more severe means are necessary to make a remedy. Total change might do much—where that cannot be obtained—work is the best substitute.[12]

The "severe means" appropriate to treat her sorrow involved an approach to her work which while prepared for in all her previous writing, was radically new in the degree of courage and commit-

11. August 25, 1852. Wise and Symington, IV, 6.
12. Wise and Symington, II, 349.

ment it demanded. Each of her fictions had been deeply personal. They had become successively more self-analytical and autobiographical. *The Professor,* with its unresolved compromises, between romance and reality, its awkwardly shrouded truths, gave way to the integrated fairy tale of *Jane Eyre,* a psychosexual and social myth expressed through fantasy and dream. *Shirley,* ostensibly social in its choice of subject, had been—in its unabashed dependence upon personal feelings, relationships, and experiences—the most autobiographical of all. Here Brontë had considered the pressures exerted upon the individual by the forces of the culture. Now her consideration moved her from the oppressive society to the repressed individual—to herself. Romantic allegory was no longer an adequate mode of expression. It had liberated her initially but a deeper form of introspection was necessary. The creating consciousness itself had to be analyzed. The functioning of will, the possibility of choice, the action of "fate" had become for her psychological as well as philosophical problems.

In *Villette* the confrontation of the self by the self is as extraordinarily uncompromising as it must have been painful. That Brontë found this novel unusually difficult to write is a matter of record. Her letters are full of references to periods of depression and illness in which work was impossible. "Certainly the past winter has been to me a strange time, had I the prospect before me of living it over again, my prayer must necessarily be, 'Let this cup pass from me.' "[13] That these were also periods of intense psychological conflict it seems reasonable to assume. Modeling her heroine upon herself, dwelling upon the buried knowledge of the past while attempting to deal effectively with the problems of the present, always forced to confront the truth of her own personality, Brontë sought to bring the unconscious into consciousness and tried to unify the fragmented pieces of the self.

Lucy Snowe is a faithful self-portrait. The contradiction contained in the juxtaposition of her two names (cold, on the one hand, the warmth of light on the other) suggests the form of her "malaise."[14] Seemingly impassive, Lucy is in fact abnormally

13. February 6, 1852 to Elizabeth Gaskell. Gaskell, p. 351.

14. Charlotte Brontë wrote to W. S. Williams (November 6, 1852. Wise and Symington, IV, 18.)

As to the name of the heroine, I can hardly express what subtlety of thought made me decide upon giving her a cold name; but at first I called

sensitive, unusually emotional. Because her needs have been un-
satisfied, her hopes thwarted, she withdraws from society: rejecting relationships because she herself fears rejection. Hostility and
anger are her defenses against the pain of deprivation. A stance of
superiority, postures of righteous judgement, insulate her feelings.[15]

How could Brontë portray most effectively this tortured,
oddly unsympathetic woman for whom, by her own wry admission, she felt significantly little affection? How best to create a
character whom the reader would at first reject as Lucy and Charlotte Brontë herself were always rejected by casual acquaintances? How to make accessible an individual defined by inacces-
sibility? How to win understanding and respect for this fiercely
private personality which refused to show itself—which barely
knew itself? To succeed was as crucial to Brontë personally as it
was important to her as a writer.

The plan was brilliant. It marked the extent of her artistic
progress since *The Professor.* The narrating voice would be
Lucy's own. The central consciousness would belong to her. The
technique was superficially similar to that of *Jane Eyre,* but for
the guilelessness, the straightforward self-awareness, the friendly
openness of Jane would be substituted indirection, neurotic rationalization, and narrative "unreliability."[16] A comparison of the
opening sections of the two novels makes the differences dramat-
ically clear. Jane is discovered as a child at Gateshead, her

---

her Lucy Snowe (spelled with an "e") which Snowe I afterward changed
to "Frost." Subsequently I rather regretted the change and wished it
"Snowe" again. If not too late I should like the alteration to be made now
throughout the MS. A cold name she must have; partly perhaps on the *lucus
a non lucendo* principle—partly on that of the fitness of things for she has
about her an external coldness.

15. An interesting parallel might be drawn between Lucy Snowe and Jane
Austen's Fanny Price in *Mansfield Park.* Fanny assumes a similar posture of
righteous superiority in order to protect herself against her threatening feelings
of inferiority. She too is deprived of economic and social status. Plain, she is
virtually deprived of sexual definition as well. The crucial difference, of course,
lies in authorial attitude. Jane Austen seems largely unconscious of pressures
which create the personality configuration and identifies uncritically with her
heroine. Charlotte Brontë comprehends these pressures fully and, refusing to
make virtues of the mechanisms of defense, identifies them as neurotic.

16. Charlotte Brontë probably learned many of the possibilities of "unreliable narration" from Emily's use of Lockwood and Nelly Dean in *Wuthering
Heights.*

unhappy story is quickly told, the quality of her mind and the intensity of her feelings directly established. The process of "education" is described by a mature narrator who understands its implications at every point and shares them with the reader. Lucy, on the other hand, is a girl of fourteen at the beginning of *Villette*. She is a temporary visitor in the home of her godmother, Louisa Bretton, who takes notice of her "in a quiet way." Her past is darkly obscure. She lives, for the moment, with "kinfolk" who remain unidentified. The future casts a shadow upon her which "imparts unsettled sadness." The story she tells is ostensibly her own, but she is not its subject.

Lucy hints at the reason for this displacement when she says at the outset, "I liked peace so well, and sought stimulus so little, that when the latter came I almost felt it a disturbance, and wished rather it had still held aloof."[17] Lucy, like her creator, is a "survivor." Her identification is more with the dead than the living. She has already been so hurt by her circumstances that she is unable to talk about her past. She is already so afraid of feeling that she would rather not participate in life at all. Psychologically, she has closed herself off.[18] To the extent that she must play a role, she prefers to be a spectator, a "voyeur." And so she begins exploring her life by telling the reader of Pauline Home, who arrived in Bretton during Lucy's own visit there. As Lucy tells Polly's story, revealing the nature of her identification with the child, as we remark upon the things she chooses *not* to tell us, we first divine the traces of Lucy's singularly defended and complex personality.

Paulina is brought to Bretton by her father, whom she adores. Her mother has died ("a giddy, careless woman, who had neglected her child, and disappointed and disheartened her husband") and Mr. Home is about to embark on a journey to France,

17. Charlotte Brontë, *Villette* (Boston: Houghton-Mifflin, 1971), p. 6. All subsequent references are to this edition and will be given in the text.

18. Lifton (p. 163), speaking of the survivor, observes:

Psychic closing-off is thus related to the defense mechanisms of denial and isolation, as well as to the behavioral state of apathy . . . it enables the organism to resist the impact of death—that is, to survive psychologically in the midst of death and dying. It may well represent man's most characteristic response to catastrophe: one which is at times life-enhancing, or even, psychologically speaking, life-saving; but at other times, particularly when prolongated and no longer appropriate to the threat, not without its own dangers.

intended to relieve his depression. It is the way in which the small child deals with her loss, the way in which she expresses and controls the intensity of her feelings, and, finally, the way in which she risks herself, despite her vulnerability, in a new relationship of devoted love that repels, frightens, and fascinates Lucy. At first the reader is surprised, even appalled by Lucy's coldness. The words she uses to characterize Polly ("creature," "doll," "busy-body," "the child") serve to objectify the little girl. Lucy seldom describes any direct form of interaction between them. She rather presents Polly as she—Lucy—thinks about her: from a distance. It gradually becomes clear, however, that Lucy employs this technique of narration for the same reason that she had employed this technique of interaction: not because she is unable to feel, but because she feels too much; not because she cannot identify with Polly but rather because the degree of her identification is extreme.

Her responses to Polly's open emotionality are disproportionate. For Lucy, the expression of feeling cannot be understood as a healthful, restorative release. She sees it instead as a danger which can overwhelm and obliterate the self and she refuses to relive, through identification with the little girl, the circumstances surrounding her own grief. So, when Lucy hears Polly moaning pathetically, "Papa! Papa!," she explains: "I roused myself and started up, to check this scene while it was yet within bounds" (p. 10). Lucy is intent upon controlling Polly as she has learned to control herself and she does it more for her own sake than for the child's. She has learned what price might be demanded for love, if love is lost or denied. She reveals how deeply fearful that lesson has made her when she observes of Polly's suffering after Mr. Home's departure, "She went through, in that brief interval of her infant life, emotions such as some never feel; it was in her constitution: she would have more of such instants if she lived" (p. 19). And although she betrays her belief that emotional and psychological pain can, in their intensity, destroy life itself, she adds in describing the scene: "I, Lucy Snowe, was calm."

This is the illusion which she must maintain in order to keep her own sanity. Repressing feeling—rejecting, therefore, a past too threatening to be confronted—Lucy appeals to "reason" which gives to repression both justification and authority. "How will she get through this world, or battle with this life?'' Lucy asks. "How will she bear the shocks and repulses, the humiliations and desolations, which books, and my own reason tell me are prepared for all flesh?'' (p. 29). From her "books'' (one notes that she does not cite experience) Lucy has gathered a "tolerable stock'' of philosophical maxims which guide her behavior. These she would share with Polly, who endangers herself still further by becoming attached to Graham Bretton, a charming boy, Lucy's contemporary, who enjoys—somewhat erratically—the attentions of the younger child. The principal "maxim'' is "don't fret, and don't expect too much of him, or else he will feel you to be troublesome, and then it is all over'' (p. 28). So Lucy herself behaves toward Graham, whom she grudgingly praises as being "not quite as other boys are'' (p. 24), but whom she obviously admires from a distance. So she behaves toward everyone (as Brontë always behaved to those outside her family circle), never demanding; reticent and withdrawn, yet always watching, priding herself on being an amused observer of character. And as she represses the pain of rejection (Polly has, after all, appropriated Lucy's place in her godmother's house) so also does she repress the anger, allowing it expression only in the coldness of her tone, in her judgmental attitude, in her uneasy air of intellectual superiority.

It is Lucy's ambivalence, then, which accounts for what might be called the tonal distortions of the Bretton section of the novel. Because Lucy is the anesthetized survivor, passion is described dispassionately: a household warmed by love—by Mrs. Bretton's adoration of her son, by Polly's idolatry first of her father and then of Graham, by Graham's easy affectionate nature—this household feels chill and sterile to the reader. Similarly, it is because of Lucy's will to repression—because of her need to tell another's story as a substitute for her own—that the novel's structure is initially disorienting. Chronicling incidents which are representative of her own circumstances, Lucy compromises a reticence morbid in its intensity. But that reticence continues to express itself in her defensiveness, elusiveness, hostility, and inconsistency. The form of *Villette* is the form of Lucy's neurosis: a representation of the novel's subject. The narrative is as difficult and as indirect as is the heroine's attempt to defeat loneliness by learning to accept and even to reinvent herself.

In this first section Lucy grieves for the natural tendencies of Polly's personality:

> This, I perceived, was a one-idea'd nature; betraying that monomaniac tendency I have ever thought the most unfortunate with which man or woman can be cursed. (p. 11)

What she recognizes in Polly, she must recognize in her own self: an overwhelming need and capacity for love. But instead of condemning it as monomaniacal, she must learn to acknowledge it as the foundation stone upon which she can reconstruct her ego to fill the void of abandonment.

Lucy similarly grants to Polly another quality of mind which she is unprepared to recognize as her own:

> I, Lucy Snowe, plead guiltless of that curse, an overheated and discursive imagination; but whenever opening a room-door, I found her seated in a corner alone, her head in her pigmy hand, that room seemed to me not inhabited, but haunted. (p. 11)

Of course, the description which follows the disavowal effectively contradicts it. But the contradiction is unconscious on Lucy's part and it is not until she learns to trust her imagination as she must trust her feelings and intuitions that she can become "reliable" as a narrator; "whole" as a woman. In a remarkably contemporary way, the fiction strives for its form as the heroine searches out her identity. The concept of narration was too sophisticated to be genuinely appreciated or even understood by Brontë's contemporaries. Her publisher and critics thought the apparent shift of focus from Polly to Lucy a serious aesthetic flaw. Readers into the twentieth century continued to concur. Only now do we begin to recognize the nature of the genius that urged Brontë to accept the risk and challenge of her art.

II

It is as difficult for Lucy to speak of the events which follow her stay at Bretton as it was for her to describe the events which preceded it. As she found an acceptable metaphor in Polly's experience for her own early deprivation, so does she find in the indirect allusiveness of language and imagery a way of expressing the pain of the eight years of tragedy which changed her from an adolescent of fourteen to a young woman of twenty-two.

> I will permit the reader to picture me, for the next eight
> years, as a bark slumbering through halcyon weather, in a har-
> bour still as glass . . .
>
> Picture me then idle, basking, plump, and happy,
> stretched on a cushioned deck, warmed with constant sun-
> shine, rocked by breezes indolently soft. However, it cannot
> be concealed that, in that case, I must somehow have fallen
> over-board, or that there must been wreck at last. I too well
> remember a time—a long time, of cold, of danger, of conten-
> tion. To this hour, when I have the nightmare, it repeats the
> rush and saltness of briny waves in my throat, and their icy
> pressure on my lungs. I even know there was a storm, and that
> not of one hour nor one day. For many days and nights neither
> sun nor stars appeared; we cast with our own hands the tack-
> ling out of the ship; a heavy tempest lay on us; all hope that we
> should be saved was taken away. In fine, the ship was lost, the
> crew perished. (pp. 29–30)

Here is the deluge which Brontë metaphorized in describing to
Williams the tragic experience of her life. Sea and storm imagery
are used throughout the novel, as they were used in *Jane Eyre,* to
suggest the psychological torment which is a response to separation and loss. Most important of all is Lucy's presentation of herself as the sole survivor of a shipwreck in which all whom she
loves are destroyed.[19] Although the actual circumstances of her
tragedy are never revealed to us, the emotions which accompanied them are always just beneath the surface, waiting to be
summoned, exerting their pressure. There is, of course, sorrow—
and desperate loneliness. But there is also the guilt, the anxiety,
the sense of inadequacy which had been expressed in Charlotte's
own childhood dreams of the dead Maria and Elizabeth: the survivor's sense of unworthiness which was as central in Brontë's
character as it is dominant in Lucy Snowe's.[20] And there is also

19. Although Brontë is not faithful to her own experience in the chronology and details of Lucy's circumstances, she does suggest the stages of loss
which she endured as well as the nature of her response to the tragic events.

20. From Roe Head, Charlotte had written to Ellen Nussey (Gaskell,
p. 95.):

> You have been very kind to me of late, and have spared me all those little
> sallies of ridicule which, owing to my miserable and wretched touchiness
> of character, used formerly to make me wince, as if I had been touched
> with a hot iron; things that nobody else cares for, enter into my mind and
> rankle there like venom. I know these feelings are absurd, and therefore I
> try to hide them, but they only sting the deeper for concealment.

depression, for the misery of the past conditions the expectations of the future. The deluges of life, as Brontë knew, are all too likely to return again. So Elizabeth Gaskell wrote, after her friend's death: "In after-life I was painfully impressed with the fact that Miss Brontë never dared to allow herself to look forward with hope; that she had no confidence in the future,"[21] and Lucy admits:

> Oh, my childhood! I had feelings, passive as I lived, little as I spoke, cold as I looked, when I thought of past days, I *could* feel. About the present, it was better to be stoical; about the future—such a future as mine—to be dead. And in catalepsy and a dead trance, I studiously held the quick of my nature. (p. 93)

The impulse is to resist change, to avoid involvement, to live as if one had also died.

Psychic withdrawal bound Brontë to her home and imprisoned her in the cavern beneath the sea: the tiny space which was the vestige of the surviving self—drowned yet still alive. Psychic withdrawal makes Lucy welcome the undemanding emotional life at Bretton and ultimately it causes her to accept, when it is offered, the position of companion to Miss Marchmont. Here too the dwarfed and stifled ego finds security in the narrow boundaries of claustrophobic space.

> Two hot, close rooms thus became my world; and a crippled old woman, my mistress, my friend, my all. Her service was my duty—her pain, my suffering—her relief, my hope—her anger, my punishment—her regard, my reward. I forgot that there were fields, woods, rivers, seas, an ever-changing sky outside the steam-dimmed lattice of this sick-chamber; I was almost content to forget it. (p. 31)

In forming this attachment, Lucy comes as close as she can to expressing her identification with those who have died while still asserting a minimal commitment to life. But because a bond does form between her and Miss Marchmont, because there is mutual respect and even affection between them—never openly and therefore never threateningly expressed—these two rooms become in fact a new world for Lucy to discover. Here she learns that she can be more than a self-effacing shadow, that she can be a rock upon which another's life can rest: a source of comfort and

21. Gaskell, p. 77.

aid. Here she has confirmed for her the value of stoicism; the importance even of thwarted love. When Miss Marchmont dies in still another storm (first she shares with Lucy her memory of a profound romantic attachment which, while lost in youth, gave her life its meaning) Lucy is once again a survivor, but now—instead of withdrawing further into herself—she begins to enlarge her existence. Although she has been deprived of a surrogate mother, she knows that she had truly earned the place of "daughter": that she had begun to reconstruct for herself the context of a family. From this knowledge she derives her first store of strength.

> I had wanted to compromise with Fate: to escape occasional great agonies by submitting to a whole life of privation and small pains. Fate would not be so pacified; nor would Providence sanction this shrinking sloth and cowardly indolence. (p. 32)

Still using the language of passivity ("Fate," "Providence") Lucy does, for the first time, admit the possibility of a determining personality. Thus she can begin her journey from withdrawal to self-discovery. It is not an allegorical journey and the symbols of opposition are not fixed as clearly as they were in *Jane Eyre* (the red-room—Helen Burns; Rochester—St. John Rivers; resolution at Ferndean). The movement does not follow a neatly repetitive dialectical pattern. It is more fluid, with regressions and progressions, a process in which it is more difficult to perceive linear development because the personal past impinges continually on the present: changing, redefining, distorting. A simplistic antagonism between reason and emotion can be identified again as the basic source of conflict, but the meaning of these terms is more complex and more elusive. Their context is more openly psychological than it was in *Jane Eyre*. Reason is identified predominantly with repression and the "feeling" intuitive self is accepted less fearfully as authentic.

As Lucy enters a strange world which will test her into growth, her public self—sensible and controlled—contends with her aspiring, private being. She notes that "there is nothing like taking all you do at a moderate estimate: it keeps mind and body tranquil; whereas grandiloquent notions are apt to hurry both into fever" (p. 38). But she responds to London as Brontë had herself: finding there an alternative to the claustrophobic space to which she was accustomed, by which she had previously been comforted:

> While I looked, my inner self moved; my spirit shook its always-fettered wings half loose; I had a sudden feeling as if I, who had never yet truly lived, were at last about to taste life.
> (p. 40)

Discovering independence, she lives, in walking London's streets, a "prodigious amount of life." She wanders in an "ecstacy of freedom and enjoyment": stimulated, vital, excited; hungry for the first time in many years. In her awakening, Lucy decides to leave England for Brussels. Pushing herself into activity which prohibits withdrawal, making herself deeply vulnerable, she acts not out of desperation but hope:

> . . . peril, loneliness, an uncertain future, are not oppressive evils, so long as the frame is healthy, and the faculties are employed; so long, especially, as Liberty lends us her wings, and Hope guides us by her star. (p. 48)

Allowing herself to "feel," she can also allow herself the liberty to imagine. The river she rows on to reach the boat which will take her to the continent reminds her of the river Styx. Her soul, awaiting rebirth, quivers in anticipation and she is brought to the admission that, "I must possess something of the artist's faculty of making the most of present pleasure" (p. 51).[22] Her freedom is confirmed in Brussels, as Crimsworth's had been. As a foreigner, an Englishwoman, a Protestant (without money, position, or beauty) she is without conventional restraints, automatically accepted as eccentric, granted a special status. Still, despite the fact that "my fancy budded fresh and my heart basked in sunshine," although the present and future seemed rich in possibilities never before dreamt of, threats from the past are always potentially present:

> . . . the secret but ceaseless consciousness of anxiety lying in wait on enjoyment, like a tiger crouched in a jungle. The breathing of that beast of prey was in my ear always; his fierce

---

22. Brontë's return to Brussels is described by Mrs. Gaskell, (p. 159) in much the same terms as Lucy's journey is presented.

heart panted close against mine; he never stirred in his lair but I felt him: I knew he waited only for sun down to bound ravenous from his ambush. (p. 52)

The juxtaposed images of Brontë's childhood dream are echoed here: the fragile sea-cavern threatened by pounding waves and the attacking lion in the desert—claustrophobic space and the fear of negation.

But although she is frightened, Lucy does not surrender to anxiety. In a new situation, assigned different roles by the teachers and students at Madam Beck's Pensionnat, Lucy finds that instead of being deprived of an identity she has protected with such difficulty, she can define herself in a number of different ways, playing a variety of roles, responding to other people's expectations of her. Ginevra Fanshawe, the beautiful and flighty young English girl, summons Lucy's independence by making her strong in her assertion of disapproval. Ginevra's excessive femininity elicits the masculine side of Lucy's personality, the "crust and rind of my nature" (p. 402). The triviality and pettiness of her values allow Lucy to express with unusual openness, her impatience, resentment, and jealousy. Ginevra represents a world of fashion and sexual role-playing, a world of values unearned. Lucy scorns those values and that world but, as an outsider who has herself been scorned, she cannot help feeling envious of those who "belong." It is, in part, this ambivalence toward society which draws her to Ginevra and allows her to indulge the girl as she would a child:

I don't know why I chose to give my bread rather to Ginevra than to another: nor why, if two had to share the convenience of one drinking-vessel . . . I always contrived that she should be my convive, and rather like to let her take the lion's share, whether of the white beer, the sweet wine, or the new milk: so it was, however, and she knew it; and, therefore, while we wrangled daily, we were never alienated. (pp. 200–201)

But there is also another, more simple and appealing reason for their friendship. Charlotte had said to Ellen Nussey, explaining her propensity for easy attachments: "If anybody likes me, I can't help liking them."[23] Lucy might say the same. Because

23. January 4, 1838. Wise and Symington, I, 164.

rejection has been the rule, her need responds to Ginevra's warmth and respect. Acceptance, though it be predicated on misunderstanding, cannot go unanswered.[24]

Madame Beck, the school's headmistress, also elicits hidden aspects of Lucy's personality. Regarding the young woman as one of those "Anglaises," who will dare anything, Madame Beck continually challenges Lucy to assume roles which express her capacity for leadership, which evoke her Protestant "individualism," her fierce integrity, her pride. When Madame Beck asks her to assume charge of a classroom, Lucy recognizes that she has been offered a "challenge of strength." She meets the test: "I suddenly felt all the dishonor of my diffidence—all the pusillanimity of my slackness to aspire" (p. 66). And she does aspire. She finds that she can be aggressive. But the cost is high, comparable to that which Brontë herself had to pay in the coldness of the public self which she formed to protect her vulnerability.[25] Lucy respects Madame Beck's shrewdness, her cold rationality, her open commitment to self-interest. And she recognizes that Madame Beck might beat her at her own game for, if she watches Madame Beck, Madame Beck also watches her. If voyeurism is Lucy's route to power (judging, she feels herself su-

24. One is reminded here of Charlotte Brontë's lifelong relationship with Ellen Nussey: a relationship which seems so strange because of the inequality of the partners. Brontë wrote to W. S. Williams about the friendship (January 3, 1830. Wise and Symington, III, 63.):

> When I first saw Ellen I did not care for her—we were schoolfellows—in the course of time we learnt each other's faults and good points—we were contrasts—still we suited—affection was first a germ, then a sapling—then a strong tree: now, no new friend, however lofty or profound in intellect—not even Miss Martineau herself could be to me what Ellen is, yet she is no more than a conscientious, observant, calm, well-bred Yorkshire girl. She is without romance—if she attempts to read poetry—or poetic prose aloud—I am irritated and deprive her of her book—if she talks of it I stop my ears—but she is good—she is true—she is faithful and I love her.

It is not without significance that Brontë kept from Ellen the secret of her authorship until it was general knowledge and that her letters to Elizabeth Gaskell and particularly to W. S. Williams were more intimate in nature as well as more intellectual than those which she wrote in these same years to Ellen.

25. Rosamund Langbridge (p. 94) commented:

> Very few people were ever to understand Charlotte Brontë, for it is seldom that such appealing weakness is leashed to such appalling strength. All that most people saw of her was that aspect of slight mercilessness which was aimed, in reality, at crushing her own weaker self, and not, as they supposed, at their inferiority.

perior) spying is, for Madame Beck, a way of maintaining the power which she already possesses. More to the point, because Lucy is Madame Beck's employee, her subordinate and victim, it is only by becoming Madame Beck's complicitor, by allowing herself to *be* watched, her possessions to be examined, her secrets to be explored, that Lucy can maintain the illusion of control.

Thus, when Lucy discovers Madame Beck looking carefully through her bureau, she watches her "with a secret glee," admiring her care. Lucy knows that the headmistress suspects her of a romantic intrigue and she exults in the little woman's error. "Loverless and inexpectant of love, I was safe from spies in my heart-poverty, as the beggar from thieves in his destitution of purse" (p. 101). And as Lucy flees so that *she* will not be discovered, she laughs:

> Yet as the laugh died, a kind of wrath smote me, and then bitterness followed: it was the rock struck, and Meribah's waters gushing out . . . I never had felt so strange and contradictory an inward tumult as I felt for an hour that evening: soreness and laughter, and fire, and grief, shared my heart between them. I cried hot tears; not because Madame mistrusted me—I did not care twopence for her mistrust—but for other reasons. Complicated, disquieting thoughts broke up the whole repose of my nature. However, that turmoil subsided: next day I was again Lucy Snowe. (p. 102)

But it is no longer possible for her to suppress turmoil completely, to "be Lucy Snowe," veiling insecurity beneath a pretense of power. Lucy is not like her employer who "devoid of sympathy, had a sufficiency of rational benevolence" (p. 63). Because her repressed self has been awakened, because she has become active and feels what it means to have a stake in life, she is forced to admit—as Brontë admitted to Ellen—that self-alienation, the assumption of a role that does not express her own identity, is insupportable.[26] Lucy finds it increasingly difficult to "hold the quick of her nature in a dead trance" (p. 93). The tran-

26. ". . . What dismays and haunts me sometimes is the conviction that I have no natural knack for my vocation—if teaching only were requisite it would be smooth and easy—but it is the living in other people's houses—the estrangement from one's real character—the adoption of a cold, frigid apathetic exterior that is painful." Charlotte wrote this, when she was a governess, to Ellen Nussey, August 17, 1841 (Wise and Symington, I, 241).

scendent world summons her from the musty enclosures of her limited experience. Her buried self awakens when the storms come and she is "roughly roused and obliged to live." Then she rejects the narrow, interior spaces:

> I did long, achingly, then and for four-and-twenty-hours afterwards, for something to fetch me out of my present existence, and lead me upwards and onwards. (p. 93)

The violent imagery used to describe her consequent repression of feeling, the necessary containment of the beast awakened, suggests the cost to Lucy of momentary peace:

> This longing and all of a similar kind, it was necessary to knock on the head; which I did, figuratively, after the manner of Jael to Sisera, driving a nail through their temples. Unlike Sisera, they did not die: they were but transiently stunned, and at intervals would turn on the nail with a rebellious wrench; then did the temples bleed, and the brain thrill to its core. (p. 94)

Growing knowledge and sensitivity make continuing self-denial increasingly difficult. Finally, when she is left alone at the school during summer vacation (as Charlotte had been left by the Hegers in the summer of '43, when they went off with their children to the seashore) Lucy finds her "self" completely undefended. Deprived of her usual tasks, unable to play her accustomed roles, kept from exploring the terrain of her expanding personality, Lucy endures an experience similar to the one which Charlotte had described to Ellen: "I tried to read, I tried to write; but in vain. I then wandered about from room to room, but the sounds and loneliness of all the house weighs one's spirits like lead."[27]

For all the others, students and teachers alike, this is a time of rest and companionship. For most there is love to enjoy. For

---

Two years earlier when she was a governess for the Sidgewick family, she had written to Emily (June 8, 1839. Wise and Symington, I, 178.):

> I said in my last letter that Mrs. Sidgewick did not know me. I now begin to find that she does not intend to know me, that she cares nothing in the world about me except to contrive how the greatest possible quantity of labor may be squeezed out of me . . . I see now more clearly than I have ever done before that a private governess has no existence, is not considered as a living and rational being except as connected with the wearisome duties she has to fulfill.

27. To Ellen Nussey, November 15, 1843. Wise and Symington, I, 309.

some, like Ginevra, adored by Dr. John, there is still greater love to anticipate. But for Lucy there is regression to the suffering of the past. She is a survivor once again. She knows depression and despair. There is the grueling dependence of the barely human "cretin" assigned to her care; their relationship a nightmarish parody of her situation with Miss Marchmont and a bizarre echo of Jane Eyre's ambivalent dream of carrying the fretful, burdensome child to its death. Then there is Lucy's terrible dream of visitation and rejection from eternity: "the well-loved dead, who had loved *me* well in life, met me elsewhere, alienated: galled was my most inmost spirit with an unutterable sense of despair about the future" (p. 137–38).[28] She is forced once more into the position of voyeur. Her profound need for love finds expression in her identification with Ginevra's imagined love for Dr. John. Her fantasy of their sexual connection recalls Jane's orgasmic awareness of Rochester:

> I conceived an electric chord of sympathy between them, a fine chain of mutual understanding, sustaining union through a separation of a hundred leagues—carrying, across mound and hollow, communication by prayer and wish. (p. 137)

The crisis of feeling, previously repressed, must now be acknowledged. Her pain cannot be borne alone. In turning, upon an impulse, to the comfort of the Catholic priest, she acknowledges implicitly the failure of reason, of discipline, of Protestantism itself: the necessity of recognizing a part of herself too long rejected and denied. That expression should take the form of confession seems appropriate, since in Lucy deprivation has caused guilt and anxiety: feelings of unworthiness and shame. For her, self-expression is tantamount to sin.[29] Lucy does find relief in the

28. The parallel with Brontë's dream of her dead sisters is obvious.
29. On September 1, 1843, in a state of mind of which Lucy's is a reflection, Brontë herself confessed to a Roman Catholic priest in the Cathedral of Ste. Gudule. Writing to Emily on the following day, she explained that the priest refused at first to listen to the confession of a Protestant, "but I was determined to confess, and at last he said he would allow me because it might be the first step toward returning to the true church. I actually did confess—a real confession . . . the adventure stops there, and I hope I shall never see the priest again. I think you had better not tell papa of this. He will not understand that it was only a freak, and will perhaps think that I am going to turn Catholic!" (Wise and Symington, I, 304.)
One can imagine that Brontë's own feelings of sexual longing and jealousy were so much greater than those pictured here in Lucy's vague admiration of Dr.

cathartic experience: "The mere pouring out of some portion of long accumulating, long pent-up pain into a vessel whence it could not be again diffused—had done me good. I was already solaced" (p. 140). Although she fears her own vulnerability too much to accede to the priest's invitation to return to him for help, she has been, to a limited extent, freed. Before she collapses on the darkened street, she has rediscovered the courage and strength, and will to live, which had before carried her to Belgium. She expresses the same wish for transcendence—linked before to sexual experience—that had been Brontë's, as it had also been Jane's: "My heart did not fail at all in this conflict; I only wished that I had wings and could ascend the gale, spread and repose my pinions on its strength, career in its course, sweep where it swept" (p. 141).

The further implications of release become clear when Lucy regains consciousness. The fainting fit does not simply mark a transition to a new level of awareness, her readiness for a new stage of experience, as did similar episodes in *Jane Eyre* (the red-room, the recuperative sleep at the Riverses' home). Now—the parallel with psychoanalysis again suggests itself—Lucy can be moved into the future only through the medium of the past. Lucy wakens to the beginning: the only beginning she has been able to record: the house at Bretton. She is carried back ten years by the ornaments and decorations of the room in which she lies. It is now that we learn that she is twenty-four: that she was only fourteen when the first incident of the novel took place. And as she attempts to orient herself, looking at a portrait of Graham Bretton which hangs upon the wall, we discover how deeply she herself had cared for the young boy, to what extent Polly was not only her surrogate, but her competitor as well.

> "Ah! that portrait used to hang in the breakfast-room, over the mantel-piece: somewhat too high, as I thought. I well remember how I used to mount a music-stool for the purpose of unhooking it, holding it in my hand, and searching into those bonny wells of eyes, whose glance under their hazel lashes seemed like a pencilled laugh; and well I liked to note the

John and envy of Ginevra, and her feeling of guilt about her emotional involvement with Heger—only in the early stages of recognition—much more intense. *Her* impulse to seek the comfort of confession is therefore even more readily understandable.

colouring of the cheek, and the expression of the mouth." I
hardly believed fancy could improve on the curve of that
mouth, or of the chin, even *my* ignorance knew that both were
beautiful, and pondered perplexed over this doubt: "How it
was that what charmed so much, could at the same time so
keenly pain?" (pp. 146–47).

In this brilliantly convoluted plotting, possessed of such psychological validity, Brontë reveals that Lucy had recognized Graham
Bretton in Dr. John—Ginevra's suitor and the school's doctor—
and had neither shared her secret with him nor with the reader.
We accept Brontë's artifice because we are familiar with Lucy's
fear of rejection, with her extreme vulnerability, and with her
consequent unreliability as a narrator.

Finding herself in the Bretton's home as it has been reestab-
lished in Brussels, cared for by her godmother and treated with
affection and kindness by Graham, Lucy can, in fact, continue to
build on the possibility for a relationship begun with her "confession"—the first presentation of herself to another. She imagines
that "my calm little room seemed somehow like a cave in the
sea":

When I closed my eyes, I heard a gale, subsiding at last, bearing upon the house-front like a setting swell upon a rock-base.
I heard it drawn and withdrawn far, far off, like a tide retiring
from a shore of the upper world—a world so high above that
the rush of its largest waves, the dash of its fiercest breakers—
could sound down in this submarine home, only like murmurs
and a lullaby. (pp. 155–56)

The image is again drawn from Brontë's childhood dream and
suggests the tenuousness of her security. Lucy realizes that she
must call on Reason in her struggle with feeling so that her life
will at least *seem* to "be better regulated, more equable, quieter
on the surface, and it is on the surface only the common gaze will
fall" (p. 153). But although she resubmits out of pride to Reason,
she struggles more honestly for expression, allowing herself to
believe more intensely in the integrity of feeling. A welter of
psychic experience replaces the analytical dialectic which traced
the self-discovery of Jane Eyre. If Reason would crush her, cow
her, break her down, if it is as "vindictive as a devil" and "en-
venomed as a stepmother," imagination is her "divine love," "a
goddess representing Help and Hope" (p. 196). Later, in answer-

ing Graham's letters, Lucy writes one message to satisfy Reason, which she sends to him, and one which expresses her feeling, which she keeps for herself. It is a recognition of her own needs as well as of society's demands; a compromise with her understanding of Graham which allows her to maintain a personal integrity newly discovered. The self is protected so that it need not be sacrificed. Only when Graham has encountered Polly once again and has fallen in love with her, does Lucy allow Reason to persuade her of what she has always dimly known: that this "true young Englishman," whom nature has made good enough for a prince, could not find in *her* a fit mate. So she seals her letters in a bottle and buries them in a garden. ("People who have undergone bereavement always jealously gather together and lock away mementos: it is not supportable to be stabbed to the heart each moment by sharp revival of regret" (p. 251). She compares the impulse which compels her to this action to that which moved her to visit the confessional. Both are acts of self-preservation. Self-control is healthfully born of self-knowledge.

If Lucy's attraction to Graham persists despite repression ("Was this feeling dead? I do not know, but it was buried." [p. 307]), it persists because of the power of her ambivalence—not unlike Brontë's ambivalence toward George Smith, Graham's model. Ambivalence grows out of Lucy's recognition that if she cannot be a satisfactory mate for Graham, the fault is as much a function of the defects in *his* character as it is a result of her own inadequacy. Because she cannot rid herself of her sense of the second any more than she can deny her knowledge of the first, the conflict remains unresolved.

> Reader, if in the course of this work you find that my opinion of Dr. John undergoes modification, excuse the seeming inconsistency. I give the feeling as at the time I felt it: I describe the view of character as it appeared when discovered. (p. 164)

Lucy knows that she is plain. (The reader believes in that plainness as it was impossible to believe in Jane's.) Her knowledge is corroborated for her many times. Ginevra, for example, is cruelly critical when she insists upon comparing their mirror images, finding her own to be infinitely superior.[30] On a more

---

30. The incident is reminiscent of one which took place when Charlotte Brontë and Mary Taylor were students at the Roe Head School. Mary Taylor described it to Elizabeth Gaskell (Gaskell, p. 66):

important occasion, Lucy is forced "to see herself as others see her," when she comes unexpectedly upon her own reflection as she stands with Mrs. Bretton and Graham. Then she remarks, "It brought a jar of discord, a pang of regret; it was not flattering, yet, after all, I ought to be thankful; it might have been worse" (p. 180). Although her "feeling self" would probably respond in a tone more anguished than this one struck by Reason, Lucy does know that Graham is a man who can't see far beneath the surface, who can't penetrate further than his own hopes and illusions. To him, she is only "quiet Lucy Snowe," a being "inoffensive as a shadow." His public self—generous, benevolent, modest—approves her: to his private self—vain, selfish, full of masculine egotism—she is unacceptable.

> With now welcome force, I realized his entire misapprehension of my character and nature. He wanted always to give me a role not mine. Nature and I opposed him. He did not at all guess what I felt: he did not read my eyes, or face, or gestures; though, I doubt not, all spoke. (p. 270)

Polly, who molds herself to the needs of those for whom she cares, will not betray Graham's illusions. Because she is also rich and beautiful she will not threaten his vanity. Lucy acknowledges that "society must approve—the world must admire what he did, or he counted his measures false and futile" (p. 313), and she can't help wondering if he might have treated her better had her wealth and station been different.

Lucy's ambivalence remains up to their last encounter in the novel—and beyond. When Lucy sees Graham at the "fete" and entreats him with her eyes not to reveal her presence there, they exchange a glance which reawakens those feelings long buried:

> He resumed his seat, nor did he again turn or disturb me by a glance, except indeed for one single instant, when a look, rather solicitous than curious, stole my way—speaking what

---

It was about this time I told her she was very ugly. Some years afterwards, I told her I thought I had been very impertinent. She replied, "You did me a great deal of good, Polly, so don't repent of it."

Gaskell (p. 380) suggests that Brontë never did overcome an agonizing self-consciousness which derived from her feelings of insecurity:

> Much of this nervous dread of encountering strangers I ascribe to the idea of her personal ugliness, which had been strongly impressed upon her imagination early in life, and which she exaggerated to herself in a remarkable manner.

somehow stilled my heart—"like the south-wind quieting the
earth." Graham's thoughts of me were not entirely those of a
frozen indifference, after all. I believe in that goodly mansion,
his heart, he kept one little place under the skylights where
Lucy might have entertainment, if she chose to call . . . I kept
a room for him, too—a place of which I never took the measure, either by rule or compass: I think it was like the tent of
Peri-Banou. All my life long I carried it folded in the hollow of
my hand—yet, released from that hold and constriction, I
know not but its innate capacity for expanse might have mag-
nified it into a tabernacle for a host. (p. 386)

Graham is her adolescent hero, the romantic love unmasked, but
tempting still. The immature longing remains, but it is contained
by an ego increasingly capable of assertion and control.

Although Lucy is fond of the matured Polly, seeing in the
girl's capacity for feeling, in her quiet pride and self-respect,
reflections of her own personality, and while she needs still to
identify herself with the privileged and blessed, Lucy openly refuses to allow Polly to share with her confidences about her love
for Graham. When Polly asks her: "Do other people see him with
my eyes? Do you admire him?", Lucy replies, with wry honesty,
"I *never see* him," and she goes on to explain to the reader: "It
was best to answer her strongly at once, and to silence for ever
the tender, passionate confidences which left her lips, sweet
honey, and sometimes dropped in my ear—molten lead" (p.
359). The sentiment is, in its way, harsh but it is honestly self-
protective. If Polly, with the "infatuated egotism" common to
lovers "must have a witness to (her) happiness, cost that witness
what it may" (p. 359), Lucy with a clear understanding of her
own needs, knows that it is not in *her* interests to serve that purpose. In rejecting voyeurism, she asserts her right to a life of her
own.

III

Having explored the frustrations of her current relationship
with George Smith, Brontë went further back—to that more profound and traumatic relationship which had sparked her to growth
and to despair. The movement is progressive in psychoanalytic
terms, but regressive in its suggestion that the idealized professor
in Brussels became again for Brontë the standard by which all

other men had to be judged. It is, of course, through her love affair with Paul Emanuel, the schoolmaster modeled upon M. Heger, that Lucy ultimately realizes herself. The pattern of their interaction is similar to that of the "Jane" poem, which had been repeated in Frances's relationship to Crimsworth, in Jane's relation to Rochester, in Shirley's relation to Louis. Now the psychological process that shaped the pattern is more insightfully presented and the emotional power that informed Brontë's love for her "maitre" finds expression.

M. Paul has undeniable connections with the Byronic hero. He is "a dark little man . . . pungent and austere" (p. 110), fiery and grasping. He has dark hair, a "broad, sallow brow" and thin cheek, a "wide and quivering nostril." He utters groans of scorn and fierce hisses of rage. Lucy, seeing his love of power, compares him to Napoleon. She comprehends his capacity for deep and irrational passion, the volatility of his temper, his jealousy. A rebel at heart, he fervently opposes tyranny and resists whatever is obligatory. But there is another side to his character. He is benevolent and charitable, given to acts of extraordinary kindness. If "he was as capricious as women are said to be" (p. 279), he is also as emotional, as sympathetic, as impulsive, and intuitive.

> [His heart] was not an ossified organ: in its core was a place, tender beyond a man's tenderness; a place that humbled him to little children, that bound him to girls and women: to whom, rebel as he would, he could not disown his affinity, nor quite deny that, on the whole, he was better with them than with his own sex. (p. 287)

His is an androgynous nature: not confused and blocked as Hunsworth's was, not insecure as Crimsworth's; but complex and whole. He is the romantic hero humanized, offering a promise of equality. Once he trusts Lucy he is not afraid to reveal to her his vulnerability, to confess that "there is a fund of modesty and diffidence in my nature" (p. 308), to express that about himself which is tender and nurturing. Finding Lucy asleep at her desk he covers her with a warm shawl and explains to her, when she awakens: "You need watching, and watching over, and it is well for you that I see this and do my best to discharge both duties" (p. 307). He is not only the "maitre," the father-lover who haunts all of Brontë's novels. He is also a maternal figure—and, in his stubborn impulsivity and petulance, a child. To Lucy who has had no relationships, he offers all.

Because Monsieur Paul's is such a comprehensive and vital personality, he evokes and even demands a wide range of responses. Although he likes to dominate, his is not an ego which blocks response. His empathetic nature allows him to define himself through interaction. It is revealing that he should feel an affinity with the theatre and choose to direct amateur performances. It is important that he should persuade Lucy to take part in a school production. Her assigned role is one which she despairs at first of playing properly. She is to be a man: Ginevra's suitor, a fop. But she discovers it to be a part that she can not only play well, but can play "with relish." Imagining that Graham is her rival, responding to Ginevra's flirtatiousness, to the girl's clear preference for herself, Lucy becomes instinctively the dandy, deHamal, with whom Ginevra eventually elopes. In the process she learns something about each of them and, most importantly, she learns to explore and release some hidden androgynous aspect of her own personality. The knowledge she gains is frightening. The possibility she feels makes her wish to withdraw again into the more limited spaces of herself. "A keen relish for dramatic expression had revealed itself as part of my nature; to cherish and exercise this new-found faculty might gift me with a world of delight, but it would not do for a mere looker-on at life" (p. 121). Her reaction is composed of the same elements of attraction and repulsion that she experiences when she later goes with Graham to see Vashti, the great actress.[31] In Vashti's per-

31. This incident is modeled on Charlotte Brontë's experience with the French tragedienne, Rachel (Elisa Felix), whom she saw in Scribe's *Adrienne Lecouvreur* and Corneille's *Les Trois Horaces* in London, in June 1851. She wrote to James Taylor of her response (November 15, 1851. Wise and Symington, III, 289.):

Rachel's acting transfixed me with wonder, enchained me with interest, and thrilled me with horror. The tremendous force with which she expresses the very worst passions in their strongest essence forms an exhibition as exciting as the bull-fights of Spain and the gladiatorial combats of old Rome, and (it seemed to me) not one whit more moral than those poisoned stimulants to popular ferocity. It is scarcely human nature that she shows you; it is something wilder and worse; the feelings and fury of a fiend.

formance she finds the very image of passion. She is almost un-
bearably moved by the "marvelous sight: a mighty revelation
. . . a spectacle low, horrible, immoral" (p. 220). Through
Vashti is revealed the range of passions available to the human
spirit. The actress's power is "like a deep, swollen winter river,
thundering in cataract," which plucks Lucy's soul "like a leaf,
on the steep and steely sweep of its descent" (p. 222). And when
the force of Vashti's conflict, the depth of her passion, becomes
in fact too much for Lucy to bear, the theatre bursts into flames,
much like the mystery of fire which flickers through *Jane Eyre*.

Although Lucy deeply fears such a loss of rational control,
she is magnetically drawn by the potential for extension and self-
exploration which the irrational seems to hold out to her. Paul
Emanuel does not present her with a range of possibilities as vast
as those implied by Vashti's performances. These would overwhelm Lucy, as the fire symbolically suggests. He does, however, continue to place her in role-playing situations which prevent her from becoming again "a mere looker-on at life." Lucy
initially makes the mistake of thinking that Paul Emanuel is simply like all of the others who project upon her roles which express
their sense of her and freeze her into false postures;

> Madame Beck esteemed me learned and blue; Miss Fanshawe,
> caustic, ironic and cynical; Mr. Home, a model teacher, the es-
> sence of the sedate and discreet: somewhat conventional per-
> haps, too strict, limited and scrupulous, but still the pink and
> pattern of governess-correctness; . . . (p. 257)

In fact, M. Paul can read Lucy's eyes, her face, her gestures—
and he responds to the spark of her being instead of the shadow of
her seeming. It is a new experience for her, as she observes with
some amazement to herself: "You are well habituated to be
passed by as a shadow in Life's sunshine: it is a new thing to see
one testily lifting his hand to screen his eyes, because you tease
him with an obtrusive ray" (p. 284). Initially, responding to her

---

She also wrote:

> I neither love, esteem, nor hate this strange being, but (if I could bear the
> high mental stimulus so long) I would go every night for three months to
> watch and study its manifestations. (David Isenberg, "Charlotte Brontë
> and the Theatre," in *Brontë Society Transactions*, 15, No. 3 (1968), p.
> 239.)

strength, her "Protestant independence," Paul sees her as a competitor, "one of those beings who must be *kept down*" (p. 133). His urge to dominate, inspires her resistance, "(gives) wings to aspiration" (p. 298). His belief that she is more learned than she in fact is and his fear that she will use her learning as a weapon against him, stimulate her confidence. His excessive emotionality (so like her inner self) releases her into perverse playfulness and his mercurial disposition makes her "placid and harmonious," almost maternal. So too, his jealousy of Graham, which moves him to petulant accusations concerning her "frivolity" and "vanity," amuses her while awakening a sense of the power of her own femininity. Asserting herself in opposition to him, Lucy discovers a range of responses, feelings, opinions, and ideas which will not be confined to the narrow space of a submerged personality. He sparks her to growth—as Hunsden incites Frances, as Rochester stimulates Jane. But he does not—in the manner of his predecessors—frustrate the spirit he arouses.

As M. Paul becomes aware that Lucy's capacity for passion makes her vulnerable as well as strong, he allows himself to substitute sympathy and support for anger. More secure, he can overcome his suspicions and assure her that "we worship the same God, in the same spirit, though by different rites" (p. 323). His avowal is not a simple assertion of religious tolerance. It is, in its admission of equality, a genuine offer of friendship: an advance towards psychic confrontation: the beginning for each of emotional fulfillment. To acknowledge religious kinship Paul and Lucy must accept the manifestations of each other in themselves for their religions define the dominant aspects of their personalities. Reason and imagination, control and expression, must be placed in appropriate relationship.

Lucy fears Catholicism because she equates its apparent excesses of feeling with loss of self. She fears it because it offers her, as an alternative to the familiar agony of alienation, the self-contained world of religious fanaticism. She knows that if she had returned to Père Silas after the night of her impulsive confession, "I might just now, instead of writing this heretic narrative, be counting my beads in the cell of a certain Carmelite convent on the Boulevard of Crecy in Villette" (p. 141). Lucy prefers Art—the rational ordering of intuition and emotion—to the mystical transfiguration which leaves reality behind. But the power of aversion measures the force of attraction. There is that in Catholicism to which she profoundly responds—both in the sublimity of nature and in the mysticism of her own soul; feelings which represent spiritual and erotic transcendence: the dual temptations of the romantic experience.

For Jane, these feelings were focused in a series of fiery images projected first in the red-room of her childhood; later associated with the vampire, Berthe. Lucy's fear is typically one of deprivation rather than anticipation. It finds its object in the ghostly figure of the nun who haunts her at the Pensionnat. But we are aware of its presence earlier in the novel: when Lucy first begins to confront herself after Miss Marchmont's death. It is then that she unexpectedly meets an old school friend:

> . . . What a beautiful and kind-looking woman was the good-natured and comely, but unintellectual girl become! Wifehood and maternity had changed her thus, as I have seen them change others even less promising than she. Me she had forgotten. I was changed, too; though not, I fear, for the better. (p. 37)

The girl's life contrasts sharply with the one Lucy has led as nurse to the invalided old woman. Lucy allows herself to feel regret as she looks at the young mother, believing that this kind of transformation will never be hers; that she, Lucy Snowe, can have no hope of wifehood and maternity. And yet—she cannot live contentedly with the certainty of that impossibility.

Later, at the Pensionnat, as she cares for Madame's children, to whom she is "only a governess," she does often seem (as the billet-doux intended for Ginevra describes her) "revêche comme une religieuse" (p. 95). It is understandable that she would identify with the nun who is said to haunt the house, the ghost of a girl who had been buried alive "for some sin against her vow" (p. 90). Lucy has also been "buried alive," and the specter is the dread shape of the imprisoned, undeserving self of the past: the sterile and isolated self of the future. The chill form of enforced virginity hovers prophetically over Lucy, as Berthe—unleashed sensuality—had menaced Jane. Both are the perverse offspring of sexual desire and the repression which results from guilt and fear. Both represent the wish for union and the horror of negation. In aspect, Berthe is the projection of Jane's expectant sexuality which is passionate though fearful. The figure of the nun expresses Lucy's only nascent sexuality, anticipatory of rejection and sterility.

When Lucy reads Graham's first letter, her intense joy is countered by terror at the depth of her own happiness: a fear of risk, a resurgence of insecurity. It is then that she first sees the nun. Panicked, she asks: "Are there wicked things, not human, which envy human bliss?" (p. 210). And when she decides at last to bury Graham's letters—repressing feelings that can only cause her pain—the apparition offers itself again, apparently validating her belief that "If life be a war, it seemed my destiny to conduct it single-handed" (p. 253).

As Lucy's relationship with Paul begins to flourish, the specter returns as a warning. But now Paul sees it as well and their kinship is expressed in their shared sensitivity, derived from a surprising similarity of personal history. For him, too, the nun has had a special significance. He associates her with Justine Marie, a young woman who had died in the convent in which she had been placed because of him, by relatives who thought him unsuitable as a lover. The power the girl exerts over him in death creates for Paul a life which is as stunted as the one which the nun seems to prophesy for Lucy. Faithful to Justine's memory, trapped in guilt and sentimentality, Paul has sacrificed everything to her family and friends, demonstrating his worthiness repeatedly. To Madame Walravens and Père Silas he has given his energy, his wealth, his hopes for an independent life. He, too, has been a survivor—identifying with the dead. He has lived as a monk, in a space as limited as the one which enclosed Lucy and Miss Marchmont. Now he fears that Justine Marie has come herself, motivated by jealousy of his friendship with Lucy.[32]

The power of the nun is diminished before the secret of her identity is discovered. The Gothic motif is imparted a realism by the psychological validity of Brontë's insight.[33] Because they are functions of human fear, specters respond to assertions of human

32. One must remember that Heger was also a survivor, who witnessed the deaths of his first wife and child. By metaphorically developing this aspect of his experience, Brontë undercuts the importance of his second marriage—and second family.

33. For a useful discussion of Charlotte Brontë's adaptation of Gothic forms and technique to psychological purposes, see Robert B. Heilman, "Charlotte Brontë's New Gothic," in *From Jane Austen to Joseph Conrad*, ed. Robert C. Rathburn and Martin Steinmann, Jr. (Minnesota: University of Minnesota Press, 1958), pp. 118–32.

will. Superstition is dispelled as Lucy and Paul's belief in one another is substantiated. Learning of Paul's past fidelity and magnanimity, experiencing his tenderness and sympathy, Lucy surrenders to the force of her feeling and to the promise of romance. When they exchange their vow of friendship she believes that she might evade her fate after all: "I envied no girl her lover, no bride her bridegroom, no wife her husband" (p. 344). Despite his Catholicism, Paul has become for her a "Christian hero." He is Apollyon, Great Heart, "my Champion."

But although Lucy's happiness seems less threatened by the mysterious forces within, it is threatened still by the jealousy and selfishness of Paul Emanuel's "friends," as well as by Paul's own fanatic self-sacrifice: his apparent inability to assert himself in behalf of his own needs. Succumbing totally to irrational fear, Lucy perceives Père Silas, Madame Walravens, and Madame Beck as the malicious villains of a Gothic tale in which she and Paul are cast as helpless victims. It is in the distorting mirror of Lucy's Protestant prejudices that the reader perceives Père Silas, the bigoted, devious priest and Madame Walravens, who is "Cunegonde, the sorceress! Malevola, the evil fairy" (p. 329). But if the colors Lucy uses to paint their portraits are lurid, the plan she attributes to them is real. With Madame Beck, they do intend to send Paul Emanuel off to the West Indies for three years on a final "errand of mercy." There he will be secured from her heretical influence while looking after their material interests. In Madame Beck's jealous opposition to their love, we hear the outrage of Madame Heger,[34] and in Lucy's wordless desperation as she waits for Paul's last visit, in her sense of impotence before feeling, we feel the passion which Brontë had never before expressed so openly. Because Lucy is secure in Paul's feeling for her as Brontë could never have been in M. Heger's, she is finally able to overcome her passivity, confronting her rival and un-

34. Writing to Ellen of Madame Heger's coldness towards her, Charlotte comes as close as she did in any of her existing letters to sharing her secret infatuation (November 15, 1843. Wise and Symington, II, 309.):

You will hardly believe that Madame Heger (good and kind as I have described her) never comes near me on the occasions . . . I own, I was astonished the first time I was left alone thus . . . you remember the letter she wrote me when I was in England? How kind and affectionate that was! is it not odd? I fancy I begin to perceive the reason of this mighty distance and reserve; it sometimes makes me laugh and at other times nearly cry. When I am sure of it I will tell you.

masking her ("I saw underneath a being heartless, self-indulgent, and ignoble."[p. 377]).

Madame Beck's attempts to keep Lucy and Paul separated are self-defeating. The drug which she administers to make Lucy sleep sharpens her senses and intensifies her perceptions. It arouses her, moves her to definitive action.[35] Lucy seeks freedom again as she had sought it before, but now she gives herself completely to her quest. It is a holiday evening and everyone she knows has gathered in the spacious park—radiant with moonlight, alive with the promise of celebration. It is a fitting place for her to seek an encounter with Paul, another of the meetings which have taken place in natural settings, in moonlit gardens, in the open air where the limits of the self are expanded: where the soul can aspire and breathe. Once more a solitary voyeur, Lucy is still not lonely. She projects herself into everything around her. She denies nothing, not even, when she sees Graham, that part of her infatuation for him which always remains potentially alive. Now she searches out experience, eagerly pursuing her "fate." She is humorous and ironic, purged of bitterness. Even the reality that undercuts the melodrama of her Gothic vision insists upon recognition:

> Hail, Madame Walravens! I think you looked more witchlike than ever. And presently the good lady proved that she was indeed no corpse or ghost, but a harsh and hardy old woman; for, upon some aggravation in the clamorous petition of Desirée Beck to her mother, to go to the kiosk and take sweetmeats, the hunchback suddenly fetched her a resounding rap with her gold-knobbed cane.

> There, then, were Madame Walravens, Madame Beck, Père Silas—the whole conjuration, the secret junta. The sight of

35. Elizabeth Gaskell writes (Gaskell, chap. xxvii):
I asked her whether she had ever taken opium, as the description given of its effects in *Villette* was so exactly like what I had experienced,—vivid and exaggerated presence of objects, of which the outlines were indistinct, or lost in golden mist, etc. She replied, that she had never, to her knowledge, taken a grain of it in any shape, but that she had followed the process she always adopted when she had to describe anything which had not fallen within her own experience; she had thought intently on it for many and many a night before falling to sleep,—wondering what it was like, or how it would be,—till at length, sometimes after the progress of her story had been arrested at this one point for weeks, she wakened up in the morning with all clear before her, as if she had in reality gone through the experience, and then could describe it, word for word, as it had happened.

them thus assembled did me good. I cannot say that I felt weak before them, or abashed, or dismayed. They outnumbered me, and I was worsted and under their feet; but, as yet, I was not dead. (p. 388)

The most crucial recognition comes in relation to Paul Emanuel. When she sees him there with his goddaughter, whom she believes to be his intended bride, she responds with a degree of intensity she would never have allowed herself before: "And then—something tore me so cruelly under my shawl, something so dug into my side, a vulture so strong in beak and talon, I must be alone to grapple with it" (p. 395). Her jealousy teaches her the depth of her love. When she returns to her room with the pain and comprehension of that knowledge, she finds once again—the nun. But the self that has penetrated to truth, and the sexual longing which is at last awakened, both disdain the imagination that builds illusion:

> Warm from illuminations, and music, and thronging thousands, thoroughly lashed up by a new scourge, I defied spectra. In a moment, without exclamation, I had rushed on the haunted couch; nothing leaped out, or sprang, or stirred; all the movement was mine, so was all the life, the reality, the substance, the force; as my instinct felt. (pp. 396–97)

In the absurd reality of the nun (a costume disguise for Ginevra's suitor) Lucy recognizes the power of the mind to create its own fears and anxieties; its own guilt, even its own prison. She knows that now she can "handle the veil and dare the dread glance." Once the harsh demands of her Protestantism are softened, the repressive ban lifted, Lucy's faith can be confirmed and the integrity of her personality preserved.

The final trial and the ultimate victory remain. Anticipating a meeting with Paul before he sails, fearing that it will not, in fact, take place, Lucy is "pierced deeper than I could endure, made now to feel what defied suppression." Forced to the center of her soul, touching the very quick of her nature, Lucy is undefended at last. When they are reunited she, who has never described herself to the reader (unexpectedly coming upon her reflection in a mirror she had seen simply "a third person in a pink dress and black lace mantle" [p. 179]), she, Lucy Snowe, risks herself totally, asking: " 'Ah! I am not pleasant to look at—? I could not help saying this; the words came unbidden: I never remember the time when I had not a haunting dread of what might be the degree of my outward deficiency; this dread pressed me at the moment with special force.' " It is a validation of her transformed self that she requires. Paul does not disappoint her:

> A great softness passed upon his countenance; his violet eyes grew suffused and glistening under their deep Spanish lashes: he started up: "Let us walk on."
>
> "Do I displease your eyes much?" I took courage to urge: the point had its vital import for me.
>
> He stopped, and gave me a short, strong answer—an answer which silenced, subdued, yet profoundly satisfied. Ever after that, I knew what I was for *him;* and what I might be for the rest of the world, I ceased painfully to care. (p.407)

With Paul she, who has always found it so difficult to speak, becomes eloquent. She who has hardly dared to tell herself her thoughts, she who has hoarded every feeling, can say, "I want to tell you all" and she can tell him freely and unbidden of her anxieties and fears. She can tell him also of her love: "I spoke. All leaped from my lips. I lacked not words now; fast I narrated; fluent I told my tale; it streamed on my tongue" (p. 412). Her capacity for love, newly discovered, newly explored, brings with it self-knowledge and expression.

In his love, Paul has also been able to find the will to self-assertion. He will make this one last journey in Justine Marie's service. Then, returning to marry Lucy, he will commit himself to life. Meanwhile, he plans to make it possible for Lucy to realize her freedom. With the home which he has rented for her and the school which he has established in her name, he offers her the impossible gift of independence. It is the gift which Crimsworth had bestowed upon Frances. But because Lucy must support herself in Paul's absence, because the school is nothing until she creates it, his gift is genuine. Its implications however, are ambiguous. The role which Paul will play in the school upon his return and the effect which that role will have upon Lucy's functioning: these are not defined. But the novel's conclusion is, in part, an attempt to come to terms with the crucial if unexpressed problems.

When they separate, Paul has demonstrated his sensitivity to Lucy's needs, his generosity in satisfying them. His personality has been softened—the more aggressive and domineering qualities purged. In Lucy's idealized vision, only those elements remain which sustain and nourish. His fidelity is proven. Still, theirs is not a relationship of equality. Lucy sees him as her king: "royal for me had been that hand's bounty: to offer homage was both a joy and a duty" (p. 410). It is only in his absence that she can and does discover the possibilities of her own strength. Her words are telling: "M. Emanuel was away three years. Reader, they were the three happiest years of my life" (p. 414). The tone is more telling still. It could be the tone of Jane Eyre. The unreliable narrator has been replaced by one who confronts her reader directly. Lucy Snowe has rejected the silences, the claustrophobic spaces, and the labyrinthian ways of anxiety and repression. She achieves with Brontë herself the maturity of her creator's art. She does not share the totality of Brontë's awareness, however; nor is she allowed the disturbance of her author's subconscious doubts.

Although Lucy can finally assert her independence to become the antithesis of a romantic heroine (neither a "little spaniel" like Polly nor a thoughtless doll like Ginevra) she is oblivious to the dangers which would confront her if Paul Emanuel should, in fact return. In this novel, as in her three earlier books, it is Brontë who must try to reconcile the heroine's independent self-realization with her need to be submerged in the powerful, masculine "other." For Brontë it had always been impossible to accommodate these two commanding impulses which psychosexual conditioning and social reality place in extreme conflict.

Harriet Martineau, the redoubtable intellectual and social reformer, mistook Charlotte Brontë for Lucy Snowe. With an obtuseness born of militancy, she overlooked the novel's psychological center and, while noting the resolution of Lucy and Paul Emanuel's relationship, did not mark the significance of the story's ending. In a review which she wrote for the *Daily News,* she evinced the kind of outrage that had typified Mary Taylor's earlier response to *Shirley:*

> All the female characters, in all their thoughts and lives are full of one thing, or are regarded by the reader in the light of one thought—love. It begins with the child of six years old, at the opening—a charming picture—and it closes with it at the last page; and so dominant is this idea—so incessant is the writer's tendency to describe the need of being loved—that the heroine

who tells her own story, leaves the reader at last with the un-
comfortable impression of her having either entertained a double love, or allowed one to supersede another without notifica-
tion of the transition. It is not thus in real life. There are
substantial, heartfelt interests for women of all ages and, under
ordinary circumstances, quite apart from love; there is an absence of introspection, an unconsciousness, a repose in wom-
en's lives—unless under peculiarly unfortunate circumstances—of which we find no admission in this book; and to
the absence of it may be attributed some of the criticism which
the book will meet with from readers who are no prudes, but
whose reason and taste will reject the assumption that events
and characters are to be regarded through the medium of one
passion only.[36]

Brontë was deeply hurt by the response of this intimidating
woman whom she had only just begun to think of as a friend:

I know what *love* is and I understand it; and if man or woman
should be ashamed of feeling such love, then there is nothing
right, noble, faithful, truthful, unselfish in this earth as I comprehend rectitude, nobleness, fidelity, truth and disinterestedness.[37]

Her words, while naively courageous, suggest her continuing inability to break free entirely of that circle of romantic idealism
which had bound her life.

Charlotte Brontë had shared Harriet Martineau's feminist outrage when she had intuitively created Elizabeth Hastings, when
she had confusedly defined Francis Henri, when she had con-
structed the mythology of *Jane Eyre* and tested it—unsuccess-
fully—against the social vision of *Shirley*. But she had never
been able to deny what remained for her the most profound of
human truths: that to be able to love and to be loved are essential
conditions of a maturely realized life. How to reach that loving
state, how to treasure it, while still maintaining independence:
here was the difficulty. Brontë could offer no clear resolution—witness her elimination of Paul Emanuel—but she would
not deny the possibility of resolution altogether. She could only
assert the incontrovertible fact of her own situation, revealing in
this way the nature and limits of her feminist consciousness. Her

36. Wise and Symington, IV, 44.
37. To Harriet Martineau, January, 1853. Wise and Symington, 42.

personal history had made it impossible for her to draw upon the kind of strengths that had carried Mary Taylor to New Zealand and had allowed Harriet Martineau to create for herself a life-style and work defined by radical action and social service. Brontë had neither the self-confidence nor the militance to leave behind the conventional patterns of her world. Her freedom was private and subjective, conceived neither in political nor collective terms. Her feminism derived from her persistent attempt to define herself autonomously, resisting predetermined cultural formulations, responding to the powerful demands of her own personality. Knowledge and growth were garnered from the metaphor of Yorkshire nature and the revelations of introspection. And, of course, for her, action was the process of writing.

As she struggled with herself to bring her novel to conclusion, Brontë wrote to George Smith:

> If Lucy marries anybody, it must be the Professor—a man in whom there is much to forgive, much to "put up with." But I am not leniently disposed to Miss Frost: from the beginning I never meant to appoint her lines in pleasant places. The conclusion of this third volume is still a matter of some anxiety: I can but do my best, however. It would speedily be finished, could I ward off certain obnoxious head-aches which, whenever I get into the spirit of my work are apt to seize and prostrate me.[38]

The words suggest that Brontë paid to the end the price of personal confrontation. She could not appoint Lucy Snowe's lines in pleasant places because she could not bury again the self which she had so painfully uncovered. Therefore, she could not resolve the conundrum raised by Lucy's situation with the illusions, evasiveness, and facility of the earlier novels.

Paul Emanuel could not return. He could not return because Brontë's fantasy relationship with Heger would not then have been laid to rest. The Belgian's idealization would not have been balanced by his irrevocable loss. The tragic circumstances of her life would have been denied. No matter how great her desire and how firm her wish to believe, no matter how unprepared she was to confront directly the irreducible fact of Heger's indifference, Brontë could not betray the larger reality of her experience.

38. November 3, 1852. Wise and Symington, IV, 16.

Then, too, Paul Emanuel could not return for a reason which Martineau would have found congenial had she been able to perceive it through her rigidly structured feminism. Always intensely personal in her writing—faithful to the truths she had learned and to the confusions which remained—Brontë knew that Lucy had come to her independence through love. She understood that for Lucy to be certain of keeping that independence, she would have to pay the price of solitude. Brontë could not be sure that there was in fact another alternative. She did not know what would happen to that emergent self if it were joined in marriage to "a man in whom there is much to forgive, much to 'put up with' ''; if it were joined in marriage, in fact, to any man. Her own marriage might have taught her the answer and the answer might well have provided her with another novel. Now she eschewed the former compromises of myth and fantasy.

Paul Emanuel's death *can* be compared to the symbolic castration of Rochester. It too represents a rejection of patriarchal forces and suggests the personal and imaginative losses which result from social failure. But Paul Emanuel cannot be reborn, as Rochester was, into a new version of psychosexual romance. Romance itself is no longer viable. It belongs to the realm of princes and princesses of Fortune: the Graham Brettons and Pauline Homeses. For Lucy Snowe, the conventions of literary form—the shroud of domesticity and the implied perpetuation of social values—are as inadequate as the social conventions which call them into being.

Lucy speaks often of lives which are blessed, of love which ends in happiness and marriage, but when she does, she refers always to the relationship between Polly and Graham and theirs is not a relationship which she herself could value. This much she had revealed to Polly:

> I shall share no man's or woman's life in this world, as you understand sharing. I think I have one friend of my own, but I am not sure; and till I *am* sure, I live solitary.

To Polly's response, "But solitude is sadness," Lucy adds, "Yes; it is sadness. Life, however, has worse than that. Deeper than melancholy, lies heartbreak" (p. 359). Because Lucy—like Miss Marchmont—has loved and been loved, the harshness of her "fate" has been softened. She need not know heartbreak, only sadness. After Paul's death, she receives at last the inheritance from Miss Marchmont. She is responsible for her school. She is of use. She pursues her talents and maintains relationships. Without hope, she is not happy, but she is strong. Virginal, she has still experienced passion. Childless, her life is full of children and will not be sterile. Alone and lonely, she is not alienated. Surviving, she need not live as a survivor. She does not have to tell the story of another. Now she can tell and understand her own.

Paul Emanuel dies at sea as he journeys home. The storm in which he perishes limns the paradox at the novel's center. It expresses as well the struggle at the heart of the romantic experience and the irony of Brontë's life and death. The expanded self is poised between knowledge and annihilation. The self that is limited and withdrawn neither risks the second nor achieves the first. For Lucy the storm has always had a double meaning. Sometimes it has brought the horror of suffocation. At other times, it has stood for explosive transcendence. Always it has involved a terrible risk. Now Lucy's growth rests—with Brontë's integrity—upon the awful inevitability of Paul's loss. It is an uncompromising vision, but within the context of this novel, which gathers together the threads of all the fictions and the fragments of the life itself, it is undeniable and right.

Birth and Death

AFTER COMPLETING *Villette* in the winter of 1852, Charlotte Brontë found herself in the position of the disappointed rock-climber who achieves a difficult and heretofore unconquered peak only to find a distressingly familiar prospect before her. The analysis to which she had subjected herself had yielded a new level of insight, but the reality she had now to confront remained remarkably unchanged. In creating Lucy Snowe, Brontë had ruthlessly dissected herself. She had recorded the effects of survivorship. She had defined the withdrawn and masochistic personality. She had shown her hostility to be a defense, and revealed repeatedly the pain of her vulnerability. But that vulnerability had not been meaningfully diminished. The insight gained had stripped away layers of repression and confusion, but since her analysis had been self-directed, it had also been self-enclosed. Perceptions turned back upon themselves, untested, in the convoluted chambers which had characterized Lucy Snowe's own inner space. Brontë had journeyed alone, without a companion to define with her a relationship which could nourish where others had left her starved. Action did not follow understanding.

Brontë's technique had been radical and was easily misunderstood. The novel was perceived by some to be flawed and disunified; by others—like Martineau—to be unabashedly sentimental. Most immediately disturbing was the effect of the story upon George Smith. By describing Lucy's unrequited love for Graham Bretton, Brontë had revealed to her publisher, with extraordinary candor, her own sense of the forces which had been at work in their relationship. She insisted upon the integrity, however ambiguous, of her feeling for Smith and the thoughtless superficiality of his attachment to her. She characterized the cloying possessiveness of his mother and claimed her right to use their lives as material for her novel. Smith, who understood the implications of the Bretton sections of the story, responded harshly. He attacked the art of the novel, he underpaid the novelist,[1] and he offered cold civility in the place of the warm relationship they had shared.

The break with Smith initiated a break with Williams as well. Further intimacy between them was difficult. Their correspondence gradually dwindled and died. Friendship with Harriet Martineau was also at an end. The acerbity of Martineau's judgment of the novel had burned a wound so deep that it could not be healed by words or time. Elizabeth Gaskell was the only "literary" friend left to her and she was hardly more than an acquaintance: a dim promise for the future.

Brontë had effectively cut her lifeline with London and the world of letters. It had not proven to be a world in which she could function without great psychological and emotional strain. At the height of her fame and success, she was more alone than she had ever been before.

She could say, with Lucy Snowe, "To see and know the worst is to take from fear her main advantage."[2] The writing of *Villette* had been an act of courage. Undoubtedly, in confronting the terrors of loneliness through Lucy Snowe, Brontë had parried the more fatal thrusts of fear. But what to do with the days of quiet desperation at Haworth? How could she apply her knowledge and her strength to these? She and her father lived side by side, but not together. She dutifully cared for him. He worried endlessly about her health. They shared few concerns and no interests. There were occasional letters written to Ellen Nussey and Margaret Wooler. Occasional letters in turn received. A correspondence still with Mary Taylor. And there was the grinding tedium of the daily routine—unrelieved by the painful emancipation of writing. Brontë had written herself to the

---

1. Brontë, as was the custom, had no contractual agreement with Smith and Elder. But she expected a payment of at least £ 700 for her new novel: a recognition of her status and position. Instead Smith paid her £ 500, the same as he had given her for *Jane Eyre* and *Shirley*.

2. *Villette*, p. 393.

depth and edge of her experience. She was an explorer sitting in a ship becalmed.

A dream saved her; a scrap of illusion, or, perhaps more fairly, the last belief which she allowed herself. "I know what *love* is as I understand it," she had written angrily to Harriet Martineau, "and if man or woman should be ashamed of feeling such love, then is there nothing right, noble, faithful, truthful, unselfish in this earth, as I comprehend rectitude, nobleness, fidelity, truth and disinterestedness."

All her life she had thought and written about love. She had learned to understand the ways in which it could be manipulative and selfish, the ways in which it could destroy, the ways in which it could offer cowardly submission and escape. But private and solitary, inward-turning as she was, she knew it to be the only alternative to solipsistic strangulation. Once love *had* been that to her. Ambiguously she writes, "I know what love is." She still could not have admitted: "I know what it is to love; but I do not know what it means to have been loved." That is the truth she refuses to penetrate—the truth from which she protected Lucy Snowe and herself. In some corner of her mind, Brontë clung still to a dream of possibility. And when that possibility offered itself—in a strange, almost incongruous form—she had become strong enough to respond to her hope, despite her doubts and disappointment. She would dare to separate—as Lucy Snowe had not—commitment from romance.

The man who did in fact love her had been her father's curate for more than seven years. For more than seven years he had barely impinged upon her consciousness. She had damned him with faint praise as Mr. Macarthey in *Shirley:* the man who replaced Malone and was "decent, decorous and conscientious. . . sane and rational; diligent and charitable."[3] Elizabeth Gaskell found him to be bigoted and stern. None found him charming or magnetic. He was never mistaken for an intellectual ·nor was he thought to have a poet's soul. Friends then and readers now shrug and wonder, mostly sighing at poor Charlotte's compromise.

And yet her decision to marry him had a motive which establishes still further the continuity of the life and work. Despite appearances, Arthur Bell Nicholls was of the same stamp as all

3. *Shirley,* p. 632.

the men who had haunted Brontë's fantasies and dominated her experience. Gaskell had insightfully observed of Nicholl's appeal:

> I am sure that Miss Brontë could never have borne not to be well-ruled and ordered. . . . She would never have been happy but with an exacting, rigid, law-giving, passionate man . . .[4]

It is a less romanticized relation of Rochester and Paul Emanuel she describes. It is a strong patriarchal figure she draws: a possible portrait of Maria Branwell's young suitor, an image of the commanding presence who marked indelibly the lives at Haworth parsonage, a reflection of the father-lover whom Charlotte sought in Monsieur Heger. He was Byron distorted, Lord Wellington diluted. He embodied the authority which Brontë needed to sustain her: the authority which a lifetime of socialization had taught her to equate with masculinity. And she recognized that, despite his unyielding presence,

> Mr. Nicholls is one of those who attach themselves to very few, whose sensations are close and deep—like an underground stream, running strong but in a narrow channel.[5]

Nicholls offered her that gift which had never in actuality been offered her before; and he offered it unbidden: continued to offer it even after it had been rejected. He offered it from the depth of his regard and the depth of his need.

It must have been his need which convinced her, for his need balanced the authority which she required but understood well enough to fear. That authority had threatened all of her juvenile heroines. It had threatened Jane and Lucy. It had incapacitated Shirley. It had made her resentful of Branwell, ambivalent toward her father, miserably dependent upon Heger, repelled by James Taylor. Nicholls's need gave her room to be herself. It suggested mutuality and allowed her self-respect.

She watched Nicholls's suffering as he delivered his last sermon. He was to leave Haworth in order to escape the continuing reminder of what he had been denied in her rejection of his first proposal:

4. To John Foster, April 23, 1854. Wise and Symington, IV, 117–18.
5. To Ellen Nussey, January 2, 1853. Wise and Symington, IV, 32.

> He struggled, faltered, then lost command over himself, stood
> before my eyes and in the sight of all the communicants,
> white, shaking, voiceless.[6]

She found in him a capacity for feeling—feeling for *her*—that
she had only imagined in Rochester and Paul Emanuel: that she
had been able to imagine in them because she had experienced it
in herself:

> I found him leaning against the garden door in a paroxysm of
> anguish, sobbing as women never sob. Of course, I went
> straight to him. Very few words were interchanged, those few
> barely articulate. Several things I should have liked to ask him
> were swept entirely from my memory. Poor fellow! But he
> wanted such hope and such encouragement as I *could* not give
> him. Still I trust he must know now that I am not entirely blind
> and indifferent to his constancy and grief.[7]

And so, after finally gaining Patrick Brontë's permission (dissat-
isfied with Nicholls's replacement, the infirm and habitually selfish old man found it preferable to "settle" for a husband than to
train an intransigent curate), Charlotte agreed to become "what
people call engaged."[8] The phrase suggests the enormous ambivalence she felt. What she had learned of Nicholls "inclined me
to esteem and if not love—at least affection."[9] Her decision was
not based upon that powerful attraction, that promise of transcendence, that is the keystone of romantic love. It was based on her
evaluation of a man capable of altruistic feeling. Her evaluation
rested, in turn, on the pride in self which had been born during
these years of success and had burgeoned as she developed the
character of Lucy Snowe who becomes at last, because of *her* capacity for love, most worthy.

Still, reservation had been written into the very structure of
Shirley. It informed the psychological insights of *Villette* and per-
vaded the author's later life at Haworth. Nicholls seemed to offer
her contradictory hope for the future but she could not help but be
troubled since her optimism rested upon so little that was tangible
and sure. It was not a decision which she could have made before
the writing of *Villette*. Did the fact that she could make it now

6. To Ellen Nussey, May 16, 1853. Wise and Symington, IV, 65.
7. To Ellen Nussey, May 27, 1853. Wise and Symington, IV, 68–69.
8. To Elizabeth Gaskell, April 18, 1854. Wise and Symington, IV, 116.
9. To Ellen Nussey, April 11, 1854. Wise and Symington, IV, 112.

mean that it was "right"? Like Shirley tamed, fearfully awaiting her wedding day, Brontë wrote: "Care and Fear stand so close to Hope, I sometimes scarcely can see her for the shadows they cast."[10] Remembering the specters of Berthe and the nun, we can only guess the causes of her "care and fear." A permanent commitment where there was respect but not love? A surrendering of privacy always essential to her inner life? Risking her success and fame? Giving to another her time, her thoughts—her body, so long virginal? How easily as a girl she had written of passionate, sexual love. How odd a contrast with those romantic fantasies is this oblique and guarded letter, sent to Ellen while she was on her wedding trip:

> Dear Nell—during the last six weeks—the colour of my thought is a good deal changed: I know more of the realities of life than I once did. I think many false ideas are propagated, perhaps unintentionally. I think those married women who indiscriminately urge their acquaintance to marry—much to blame. For my part—I can only say with deeper sincerity and fuller significance—what I always said in theory—Wait God's will. Indeed—indeed Nell—it is a solemn and strange and perilous thing for a woman to become a wife. Man's lot is far—far different.[11]

Where innocence had spoken, experience is still. The new relationship must have been traumatic and disorienting. As a consequence, she returns to a dependency that had been submerged in the confidence of recent years. The pleading tone and childlike diction of this note to Ellen belie the relief she tries to suggest:

> My husband is not a poet or a poetical man—and one of my grand doubts before marriage was about "congenial tastes" and so on. The first morning we went out on to the cliffs and saw the Atlantic coming in all white foam, I did not know whether I should get leave or time to take the matter in my own way. I did not want to talk—but I *did* want to look and be silent. Having hinted a petition, license was not refused— covered with a rug to keep off the spray, I was allowed to sit where I chose—and he only interrupted me when he thought I crept too near the edge of the cliff. So far he is always good in this way—and this protection which does not interfere or pre-

10. To George Smith, April 25, 1854. Wise and Symington, IV, 119.
11. To Ellen Nussey, August 9, 1854. Wise and Symington, IV, 145–46.

tend is I believe a thousand times better than any half sort of pseudo sympathy. I will try with God's help to be as indulgent to him whenever indulgence is needed.[12]

The ambivalence remains when they return to Haworth. The days are busy, filled with activity, adjustments. The letters Brontë writes to Nussey and Wooler are ambiguous, lending themselves to contradictory interpretations. But a new cheerful tone does seem to gain ascendance, and a new tinge of equality appears to establish itself in their relationship.

The problem which she describes as pressing most upon her is one of time. She repeats, in various contexts, in different ways, that her time is not her own:

> Someone wants a good portion of it—and says we must do so and so accordingly, and it generally seems the right thing— Only I sometimes wish that I could have written the letter as well as taken the walk.[13]

But she had written so many letters as substitutes for conversations and had walked so many miles in solitude, that she could not undervalue her husband's company and concern. The "doing" was good for her. It enlarged her interests and occupied her mind without disturbing the continuity of her life.

Haworth had always been her home. Her tragic history— much of which her husband had watched unfold—bound her there. Always before she had been a stranger in the town. Only Branwell had not kept himself apart. The duties she had observed as the minister's daughter, she had now to assume as the minister's wife. Her new status allowed her to enter society with a confidence freshly experienced. There was pleasure to be derived from sharing and participation. She came to feel that "it is not bad for me that his bent should be so wholly towards matters of real life—so little inclined to the literary and contemplative."[14] Because he was neither intellectual nor poet, because he was not her "maitre" or competitor, she was free still to range in that other, private world. Sharing his interests would earn for her that

12. To Catherine Winkworth, Cork, July 27, 1854. Wise and Symington, IV, 137–38.

13. To Margaret Wooler, August 22, 1854. Wise and Symington, IV, 148.

14. To Margaret Wooler, September 14, 1854. Wise and Symington, IV, 153.

stake in life for which she had so longed and although she acknowledged that "If true domestic happiness replace Fame—the
exchange will indeed be for the better,"[15] she had begun to write
another novel,[16] and had not abandoned her literary aspirations.

Five months after the wedding anticipated with so much
doubt, Brontë wrote to Margaret Wooler:

> It is long since I have known such comparative immunity
> from head-ache, sickness and indigestion, as during the last
> three months.
> My life is different from what it used to be. May God
> make me thankful for it! I have a good, kind attached husband
> and every day makes my own attachment to him stronger.[17]

Brontë's pleas, "May God make me thankful for it!" may pose
uneasy questions for us—but the difficulty of interpretation is
slightly eased by the fact of her physical well-being: an indication
more important than any other that Brontë had begun to find the
peace that comes with an integrated life, relatively freed from
anxiety.

The constant note of sadness which sounded through her earlier letters was replaced by varying tones of humor and tolerance.
Her husband's stern seriousness amused her. Increasingly sure of
herself and him, she grew less dependent upon the paternal
aspects of his personality. Their relationship seemed to grow in
mutuality. Finally she was the mistress of her home. Arthur Nicholls was, in many ways, Patrick Brontë's temperamental son
and had inherited the mantle of the aging minister. Her husband's
presence enabled Charlotte to complete the movement to independence begun ten years earlier when Patrick's vision
failed. Now, as she made the transition from daughter to wife,
her relation to her father changed. Her feelings seemed largely
purged of the bitterness and resentment she had lived with and repressed for many years:

> My dear father was not well when we returned from Ireland—I
> am however most thankful to say that he is better now—May
> God preserve him to us yet for some years! The wish for his

15. Ibid.
16. See *Emma*, this novel fragment, printed with an introduction by
W. M. Thackeray, "The Last Sketch," *Cornhill Magazine* 1 (April 1850), pp.
485–98.
17. November 15, 1854. Wise and Symington, IV, 160.

> continued life—together with a certain solicitude for his happi-
> ness and health seems—I scarcely know why—stronger in me
> now than before I was married.[18]

The oedipal struggle was at least calmed. The long years of neurotic illness and depression gave way to healthier activity and
perhaps—one hopes, but does not know—to a satisfactory sexuality.

But the elements in Brontë's life which were conducive to
tranquility were inhospitable to other kinds of psychic growth.
Recognitions yielded by the writing of *Villette* had not released
new energies. The analysis begun was not, apparently, continued. Life moved regressively. In marrying Nicholls, Brontë
risked less than she would have risked in most other marriages.
Risking less, she could dare little. Remaining at Haworth, a
daughter still, married to a father substitute, reenacting now the
role of her mother, Brontë took refuge in a version of the past.
Lulled by the deceptions of the familiar patriarchal trap, she
waited there, unarmed, for the crucial trial which was to come.

II

There was another facet to marriage. Not one which middle-
class Victorians spoke of any more openly than they did of sex itself. Not one which Brontë herself discussed, although it might
well have been in her mind when she wrote of the "care and
fear" which obscured the hope of her approaching union. To be a
wife meant also to be a mother. The mysteries and dangers surrounding childbearing made the prospect fearful for most women:
even for those whose lives had best prepared them for maternity.
But for Brontë the problems were particularly difficult: long-
lived, complex.

As children, all desire union with the mother who gives and
sustains life. Later, each girl seeks reconciliation with the mother
after whom she has modeled herself, from whom she strives to
separate herself, whom she even tries to replace. Finally, to
achieve maturity and freedom, every woman must discover—often through her own maternity—the mother that dwells within.

---

18. To Margaret Wooler, August 22, 1854. Wise and Symington, IV,
149.

This pattern can be traced in Brontë's life as she traced it in the lives of her heroines.

Orphaned, all the central figures of the novels and the novelist herself are snatched from the vital source of nurturance. All find temporary surrogates who are more or less effective in providing them support. For Frances there is an aunt; for Jane, there is Maria Temple; for Caroline, Hortense Moore; for Shirley, Mrs. Pryor; for Lucy, Miss Marchmont. For Charlotte Brontë herself there had been her Aunt Branwell; her housekeeper, Tabby; Miss Wooler, her teacher and friend. None had satisfied her. In *Jane Eyre* and *Villette,* Brontë gives her heroines adversaries who are representative of the mother who stands between them and the father-lover. For Jane, Berthe plays such a role; for Lucy, Madame Beck. For Charlotte there was Madame Heger. Seeking the guiding spirit in themselves, all of Brontë's heroines turned to nature as their intermediary—much as Emily, Anne, and Charlotte had found on the moors and in the open skies of Haworth, the irreplaceable sources of spiritual renewal. Caroline, of course, finds her mother *in fact* and, after her discovery, regresses to a position of dependence which her marriage only confirms. Shirley's development is truncated as well. Its correlative is presented in the confused and contradictory mythologies she creates. Only in *Jane Eyre* and *Villette* do the heroines reach the third and final stages of their quests. But in the allegorical formulation of Brontë's second novel and in the rapid conclusion of her fourth, success is assumed and not really demonstrated. Never achieving full integration, Brontë could not herself have satisfactorily explored its meaning.

The years of professional success and growing fame gave her confidence which she had not known before. In the writing of *Villette* she had confronted her public and private selves. But there was still to be borne the effects of a lifetime of failed relationships. The neurotic interaction with a domineering father who had never loved her enough. Her own rejection of Branwell, essential to her growth but profoundly troubling. The tragic loss of her sisters—her feeling complicated by her recognition that she had always stood outside of their charmed circle, an awkward third, as they had stood outside the gates of Angria. And then the rejections of Heger and Smith; her frustrating indecision about James Taylor—his advances and withdrawals. There was only

Nicholls's unquestioning devotion to balance thirty-eight years of humiliation and self-doubt. Indeed, the feelings which that devotion had begun to induce in her were sufficiently optimistic to illumine, however dimly, the dark and menacing psychic recesses that the past had slowly and painfully etched. In the growing tenderness of her relationship with Nicholls, "my dear boy," Brontë had begun to discover and trust the maternal principle in herself. But many doubts remained. Autonomy, defined in agony, was threatened everywhere. Her personal independence had not yet been truly won. Her professional freedom was still in question. In her writing and in her experience she had wrestled with the life-defeating forces of romantic mythology and personal history. She had described them. She had confronted them. But, Antaeus-like, they seemed to reappear—renewed by the social powers by which they had been formed.

Seven years earlier Brontë had given to Jane Eyre a dream which she herself had dreamt recurrently. Jane, we recall, is fleeing from the ruins of Thornfield in pursuit of Rochester. A strange child clings to her neck, almost strangling her in its terror. And as Jane scrambles up the rocks to watch her lover disappear beyond the hills, the baby falls from her arms and she awakens. The dream had been relevant to Jane's experience—to her anxieties and fears—as it had been and remained relevant to her author's. Brontë—like Jane—seems simultaneously to be child and mother. Her anxiety belongs to the helpless waif and the dependent wife. She fears the loss of the protective male, the loss of the child whom she must fail, the loss of herself—unable to assume the responsibilities of mature womanhood.

The dream is prophetic. Perhaps, in time, Nicholls would have been able to help erase the survivor's guilt and shame. Perhaps in learning to be a wife, in gaining assurance as a person, Brontë would have learned also to anticipate maternity. Perhaps in her own growing strength, she would have found the confidence to sustain another. It is more likely, however, that the unresolved ambivalence of her relationship with Nicholls and the regressive circumstances in which she lived, militated against the development which could have freed her psychologically as she had been liberated intellectually. Her fears had, after all, conspired in the construction of this—her final prison. At Haworth still, she would have felt more powerfully the effects of Maria

Branwell's last dreadful illness, associated always in her mind with childbearing. The signs are there in her persistently negative expectations of childhood, in her sense of helplessness before it. Never having resolved the traumas of her own childhood, Brontë continued to find all children strangers, impossible to relate to, certainly difficult to care for.[19] She had to feel the child that was herself mature before she could shelter in her womb another life.

Nine months after her marriage, Charlotte Brontë conceived a child and fell ill of the conception: sickened, apparently by fear.[20] It was the last of her neurotic illnesses; the last of her masochistic denials. Love had come too late, too briefly, in too ambiguous a form. The past was the deluge which had long threatened—which had been long and courageously resisted. Now it overwhelmed her and she drowned. On March 31, 1855, at thirty-eight years of age, in the early months of pregnancy, Charlotte Brontë died. She could not bring to birth the self she had conceived.

19. Brontë had written to Gaskell of her children (Gaskell, p. 343):
Whenever I see Florence and Julia again, I shall feel like a bashful suitor, who views at a distance the fair personage to whom, in his clownish awe, he dare not risk a near approach. Such is the clearest idea I can give you of my feeling toward children I like, but to whom I am a stranger;—and to what children am I not a stranger? They seem to me little wonders; their talk, their ways are all matter of half-admiring, half puzzled speculation.

20. Gerin comments that "the sickness of early pregnancy was quite disproportionate in Charlotte's case" (*Charlotte Brontë,* p. 562), and Philip Rhodes has added this enlightening explanation ("A Medical Appraisal of the Brontës," p. 107):
The evidence is quite clear that she died of hyperemesis gravidarum . . . an excess of the nausea and sickness which most women suffer in early pregnancy. This morning-sickness, so-called, is probably due to the effects of the hormones from the conceptus affecting the nervous centres in the brain which control vomiting. The disease only seems to become excessive in those who display neuroticism, and they require firm, kind treatment to get them better. But this was not known in 1855. The constant vomiting depletes the body of water and sodium and chlorides, as well as potassium and other electrolytes. The deficiency of sodium chloride leads to increas-

ing apathy, drowsiness and inability to concentrate on anything, and gives a feeling of lassitude. Moreover, the electrolyte loss is probably a cause of stasis of the gastric contents leading to further dilation of the stomach and nausea with vomiting. It is a terrible malady when unchecked and yet it is so easy to nip in the bud when the pathology is understood.

The point is that Brontë's condition, while not unfamiliar in our own time, is responsive to modern medical and psychological treatment.

Selected Bibliography

I Primary Texts

Brontë, Charlotte. *Emma: A Fragment by Currer Bell with "The Last Sketch,"* by William Makepeace Thackeray in *Cornhill Magazine*, 1 (1866), 485–98. Reprinted in *Brontë Society Transactions*, 2 (1899), 84–101.

——. *Five Novelettes*. Transcribed and edited Winifred Gerin. London: The Folio Press, 1971.

——. *Jane Eyre*. Ed. Jane Jack and Margaret Smith. London: Oxford University Press, 1969.

——. *Legends of Angria*. Compiled by Fannie E. Ratchford and William Clyde DeVane. New Haven: Yale University Press, 1933.

——. *Shirley*. London: Oxford University Press, 1969.

——. *The Professor*. London: Oxford University Press, 1967.

——. *Villette*. Ed. Geoffrey Tillotson and Donald Hawes. Boston: Houghton Mifflin, 1971.

Brontë, Charlotte, and Patrick Branwell. *The Miscellaneous and Unpublished Writings of Charlotte and Patrick Branwell Brontë*. 2 vols. Oxford: Shakespeare Head Press, 1934.

——. *The Poems of Charlotte and Patrick Branwell Brontë*. Oxford: Shakespeare Head Press, 1934.

Shorter, Clement. *The Brontës: Life and Letters*. 2 vols. New York: Haskell House, 1969. First published, 1908.

Wise, T. J., and Symington, J. A., eds., *The Brontës: Their Lives, Friendships and Correspondences*. 4 vols. Oxford: Shakespeare Head Press, 1932.

II Secondary Sources

Adler, Alfred. "Sex," *Psychoanalysis and Women*. Ed. Jean Baker Miller, M.D., Baltimore: Penguin, 1973.

Banks, Joseph and Olive. *Feminism and Family Planning in Victorian England*. New York: Schocken Books, 1964.

Beer, Patricia. *Reader, I Married Him*. New York: Barnes and Noble, 1974.

Bentley, Phyllis. *The Brontës*. London: Barker, 1947.

——. *The Brontës and Their World*. New York: Viking Press, 1969.

——. *The Brontë Sisters*. London: Longmans-Green, 1950.

Bieber, Irving, M.D. "The Meaning of Masochism." *American Journal of Psychotherapy*, No. 7 (1953).

Briggs, Asa. "Private and Social Themes in *Shirley*." *Brontë Society Transactions*, 13, No. 3 (1958).

Brown, Norman O. *Life Against Death*. New York: Random House, 1959.

Burkhart, Charles. *Charlotte Brontë: A Psychosexual Study of Her Novels*. London: Victor Gollancz, 1973.

Burns, Wayne. "Critical Relevance of Freudianism" *Western Review*, 20 (1956), 301–14.

Cavell, Marcia. "Since 1924: Toward a New Psychology of Women." *Women and Analysis*. Ed. Jean Strouse. New York: Grossman, 1974.

Cecil, Lord David. *Early Victorian Novelists*. Indianapolis: Bobbs-Merrill, 1935.

Chadwick, Ellis H. "Charlotte Brontë and Thackeray." *Brontë Society Transactions*, 4, No. 21 (1967).

Chase, Richard. "The Brontës: A Centennial Observance." *Kenyon Review*, No. 9 (1947).

Cominos, Peter T. "Innocent Femina Sensualis in Unconscious Conflict." *Suffer and Be Still: Women in the Victorian Age*. Ed. Martha Vicinus. Bloomington, Ind.: Indiana University Press, 1972.

Craig, G. Armour. "The Unpoetic Compromise: On the Relation Between Private Vision and Social Order in Nineteenth Century English Fiction." *Society and Self in the Novel*, English Institute Essays, 1955. New York: Columbia University Press, 1956.

Crandall, Norma. *Emily Brontë; A Psychological Portrait*. New York: Kraus Reprint Co., 1970.

Day, Morton S. "Central Concepts of *Jane Eyre*." *Personalist*, No. 4.

Deutsch, Helene. *The Psychology of Women*. Vols. 1 and 2. New York: Bantam, 1973.

Dooley, Lucile. "Psychoanalysis of Charlotte Brontë, As a Type of the Women of Genius." *The American Journal of Psychology*, July 1920, 31, No. 3.

Dunbar, Janet. *The Early Victorian Woman: Some Aspects of Her Life*. London: 1973.

Engels, Friedrich. *The Origin of the Family, Private Property and the State* (1884). New York: International, 1942.

Erickson, Donald. "Imagery as Structure in *Jane Eyre*." *Victorian Newsletter*, Fall 1966, pp. 18–22.

Ewbank, Inga-Stina. *Their Proper Sphere: A Study of the Brontë Sisters as Early Victorian Female Novelists*. London: Arnold, 1966.

Fletcher, Angus. *Allegory: The Theory of a Symbolic Mode*. New York: Cornell University Press, 1964.

Freud, Sigmund. *Civilization and Its Discontents*. Trans. J. Strachey. New York: W. W. Norton, 1950.

———. *Collected Papers*. Ed. J. Riviere. Vols. 1–4. New York: Basic Books, 1959.

Gaskell, Elizabeth. *The Life of Charlotte Brontë*. London: J. M. Dent, 1960. First published, 1857.

Gerin, Winifred. *Branwell Brontë*. London: Thomas Nelson and Sons, 1961.

———. "Byron's Influence on the Brontës." *Keats-Shelley Memorial Bulletin*, 17 (1966), pp. 1–19.

————. *Charlotte Brontë: The Evolution of Genius.* London: Oxford University Press, 1967.

Greg, W. R. *Why Are Women Redundant?* London, 1869.

Hays, H. R. *The Dangerous Sex: The Myth of Feminine Evil.* New York: Pocket Books, 1965.

Heilbrun, Carolyn G. *Toward a Recognition of Androgyny.* New York: A. A. Knopf, 1973.

Heilman, Robert. "Charlotte Brontë, Reason and the Moon." *Nineteenth Century Fiction,* 14 (March 1960).

Hinkley, Laura J. *The Brontës, Charlotte and Emily.* New York: Hastings House, 1945.

Holgate, Ivy. "The Structure of *Shirley.*" *Brontë Society Transactions,* 14, No. 2 (1962), pp. 27–35.

Hopkins, Annette. *The Father of the Brontës.* Baltimore: Johns Hopkins Press, 1958.

Horney, Karen. "The Problem of Feminine Masochism." *Psychoanalysis and Women.* Ed. Jean Baker Miller. Baltimore: Penguin, 1973.

Isenberg, David. "Charlotte Brontë and the Theatre." *Brontë Society Transactions,* 15, No. 3 (1968), pp. 237–41.

Knies, Earl A. *The Art of Charlotte Brontë.* Ohio: Ohio State University Press, 1969.

Korg, Jacob B. "The Problem of Unity in *Shirley.*" *Nineteenth Century Fiction,* 12 (Sept. 1957).

Kroeber, Karl. *Styles in Fictional Structure: The Art of Jane Austen, Charlotte Brontë, George Eliot.* Princeton: Princeton University Press. 1971.

Langbridge, Rosamund. *Charlotte Brontë, A Psychological Study.* London: William Heinemann, n.d.

Langford, Thomas. "The Three Pictures in *Jane Eyre.*" *Victorian Newsletter,* 31 (Spring 1967), pp. 97–98.

Lewes, George Henry. "Currer Bell's *Shirley.*" *Edinburgh Review,* 91 (1850).

Lifton, Robert. *History and Human Survival.* New York: Random House, 1961.

Marchand, Leslie A. *Byron, A Biography.* Vols. 1–4. New York: A. A. Knopf, 1957.

Marcus, Steven. *Engels, Manchester and the Working Class.* New York: Random House, 1944.

Marcuse, Herbert. *Eros and Civilization.* New York: Vintage Books, 1955.

Martin, Hazel T. *Petticoat Rebels: A Study of the Novels of Social Protest of George Eliot, Elizabeth Gaskell, and Charlotte Brontë.* New York: Helios, 1968.

Martin, Robert. *The Accents of Persuasion: Charlotte Brontë's Novels.* London: Faber and Faber, 1966.

Mill, John Stuart. *The Subjection of Women* (1889). Reprinted in *Three Essays by J. S. Mill.* London: Oxford University Press, 1966.

Millett, Kate. *Sexual Politics.* New York: Doubleday, 1970.

Moglen, Helene. "The Double Vision of *Wuthering Heights:* A Clarifying View of Female Development." *The Centennial Review,* XV (Fall 1971), pp. 391–405.

Momberger, Philip. "Self and World in the Works of Charlotte Brontë." *ELH,* 32 (Sept. 1965).

Moser, Laurence. "From Portrait to Person: A Note on the Surrealistic in *Jane*

Eyre.'' Nineteenth Century Fiction, 20 (Dec. 1965), pp. 275–81.

Neff, Wanda. *Victorian Working Women: An Historical and Literary Study of Women in British Industries and Professions, 1832–1850.* London: Cass, 1966.

Ohmann, Carol. *Charlotte Brontë: The Limits of Her Feminism,* Feminine Studies VI. Old Westbury, N.Y.: The Feminist Press, 1972.

Peckham, Morse. *Victorian Revolutionaries, Speculations on Some Heroes of a Culture Crisis.* New York: George Braziller, 1970.

Peters, Margot. *Charlotte Brontë: Style in the Novel.* Wisconsin: University of Wisconsin Press, 1973.

———. *Unquiet Soul: A Biography of Charlotte Brontë.* New York: Doubleday, 1975.

Praz, Mario. *The Romantic Agony.* Trans. Angus Davidson. London: Oxford University Press, 1970.

Quennell, Peter. *Byron in Italy.* London: Collins, 1951.

———. *Byron: The Years of Fame.* London: Collins, 1950.

Rallo, Eino. *The Haunted Castle: A Study of the Elements of English Romanticism.* New York: Humanities Press, 1964.

Ratchford, Fannie Elizabeth. *The Brontës' Web of Childhood.* New York: Russell and Russell, 1964.

Rathbun, R. C., and M. Steinmann, Jr., eds. *From Jane Austen to Joseph Conrad.* Minneapolis: University of Minnesota Press, 1958.

Rhodes, Philip. ''A Medical Appraisal of the Brontës.'' *Brontë Society Transactions,* 16, No. 2 (1972).

Rich, Adrienne. ''*Jane Eyre:* The Temptations of a Motherless Woman.'' *Ms,* II (October 1973).

Rigby, Elizabeth. ''*Vanity Fair, Jane Eyre* and the Governesses Benevolent Institution—Report for 1847.'' *Quarterly Review,* 84 (1848), pp. 153–85.

Scargill, M. H. ''All Passion Spent: A Reevaluation of *Jane Eyre.''* *University of Toronto Quarterly,* No. 9 (1949).

Sewell, Mrs. S. A. *Woman and the Times We Live In.* London: Simpkin, Marshall and Co., 1869.

Shapiro, Arnold. ''Public Themes and Private Lives: Social Criticism in *Shirley.''* *Papers on Language and Literature,* 4 (Winter 1968).

Sinclair, May. *The Three Brontës.* New York: Kennikat Press, 1967.

Spens, Janet. ''Charlotte Brontë.'' *Essays and Studies by Members of the English Association,* No. 14 (1929).

Thorslev, Peter L. *The Byronic Hero.* Minneapolis: University of Minnesota Press, 1962.

Tillotson, Kathleen. *Novels of the 1840's.* London: Oxford, 1965.

Tompkins, J. M. S. ''Caroline Helstone's Eyes.'' *Brontë Society Transactions,* No. 14 (1961).

Vicinus, Martha, ed. *Suffer and Be Still: Women in the Victorian Age.* Bloomington: Indiana University Press, 1972.

Ward, Barbara. ''Charlotte Brontë and the World of 1846.'' *Brontë Society Transactions,* 11, No. 56 (1951), pp. 3–13.

Weinstein, Fred, and Gerald Platt. *The Wish to Be Free.* Berkeley: University of California Press, 1969.

West, Rebecca. ''The Role of Fantasy in the Work of the Brontës.'' *Brontë Society Transactions,* 12, No. 4 (1954), pp. 255–67.

Winnifreth, Tom. *The Brontës and Their Background: Romance and Reality.* New York: MacMillan, 1973.

Wroot, Herbert. *The Persons and Places of the Brontë Novels.* New York: Burt Franklin, 1970. First published, 1906.

Zilboorg, Gregory. "Masculine and Feminine: Some Biological and Cultural Aspects." *Psychoanalysis and Women.* Ed. Jean Baker Miller, M.D. Baltimore: Penguin, 1973.

Index

(For references to novels and characters, see entry for Brontë, Charlotte)